# RICHARD NIXON

Richard Nixon, campaigning in California, *Fresno Bee* photograph.

# RICHARD NIXON

## Rhetorical Strategist

Hal W. Bochin

*Foreword by Halford R. Ryan*

Great American Orators, Number 6
Bernard K. Duffy and Halford R. Ryan,
Series Advisors

**Greenwood Press**
New York • Westport, Connecticut • London

**Library of Congress Cataloging-in-Publication Data**

Bochin, Hal.
    Richard Nixon : rhetorical strategist / Hal W. Bochin ; foreword
by Halford R. Ryan.
        p.   cm. — (Great American orators, ISSN 0898-8277 ; no. 6)
    Includes bibliographical references.
    ISBN 0-313-26108-3 (lib. bdg. : alk. paper)
    1. Nixon, Richard M. (Richard Milhous), 1913-  —Oratory.
2. Political oratory—Political aspects—United States—
History—20th century.   3. United States—Politics and
government—1945-  I. Title.  II. Series.
E856.B58   1990
973.924'092—dc20          89-17193

British Library Cataloguing in Publication Data is available.

Library of Congress Catalog Card Number: 89-17193
ISBN: 0-313-26108-3
ISSN: 0898-8277

First published in 1990

Greenwood Press, Inc.
88 Post Road West, Westport, Connecticut 06881

Printed in the United States of America

∞

The paper used in this book complies with the
Permanent Paper Standard issued by the National
Information Standards Organization (Z39.48-1984).

10 9 8 7 6 5 4 3 2 1

# Contents

# Series Foreword

The idea for a series of books on great American orators grew out of
the recognition that there is a paucity of book-length studies on
individual orators and their speeches. Apart from a few notable
exceptions, the study of American public address has been pursued
in scores of articles published in professional journals. As helpful as
these studies have been, none has or can provide a complete analysis
of a speaker's rhetoric. Book-length studies, such as those in this
series, will help fill the void that has existed in the study of American
public address and its related disciplines of politics and history,
theology and sociology, communication and law. In a book, the critic
can explicate a broader range of a speaker's persuasive discourse
than reasonably could be treated in an article. The comprehensive
research and sustained reflection that books require will undoubtedly
yield many original and enduring insights concerning the nation's
most important voices.

Public address has been a fertile ground for scholarly
investigation. No matter how insightful their intellectual forebears,
each generation of scholars must reexamine its universe of
discourse, while expanding the compass of its researches and
redefining its purpose and methods. To avoid intellectual torpor new
scholars cannot be content simply to see through the eyes of those who
have come before them. We hope that this series of books will
stimulate important new understandings of the nature of persuasive
discourse and provide additional opportunities for scholarship in the
history and criticism of American public address.

This series examines the role of rhetoric in the United States.
American speakers shaped the destiny of the colonies, the young
republic, and the mature nation. During each stage of the
intellectual, political, and religious development of the United States,
great orators, standing at the rostrum, on the stump, and in the
pulpit, used words and gestures to influence their audiences.
Usually striving for the noble, sometimes achieving the base, they

urged their fellow citizens toward a more perfect Union. The books in this series chronicle and explain he accomplishments of representative American leaders as orators.

A series of book-length studies on American persuaders honors the role men and women have played in U.S. history. Previously, if one desired to assess the impact of a speaker or a speech upon history, the path was, at best, not well marked and, at worst, littered with obstacles. To be sure, one might turn to biographies and general histories to learn about an orator, but for the public address scholar these sources often prove unhelpful. Rhetorical topics, such as speech invention, style, delivery, organizational strategies, and persuasive effect, are often treated in passing, if mentioned at all. Authoritative speech texts are often difficult to locate and the problem of textual accuracy is frequently encountered. This is especially true for those figures who spoke one or two hundred years ago, or for those whose persuasive role, though significant, was secondary to other leading lights of the age.

Each book in this series is organized to meet the needs of scholars and students of the history and criticism of American public address. Part I is a critical analysis of the orator and his or her speeches. Within the format of a case study, one may expect considerable latitude. For instance, in a given chapter an author might explicate a single speech or a group of related speeches, or examine orations that comprise a genre of rhetoric such as forensic speaking. But the critic's focus remains on the rhetorical considerations of speaker, speech, occasion, and effect. Part II contains the texts of the important addresses that are discussed in the critical analysis that precedes it. To the extent possible, each author has endeavored to collect authoritative speech texts, which have often been found through original research in collections of primary source material. In a few instances, because of the extreme length of a speech, texts have been edited, but the authors have been careful to delete material that is least important to the speech, and these deletions have been held to a minimum.

In each book there is a chronology of major speeches that serves more purposes than may be apparent at first. Pragmatically, it lists all of the orator's known speeches and addresses. Places and dates of the speeches are also listed, although this is information that is sometimes difficult to determine precisely. But in a wider sense, the chronology attests to the scope of rhetoric in the United States. Certainly in quantity, if not always in quality, Americans are historically talkers and listeners.

Because of the disparate nature of the speakers examined in the series, there is some latitude in the nature of the bibliographical materials that have been included in each book. But in every instance, authors have carefully described original historical materials and collections and gathered critical studies, biographies and autobiographies, and a variety of secondary sources that bear on the speaker and the oratory. By combining in each book bibliographical materials, speech texts, and critical chapters, this series notes that text and research sources are interwoven in the act of rhetorical criticism.

May the books in this series serve to memorialize the nation's greatest orators.

Bernard K. Duffy
Halford R. Ryan

# Foreword

For a quarter of a century, amidst some of the most trying times that confronted the American *polis*: the Cold War of the 1950s, the Vietnam War of the 1960s, and Watergate and the specter of presidential impeachment in the 1970s, he was at the eye of the maelstrom of political rhetoric, and in the end, like Herman Melville's Captain Ahab in *Moby Dick*, was consumed in the vortex of his own creation. What propelled him from the House to the Senate to the White House, and what ultimately contributed to his political demise, was the effect that obtained when Richard Milhous Nixon addressed the American people.

What to write about Nixon's public persuasions has been a perennial problem for rhetoric critics. The epicenter of the controversy is, of course, his famous My Side of the Story speech, or the so-called "Checkers" speech, in 1952. The hand wringers perceived in the president's later speeches to the silent majority on Vietnam and Watergate many of his successful appeals that they so hated in his 1952 apologia. The ethicists bemoaned what they believed was his disingenuousness that was first practiced in his Congressional campaigns and then polished in the Checkers speech. Logicians lamented his questionable rhetorical techniques (among the ones Nixon perfected were faulty disjunctive syllogisms, *argumentum ad personam, tu quoque,* and turning the tables) that seemed to characterize his public persuasions. And forensic coaches, eager to place before novice debaters successful speakers they could emulate, were never quite sure whether to mention Nixon as an appropriate role model.

What has galled Nixon's rhetorical critics is that he always did whatever it took to win. Rarely bothering to criticize the American people who voted Nixon into his varied political offices, commentators have been content to condemn his communications. It would be more useful for the student of public discourse to understand the nature of Richard Nixon's rhetoric, to comprehend his techniques, and to appreciate how public persuasions functioned in his era and in his hands from the 1950s to the 1970s.   Professor Hal Bochin accomplishes this needed explication admirably well.

From Jerry Voorhis's Congressional upset and Helen Douglas's senatorial campaign to Checkers, the Kennedy debates, Vietnam, and finally Watergate, professor Bochin has parsed Nixon's significant speeches and has painted a compelling portraiture of a most skilled public persuader.   Those readers expecting a lamentation on the state of political rhetoric during the Nixon years might be frustrated, but Bochin is appropriately more interested in explaining the efficacy of Nixon's logical, emotional, and ethical appeals than in blaming the persuader for the state of the American audience.   Those desiring moralizing will be disappointed, but they should be solaced by Bochin's straightforward detailing of Nixon's rhetorical strategies.   And those wanting to see in the practice of debating all the evils of intercollegiate, congressional, and presidential debates should take pause.   For, as Bochin illustrates (and as any good debater knows), hard work at research, the development and briefing of arguments and refutations, and a studied delivery are traits that Nixon mastered.   But what can be said about Nixon's audience?

When returning Roman generals paraded through the streets of Rome as conquering heroes, a slave was placed behind them to serve two functions: one was to hold the olive crown of victory over their heads and the other was to whisper in their ears: "Thou art only mortal."   It would be best if the reader kept that image in mind when reading Bochin's treatment of Nixon's oratory.   Until Watergate, Nixon wore the crown of rhetorical victory, except for his encounter with the knight from Camelot, and Bochin amply demonstrates why. Yet even Richard Nixon was a mortal when he devolved to the exigency beyond which rhetoric would not save him.   For like the Roman applause for military conquests that inadvertently helped to sap the strength of the empire, the votes the American people gave Nixon eventually enabled him to try their Constitution they elected him to preserve protect, and defend.   It is easy to cast Nixon and his rhetoric as a scapegoat, a cheap shot that is beneath Bochin.   As an audience of twenty-five years of Nixonian rhetoric, did not the American people harvest what they had helped seed and nurture?

Halford R. Ryan

# Preface

This volume examines the combination of personal characteristics and artistic choices that made Richard M. Nixon a successful, albeit highly controversial, public speaker from 1946 to the present. Based on Nixon's own writings, primary materials found in special collections, a number of rhetorical studies by communication scholars, and historical case studies, the most complete picture yet of Nixon as rhetorical strategist emerges.

The study of Nixon's rhetoric is the study of many important issues, from the threat of communism to Vietnam to Watergate, confronting America from 1946 to 1974. It is also the study of the man himself because Nixon took an active role in the composition of all his important addresses. In the repetition of certain phrases in a number of speeches (e.g. "Let me be perfectly clear") and, especially, in his impromptu farewell to the White House staff in 1974, Nixon revealed the inner man. His two greatest oratorical successes, the 1952 Checkers speech, which saved his position on the Eisenhower ticket, and the 1969 Vietnam speech, which rallied the "silent majority" to his Vietnamization plan, were entirely his own efforts and reflected his background and goals.

As a Republican campaigner, Nixon often had to appeal to independent and Democratic voters to win. He adopted a simple, but ambiguous, style and captured seven out of nine major elections. He also mastered a number of rhetorical techniques that ranged from brilliant to dishonest. Although Nixon's early political campaigns have received little attention from communication scholars, the debating techniques Nixon used in his campaigns against Jerry Voorhis in 1946 and Helen Gahagan Douglas in 1950 foreshadowed his later political activities. Nixon's awareness of audiences, his willingness to take risks, his determination to control the media and to surprise his opposition, are additional characteristics of a man who, for almost thirty years, strode the highest mountain tops and the deepest valleys of American political life. That both the highs and the lows of his career were marked by public addresses makes the rhetoric of Richard Nixon a worthy subject for anyone interested in political science, history, or persuasion.

This book could not have been completed without institutional support and the cooperation of a number of individuals.  I wish to thank the California State University, Fresno, for two major research grants and the staff of the Henry Madden Library for their invaluable assistance.  I am especially grateful for the help of Fred Klose of the National Archives (Laguna Niguel, California), who led me through the Nixon Pre-presidential Papers.  I also want to acknowledge the efforts of the entire Archives staff, who went out of their way to make my stay a pleasant one.  Shirley Stephenson gratiously helped me locate materials at the Nixon Oral History Collection at the California State University, Fullerton, and the librarians at Whittier College were most helpful.

On a more personal level, I want to acknowledge the contributions of Mike Weatherson, who read the entire manuscript and helped me clarify a number of points, Gene Anderson, who introduced me to the Macintosh computer, Carlos Aleman and Scott Vick, who assisted with a number of research tasks, and Halford Ryan, who offered encouragement and wielded an editorial pen that improved the readability of my drafts considerably.  Finally, I would like to express my thanks to my wife, Janet.  Without her typing skills, this book might still be in manuscript form.

# I
# CRITICAL ANALYSIS

# Introduction

Richard Nixon debated for the first time in the seventh grade at East Whittier elementary school.  Defending the affirmative side of the resolution, "It is more economical to rent a house than to own one," Nixon won the debate and took the first step in a public speaking career that would last more than fifty years.  Although much has been written about Nixon the man and the politician, comparatively little attention has been paid to Nixon the public speaker.  This is unfortunate, because it was through public speaking that Nixon, an introverted, private person, first captured public attention, won a seat in the House of Representatives, advanced to the Senate, held on to his vice-presidential nomination, lost and won the presidency, and eventually molded a constituency that carried him to one of the most overwhelming presidential election victories in our history.  It was also through public speaking that President Nixon attempted to defend himself against charges related to the Watergate incident and sought to save himself from impeachment.  When his rhetorical efforts failed to rouse popular support, he had no choice but to resign.[1]

A close analysis of his speaking reveals that Nixon, driven by a strong competitive nature, developed a repertoire of rhetorical strategies that can be traced from his earliest speaking efforts in elementary school to his farewell speech to the staff of the White House in 1974.  Exhaustive preparation, the willingness to support either side of an issue, the use of surprise, the mastery of emotional responses, and the recognition of the value of feedback, all have their roots in Nixon's background and education.

Born in Yorba Linda, California, on January 9, 1913, to Francis (Frank) and Hannah Nixon, Richard was the second eldest of five sons, two of whom died before he graduated from college.  When Richard was nine, the family moved to Whittier where his father opened a gas station that he soon expanded by adding a grocery store in which the entire family worked.  While he was still very young, Nixon's interest in debate was stimulated by listening to his progressive Republican father who loved to argue "with anyone about anything." A friend of Hannah recalled, "You weren't right, he was right." Some customers at the Nixon store enjoyed trading barbs with Frank, but a number of others, especially those with Democratic leanings, preferred to avoid him, hoping that Hannah or one of the boys would wait on them.[2]

A "very competitive man," Frank instilled his love of argument in his sons. Richard, especially, followed his father's example. A friend from his childhood reported: "No matter what was discussed, he would take the opposite side just for the sake of argument. I remember once we went on a picnic in the mountains. We argued all the way back about which would be more useful to take with you into the wilds—a goat or a mule. Dick said a goat, and then argued in favor of a mule." His cousin Merle West refused to become involved when Richard wanted to debate whether it was better to marry a rich girl or a smart one.[3]

Although Frank was known as a strict disciplinarian, Richard soon discovered that he could avoid his father's wrath by saying the right thing. He told one biographer that "when you got into mischief, you had to be pretty convincing to avoid punishment." Thus early in life Nixon learned to value a winning argument, one that would control the opinions and behavior of others. He would soon learn that skill in arguing could gain their admiration and respect.[4]

The first time he participated in an academic debate, Nixon had to prove that there were greater financial benefits in renting a home than in owning one. His extensive preparation foreshadowed the way he would prepare for important speeches throughout his career. Although his father believed strongly in home ownership, Nixon worked with him to develop the best possible case for renting. His preparation paid off and, with the financial data Frank provided, Richard won the debate. A short time later when seventh grade teacher Louis Cox assigned Nixon and a colleague to argue the affirmative side of the proposition, "Resolved: that insects are more beneficial than harmful," Nixon spent many hours in the library reading about insects. He also consulted with his uncle, Ernest, a horticulturist, to learn the effect of insects on fruits and vegetables. Once again extensive preparation resulted in victory.[5]

In high school, Nixon took classes in public speaking, participated in interscholastic debates, and entered public speaking contests. At Fullerton High School, where he spent his freshman and sophomore years, he earned the respect of his peers for his debating skill. As a sophomore, he won the right to represent his school in the Constitutional Oratory Contest sponsored by the Los Angeles *Times*, an accomplishment he repeated when he transferred to Whittier High School for his junior year. Nixon's forensics coach at Fullerton, Lynn Sheller, remembered Richard for "the diligence with which he worked on his speech, particularly on inflections and gestures." Sheller also recalled Nixon's "strong determination, a willingness to work, and a fiercely competitive spirit that would never say die."

Hard work rather than natural ability made Nixon a winning speaker, and he was frequently called upon to repeat his award-winning efforts at student assemblies. A classmate noted that even as a high school student, Nixon mastered the difficult task of maintaining the attention of his fellow students forced to attend such convocations.[6]

At Whittier Union High School, Nixon continued his extracurricular speaking. When he was not participating in a contest himself, he would drive into Fullerton or Los Angeles to listen to other students compete and to think of responses to the arguments that he heard. Appearing before student assemblies and at Parent Teacher Association functions, Nixon impressed his listeners with his ability to speak impromptu. When he was given a topic and required to speak on it with little preparation, he acquitted himself admirably. Nixon's speaking ability won him the respect of many students though he lost the election for senior class president by a narrow margin to a football and basketball player supported by the athletic teams.[7]

The speeches Nixon wrote to win the local level of the Constitutional Oratory Contest, sponsored by the Los Angeles *Times* in 1929 and 1930, were printed in the *Cardinal and White*, the Whittier High School yearbook. As a sixteen-year-old, Nixon spoke on "Our Privileges Under the Constitution." In it he expressed concern that rights guaranteed by the Constitution could be misused: "How much ground do these privileges cover? There are some who use them as a cloak for covering libelous, indecent, and injurious statements against their fellowmen. Should the morals of this nation be offended and polluted in the name of freedom of speech or freedom of the press?" Nixon found the answer to his question in "laws which do not limit these privileges, but which provide that they may not be instrumental in destroying the Constitution which insures them. We must obey these laws for they have been passed for our welfare." Nixon's speech captured first place at both the local and district levels.[8]

The following year Nixon won the local contest again. This time he entitled his effort, "America's Progress—Its Dependence Upon the Constitution." At seventeen Nixon was already a "strict constructionist" and he warned his listeners: ". . . if the time should ever come when America will consider this document too obsolete to cope with changed ideals of government, then the time will have arrived when the American people as an individual nation must come back to normal and change their ideals to conform with those mighty principles set forth in our incomparable Constitution." But Nixon failed to win the district competition, finishing second at the contest held at Monrovia High School. He was consoled, however, by a $10 prize from his school and $20 from the Los Angeles *Times*.[9]

In another noteworthy public appearance, Nixon participated in a play put on by the Latin Club, taking the title role of Aeneas in Virgil's epic. Helen Letts, a classmate, was not surprised that Nixon tried the stage. She thought that he made a strong debater precisely because debating was "partly acting.  He could get worked up on a point in debating and sometimes give the appearance of anger, but it was all showmanship."   Nixon's interest in the stage extended throughout his educational career and into community little theater productions.   Nixon's debate coach at Whittier High School, Mrs. Clifford Vincent, marvelled at Nixon's ability to avoid answering difficult questions.[10]

Offered a tuition scholarship to Harvard for being selected Whittier's "best all-around student" by the local Harvard Club, Nixon had to decline because he knew he could not afford the cross-country transportation costs and the housing and other expenses associated with enrolling at the Ivy League school.  Instead he decided to attend a local Quaker institution, Whittier College, where he could commute to school and where he could continue his debating career.  Ambrose argued that "it was in his debate experience, more that the classroom or the student government that he got his real education."   Debate introduced Nixon to a number of important political questions. During his four years at Whittier, Nixon argued for and against propositions calling for free trade, centralized control of industry, cancellation of interallied debts, and substantial increases in the powers of the president.  In addition to increased knowledge about significant topics, his debating experience left Nixon with the belief that few important issues were black or white.  Debate was for him "a healthy antidote to certainty."   This attitude carried over into his political life and he could champion ideas that he had previously spoken against.[11]

Nixon's competitive instinct led him to develop debating tactics that would promote success.  He learned early in his debating career that surprise could play an important role in winning.  Relying on extensive preparation to protect himself, he sought out those arguments that his opponent would be unprepared for.   Even in demonstration debates with his own teammates Nixon would argue the unexpected in order to win.   His colleague Kenneth Ball remembered that "he would come out suddenly, extemporaneously with some ideas I had not heard of before when we were going over the material for the debate."   He would "beat us down," William Hornaday, another teammate, recalled, "He would always come up with something."[12]

Another technique Nixon relied on to win was the use of emotion.  Anger and nervousness could be controlled and they could aid rather than hinder the speaker.  He told classmate Louis Valla, "To be a good debater, you've got to be able to get mad on your feet without losing your head."   To Talbert Moorehead, who was uneasy about having to speak in front of a large audience, he counseled, "You have to find one issue and concentrate on *it*—forget yourself completely— think only of that issue."  If the observations of Lois Elliott were accurate, however, Nixon's desire to win was so great that he once used an unethical tactic in a debate round.  She reported: "I was editor on the school paper covering the debate . . . in the spring of 1933.  I sat in the gallery and I saw when Nixon spoke in his rebuttal that he quoted from a blank paper. I told it later to my roommate; it was against all regulations, and very cunning. I remember it well."[13]

During the time Nixon debated for Whittier College, the forensics team competed at various campuses throughout the western United States. In his sophomore year, for example, Richard's father allowed the team to use his "eight-year-old, seven passenger Packard" for a 3,500 mile trip to debate a number of opponents in the Pacific Northwest. Not only did Nixon and his colleague, Joe Sweeney, win all of their dual-decision debates, Nixon made his first visit to a speakeasy (in San Francisco) and ordered his first alcoholic drink (a Tom Collins). That spring the team captured its league title and the Allison Speech Trophy by winning seven out of ten debates. Nixon and his partner contributed an important victory to the cause by defeating the University of Redlands team of Frost and Dean, the national debate champions. The following year the team had considerably less success. In a trip marked by a snowstorm that left them stranded for four days in Cameron, Arizona, Nixon and his colleague managed a single victory while losing to the University of Nevada, Brigham Young University, and Phoenix Junior College.[14]

An important characteristic of Nixon's speaking that first showed itself during Nixon's collegiate debating career was the importance he attached to immediate feedback. Once after losing a close debate he thought he should have won, an angry Nixon was tempted to leave the room quickly. Instead he went up to the judge and asked him to explain what he and his colleague had done wrong. The judge reported that the issues had been unclear and that the team needed to better define their position. In the next debate Nixon and his colleague "did it right." Occasionally Nixon's father drove him to his debates and sat in the back of the room. Nixon reported that on the way home, his father would "dissect and analyze each of the arguments." In his early political campaigns, Nixon relied on his wife Pat for such feedback. After every important speech he wanted to know how he had done and what he could do to improve his performance. Nixon also offered immediate feedback to his colleagues. He would pass his partner a note saying, "Pour it on at this point" or "Save your ammunition" or "Play to the judges, they're the ones who decide."[15]

Nixon's success in oratory contests continued. He entered the southern California section of the *Reader's Digest* Extemporaneous Speaking Contest in which the contestants had to speak with little immediate preparation on a topic chosen from articles that had appeared in previous months' issues of the *Digest*. Nixon was given the topic "Youth of 1933" and, according to C. Richard Gardner, he won "hands down."[16]

Nixon also spoke to a number of audiences in the community. He talked to high school students and to civic organizations about the benefits of a higher education at Whittier. While he was president of the student body during his senior year, he spoke so often that the

*Quaker Campus* offered its congratulations: "Dick spends half his life speaking to various organizations on behalf of the school; let's give him a hand."[17]

Nixon's most important speaking assignment while he was in college was a substantive rather than an educational one. As part of his campaign for student body president, Nixon promised on-campus dances, an activity supported by the students but frowned upon by many conservative Quakers in the Whittier community. Nixon's opponent in the election reported that he "knew damn well I didn't have a Chinaman's chance. It was a silver-tongued orator up against a babbling idiot. Even if he didn't say anything, it sounded good." Following his victory in the election Nixon went to the college president with his request on behalf of the students, but it was denied. In spite of the fact that he himself did not like to dance and that he did it poorly, Nixon appealed the president's decision to the board of trustees. Using the argument that since the students were going to dance anyway, it was better that they do it on campus instead of in some sleazy dance hall in Los Angeles, Nixon won approval for his proposal and additional respect from his peers.[18]

Although Nixon learned a great deal at the speaker's rostrum, he learned the important lesson of not giving up in adversity while sitting on the bench for four years with the Whittier College football team. Through football Nixon met Coach Wallace "Chief" Newman, a man Nixon admired more than any man he had ever known, with the exception of his father. "Show me a good loser," Newman once said, "and I'll show you a loser." Nixon attributed to Newman his own "competitive spirit and the determination to come back after you have been knocked down or after you lose." This determination asserted itself throughout Nixon's political career.[19]

When Nixon graduated from Whittier he ranked second in his class and he eagerly accepted a scholarship to Duke University Law School. He graduated from Duke three years later, ranked third in his class, passed the California bar examination on his first try, and was admitted to the bar in November 1937. He joined a law firm in Whittier where in 1938, while performing in a little theater production, he met Thelma "Pat" Ryan whom he married in June 1940. Shortly before the outbreak of World War II, Nixon accepted a job in Washington working for the Office of Price Administration, but he found the work unsatisfying. In 1942 he applied for a naval commission and began training at Quonset, Rhode Island. Sent to the South Pacific in 1943, he opened "Nick's Snack Shack" where transit crews could obtain free hamburgers while their aircraft were being unloaded and he became known for his prowess at the nightly poker game. In the fall of 1944 he returned to San Francisco and then to Washington as a lieutenant commander on the Navy's legal staff.[20]

Nixon's introduction to political life came in 1946 when he was selected by a committee of one hundred Republicans to contest the congressional election in California's Twelfth District, which included Whittier. His opponent, Jerry Voorhis, was a popular five-term incumbent and Nixon was a decided underdog until the Independent Voters of South Pasadena invited the candidates to make a joint appearance. Nixon immediately put Voorhis on the defensive about his alleged endorsement by political action committees dominated by communists and kept him there through a series of four more debates that attracted large and enthusiastic audiences. The Nixon-Voorhis debates are the subject of Chapter 1.

Reelected to Congress in 1948, Nixon gained much favorable publicity and an opportunity to run for the Senate through his work in exposing Alger Hiss, an eleven-year veteran of the State Department, as a perjurer. Nixon's opponent in the 1950 senatorial contest was Helen Gahagan Douglas, a liberal Democrat. Nixon argued that on more than 350 occasions Douglas had voted the same way as the only Communist member of the House, Vito Marcantonio of New York. In a campaign that is best remembered for the dirty tactics used by both sides, Nixon won an overwhelming victory. The rhetoric of the 1950 campaign is analyzed in Chapter 2.

In 1952, Nixon was selected by Dwight Eisenhower to be his running mate on the Republican ticket against Adlai Stevenson. When the New York *Post* revealed a "secret Nixon fund" supposedly donated by millionaires to buy Nixon's support, Nixon had to fight for his political life. He had to convince the public and especially Eisenhower that he was "clean as a hound's tooth." His successful defense, a radio and television address in which he detailed his financial situation from the time he entered politics and attacked the Democratic opposition at the same time, is recounted in Chapter 3.[21]

Elected as vice-president in 1952 and reelected in 1956, Nixon had little difficulty gaining the Republican nomination for president in 1960. He and his opponent, John F. Kennedy, appeared together in four nationally broadcast debates. Unfortunately for Nixon, in front of the largest television audience of the series (the first debate), he looked "like death warmed over" and his rhetoric was not persuasive. Kennedy, the unknown challenger, looked and sounded presidential. Some observers felt that the first debate cost Nixon a very close election, but a number of other factors worked against Nixon as well. An analysis of the Kennedy-Nixon debates is found in Chapter 4.[22]

Having lost the 1960 presidential election to Kennedy and the 1962 gubernatorial election in California to Pat Brown, Nixon's political career appeared to end with a press conference in which he announced that the media would not "have Nixon to kick around any more." Instead he campaigned for Republican candidates in 1964 and 1966 and was rewarded with the Republican nomination for president in 1968. In another close contest he defeated Hubert Humphrey and George Wallace. The most pressing problem facing President Nixon was the same one that had forced his predecessor, Lyndon Johnson, to forgo seeking a second term—the war in Vietnam and the accompanying antiwar protest movement. On November 3, 1969, Nixon asked the "silent majority" to support his policy of Vietnamization of the war and, in large numbers, they did

so.   Not all of Nixon's speeches on Vietnam proved so successful.
Both the successes and failures of his Vietnam oratory are examined
in Chapter 5.[23]

In 1972, Nixon won reelection by an overwhelming majority over
George McGovern.   A "third-rate burglary" attempt at the Democratic national headquarters in the Watergate office building occurred during the election campaign but had little impact on the
electorate.   Nixon's role in the Watergate affair and the attempts to
cover up what had happened slowly came to light in 1973 and 1974
through the Senate's Watergate Investigation and the House Judiciary committee's impeachment hearings.   When the House committee indicted Nixon on three grounds—covering up the Watergate
burglary and related crimes, violating the constitutional rights of citizens, and refusing to obey the committee's subpoenas to produce
recordings of his conversations—Nixon was prepared to fight the in-
dictment on the floor of the House.   The revelation of yet another tape
recording of Nixon's conversations with his staff, however, un-
dermined Nixon's defense.   In it Nixon clearly called for a coverup
effort and he lost any hope of maintaining enough political support to
prevent impeachment by the full House and conviction by the Senate.
Nixon was forced to offer his resignation on August 8, 1974, in a
nationally televised address.   Why Nixon's rhetoric could not silence
the words of his taped conversations and an examination of his
farewell speeches to the nation and to his staff are the subjects of
Chapter 6.[24]

The complete texts of eight of Nixon's most significant speeches
are given in Collected Speeches.   They are followed by a chronological
listing of all of Nixon's important rhetorical efforts.     The
bibliography, which includes primary and secondary sources, offers
an annotated listing of all the published studies about Nixon as a
communicator, a list of important works in history and political
science, and a guide to libraries and special collections that contain
important materials on Nixon's rhetoric.

# 1
# The Nixon-Voorhis Debates: Learning How to Win

When Jerry Voorhis wrote to Richard Nixon that he hoped "that we can arrange to have some joint meetings where both of us can speak," the incumbent congressman had no idea what he was getting into. The election of 1946 in California's Twelfth District offered the first of the "rocking, socking" campaigns that Nixon would wage over the next twenty-six years. In his first attempt to gain political office, Nixon combined an aggressive style, selective use of evidence, and an ability to exploit popular issues with long hours and hard work to overwhelm his unsuspecting opponent who could only respond after the election, "This fellow has a silver tongue."[1]

In the fall of 1945, a story appeared on the front pages of most of the district's newspapers: local Republicans led by Roy Day, an advertising salesman for the Pomona *Progress Bulletin*, were searching for a candidate to oppose the incumbent Democrat who would be seeking his sixth term. The Committee of 100, composed of businessmen and women, farmers, fruit ranchers, and housewives, who feared the New Deal's continuing regulation of the economy and what they considered to be the increased coddling of powerful labor unions, had written an announcement in the form of a want ad seeking: "Any young man, resident of the District, preferably a veteran, fair education, no political strings or obligations, and possessed of a few ideas for the betterment of the country at large. . . ." Most of all the Committee of 100 wanted someone who could defeat Jerry Voorhis, who symbolized for them the New Deal restrictions they thought were limiting economic growth and turning the country to socialism.[2]

In five successive campaigns, Voorhis had proven himself a formidable foe. A Phi Beta Kappa graduate of Yale, he entered politics to find a forum for his somewhat idealistic views. He had always felt guilty that his wealthy father could afford for him what few fathers could provide for their children. Registering as a Socialist in the late 1920s, Voorhis supported Upton Sinclair's End Poverty in California campaign with enthusiasm; but with EPIC's defeat at the polls in 1934, he turned to Franklin Roosevelt for leadership. In 1936 he rode Roosevelt's coattails into the congressional office he held until challenged by Nixon. Voorhis had a reputation for acting on behalf of all his constituents regardless of their political persuasion. He remembered births and anniversaries with cards; he offered a weekly newspaper column from Washington and, in later years, he presented a weekly speech over local radio. In short, he kept his political fences in good repair. Many thought he was unbeatable.[3]

To challenge Voorhis, the committee's first choice was Walter Dexter, former president of Whittier College and then superintendent of public instruction for the state of California. Dexter, however, did not want to give up a secure post on the slim chance that he might defeat Voorhis. He preferred to stay in Sacramento. Herman Perry, Whittier branch manager of the Bank of America and an old friend of the Nixon family, thought of Richard, who had once approached him about seeking a place in the state legislature, as a possible candidate. He wrote Nixon, told him about the committee's work, and asked him if he would be interested in appearing before the committee to present his ideas on campaign issues.[4]

Pat and Richard Nixon considered the proposition for two days before deciding that a life in Washington was worth the risk. They had saved $10,000 toward the purchase of a house and they agreed to spend half of it, if necessary, on a political campaign. When Nixon called Perry to tell him their decision, he was surprised to learn that the committee could not offer the Republican nomination, only its support in achieving that goal. Nevertheless, Nixon agreed to meet with the committee and scarce plane tickets were supplied by a committee member to fly the Nixons to California.[5]

On November 2, 1945, Nixon appeared in uniform before the Committee of 100 at a dinner meeting at the William Penn Hotel in Whittier. The luck of the draw made him the last of six speakers seeking the committee's support. Recognizing the need to keep his remarks brief, Nixon said that he had noticed two lines of thought about America, "One advocated by the New Deal is government control in regulating our lives. The other calls for individual freedom and all that initiative can produce." Nixon supported the latter view and reported that, having talked to a number of veterans, he knew they would not be satisfied with a "dole or a government handout." They wanted respectable jobs in private industry or they wanted an opportunity to start their own businesses. Such sentiments expressed exactly the views of the committee as did Nixon's promise that if he were selected to be the nominee, he would put on an aggressive campaign on a platform of "practical liberalism." To Murray Chotiner, one of the committee members and destined to play a large role in Nixon's later career, Nixon "seemed intelligent, forceful, and with a capacity for growth." To Day, Nixon was "salable merchandise." The young Naval officer with the short, crisp answers was exactly the type of candidate Republicans could support and not just someone used to offer a protest vote against Voorhis.[6]

The Nixons returned to Baltimore where they soon heard from Day that it looked like Nixon would get the committee's endorsement in a "landslide." On November 28, seventy-seven members of the committee met and on the first ballot Nixon received 63 votes. By previous arrangement, a motion to make the choice unanimous passed. The next step would be for Nixon to win the Republican nomination, but with the Committee of 100 solidly behind him, Nixon would have no problem.[7]

Nixon immediately started to prepare for an election that was almost a year away. He made an appointment with House Republican leader Joseph Martin and received Martin's promise to do anything he could to ensure the election of a Republican in Nixon's district. Nixon studied the *Congressional Digest* and got a copy of Voorhis's voting record from the Republican national committee. By the time of his discharge from the Navy in January, 1946, Nixon reported, "I was confident that I knew Voorhis's record as well as he did himself. As it turned out, I knew it even better." While Nixon was still in Baltimore, a campaign committee met every Saturday afternoon to discuss strategy. One of their first decisions was to hire Chotiner as a consultant for $300 a month to write a weekly news release.[8]

Nixon returned to Whittier where he rented a small house next door to what proved to be a noisy mink ranch with a "terrible stench" and opened a storefront office in downtown Whittier. With little money for furniture, he relied on friends and family to provide used desks, tables, a throw rug, a couch, and a typewriter. When Pat arrived a few weeks later, she became the office staff, typing campaign literature, taking it to the printer, stuffing envelopes, or hand delivering the materials. Richard took to the luncheon circuit to earn some name recognition. Only in Whittier could he be said to be well known. Local religious, patriotic, and service clubs soon heard what became a standard speech. Nixon discussed his experiences in the Navy and the type of men he had known overseas, "mighty good kids," who could successfully adjust to peacetime if only the government would get out of their way and let them work at a decent job.[9]

Roy Day took Nixon under his wing and offered a number of sugges-tions to improve his image. First, the officer's uniform would have to go. The public respected veterans, but there had been a lot more enlisted men than officers and not all of them thought highly of the men who led them. A shortage of men's suits forced Nixon to take an ill-fitting grey one from Johnny Evans, a local haberdasher; but when a blue one in his size became available, Nixon quickly bought it and sold the grey. The money he received went for office stationery. When Nixon selected very loud ties to wear with his new suit, Day reminded him that he wanted voters to remember his ideas not his neckwear. Noting that Nixon seemed shy with women, Day advised him to look them straight in the eyes and to smile graciously.[10]

Nixon and Pat, now noticeably pregnant with Tricia, also hit the coffee klatch circuit. Both were uncomfortable at first, but Nixon soon discovered the technique of asking those in attendance what type of government they wanted, and then directing them to the ideas he was trying to support. Although he came to handle this type of situation well, Pat limited her speaking efforts to thanking volunteers for their efforts.[11]

On Lincoln's birthday, Nixon opened the formal campaign, promising that it would be a "rocking, socking" one. Stumping the district for as many as twenty hours a day, Nixon presented speeches, met people, drank coffee, and prepared leaflets. Attempting to appear well informed on the issues, he deliberately presented his speeches without notes. On February 21, Tricia was born and Nixon received welcome publicity. A photograph of the proud parents graced the district's papers and Nixon predicted that his daughter would eventually register and vote Republican.[12]

In 1946, California primaries allowed crossfiling so that the name of the Republican candidate appeared on the Democratic ballot, and Democrat Voorhis's name was on the Republican ballot. A young lawyer, William J. Kinnett, offered token opposition to both candidates. The incumbent Voorhis was so sure of retaining his party's nomination that he did not return to California for the primary election. In his absence, a friend, V. R. "Jack" Long, tried without success to drum up enthusiasm for the Democrat. Nixon, however, benefitted from an effective precinct organization that canvassed the vast district door to door. If a resident was not home, the volunteer would return four times before giving up. Less than a month after Tricia's birth, Pat was back in the office working on the campaign. Two incidents formed indelible impressions on her and changed forever the way she would feel about campaigning. On one occasion after she had spent the better part of a day typing and running off campaign literature, she discovered that there was no money for postage and broke into tears. Another time she found herself victimized by a smooth talking "volunteer" who instead of distributing newly printed pamphlets, destroyed a large number of them.[13]

During the primaries, Nixon's stock speech warned against federal control and called for making government more efficient. The Office of Price Administration (OPA), he claimed, was controlled by leftists and government bureaucrats who wanted to bankrupt segments of the economy in order to hasten socialization of these industries. For example, some rabbit growers in the Twelfth District were faced with bankruptcy because OPA ceiling prices on feed had gone up 50 percent during the war, but the ceiling price growers received for the rabbit had undergone little change. Chicken farmers faced the same problem. Nixon summarized his primary message: "If the people want bureaucratic control and domination with every phase of human activity regulated from Washington, they should vote to retain the present New Deal administration. If on the other hand the people want a change so that a man can call his life his own once more, then my election to Congress will help bring it about." He always played up the shortages of housing, automobiles, and other consumer goods and dramatized the plight of the newly returned veterans who deserved better.[14]

With the major candidates in both parties facing little opposition, voter turnout on June 4 was light. The results showed:

|          | Republican | Democrat |
|----------|------------|----------|
| Nixon    | 23,397     | 5,077    |
| Kinnett  | 1,532      | 1,200    |
| Voorhis  | 12,125     | 25,048   |

Nixon had won the Republican nomination, but it appeared that Voorhis still had the district's loyalty. Voorhis's total vote of 37,173 overwhelmed Nixon's 28,474. Nixon was disappointed until a Los Angeles *Times* reporter pointed out to him that in the previous primary Voorhis had obtained 60 percent of the votes cast, and this time he had less than 54 percent. A newly inspired Nixon wrote Day, "All we need is a win complex and we'll take him in November." He added that he wanted Day to tell all the campaign workers "that we used none of our big guns purposely (suggesting we really are holding back some stuff—as we are)."[15]

Day, however, feared he did not have the time to direct the fall campaign so he withdrew in favor of Harrison McCall, president of the Los Angeles Testing Laboratories. McCall agreed to take over for $500 a month that he passed on to his employer to compensate for his time away from work. McCall proved less forceful than Day, and Nixon soon took control of his own campaign. With the Congressional district divided into three assembly districts, a campaign coordinator was hired for each area. Roy Crocker was appointed finance chairman and Arthur Kruse, treasurer. With Day no longer in command, campaign headquarters was moved from Pomona to Whittier and Nixon was ready to show his "stuff."[16]

Voorhis's supposed endorsement by radical groups, his voting record, his ineffectiveness as a legislator, and the inability of the Democratic administration to deal with consumer shortages formed the bases of Nixon's assault on Voorhis. As early as April 23, the Committee of 100 had issued a statement that read: "Now that the Political Action Committee has publicly endorsed Jerry Voorhis for Congress, one of the real issues of the campaign is out in the open . . . The choice now is: Shall it be the people represented by Nixon, or the PAC by Voorhis?"[17]

The Political Action Committee of the CIO (CIO-PAC) and the National Citizens' Political Action Committee (NCPAC) were founded during World War II to support Franklin Roosevelt and the New Deal. Sidney Hillman, socialist president of the Amalgamated Clothing Workers, served as chair of both groups and they shared office space in New York City. The purpose of CIO-PAC was to organize the political and financial resources of the CIO in support of liberal candidates. Union leaders dominated the national board that encouraged the formation of associate groups at the local level. Consisting primarily of literary, academic, and entertainment figures, NCPAC was open to all segments of society. Endorsement of candidates was done on the local level. It should be noted that within CIO-PAC there was a bitter fight for control between communist sympathizers and liberal members. In 1944, Voorhis had received the CIO-PAC's endorsement but it was denied him in 1946 because Voorhis had been highly critical of Russian moves in eastern Europe. In fact, the communist press on the West Coast editorialized against Voorhis, calling him a "false liberal."[18]

On the other hand, members of the Southern California section of NCPAC favored an endorsement of Voorhis and issued a memorandum supporting him. Since the national board did not have to approve local endorsements, it can be said that Voorhis was endorsed by the NCPAC (at least the *Daily People's World* reported so and, as will be seen later, Voorhis himself thought so). Nixon professed to see no difference between the two groups and during the campaign referred simply to "the PAC endorsement," hoping no doubt that his listeners would supply CIO in front of it. In La Puenta on July 26, Nixon charged that Voorhis was endorsed by the PAC and allied with "the left wing group headed by Jimmy Roosevelt which has taken over the Democratic party organization in California." On August 29 in Whittier he claimed: "There are no strings attached to me. I have no support from any special interest or pressure group. I welcome the opposition of the PAC with its communist principles and its huge slush fund." Note that this description is not appropriate for NCPAC, the group supporting Voorhis, and he never had the benefit of any "slush fund."[19]

When Voorhis finally returned to California in September, he issued a press release and bought paid advertising denying that he had a PAC endorsement. Having been warned by friendly editors what Voorhis was going to do, McCall purchased space next to Voorhis's ad to run one of his own, promising to provide proof that Voorhis had been endorsed by the PAC. The opportunity to do so was soon at hand.[20]

The Independent Voters of South Pasadena, a liberal group in a conservative community, wanted to smoke out an incumbent assemblyman and decided to hold a forum to which all the candidates running for major offices would be invited. The assemblyman they hoped to confront refused to appear, but Voorhis and Nixon were invited and they accepted. Each of the candidates would be given the opportunity to make a statement and to question his opponent. Some Nixon supporters were reluctant to see him take on the admittedly intelligent incumbent. After all, Voorhis had won his first Congressional race by challenging his opponent to debate. Nixon, however, was confident; but claiming that he had a previous engagement he had to attend, he was given permission to come late and to give the last speech. Voorhis's supporters thought he would "slaughter" his inexperienced opponent and they did not brief Voorhis for the encounter. Nixon, on the other hand, prepared carefully, going over with his advisors possible questions and how he could best answer them. His hard work paid off.[21]

Just as Voorhis reached the conclusion of his remarks, Nixon strode out on to the stage of the junior high school auditorium, greeted Voorhis, and delivered his stock campaign speech. He attacked the "mess" in Washington, the bureaucracy, the red tape. He received enthusiastic applause from the capacity crowd of fifteen hundred when he called for action against striking unions: "The time is at hand in this country when no labor leader and no management leader should have the power to deny the American people any of the necessities of life." Nixon demanded the abolition of the OPA and the end of price ceilings. Compared to Voorhis, Nixon was more direct, more conversational, and much more aggressive. Voorhis, however, thought he had the opportunity he needed to demand proof of Nixon's charge that he was a PAC endorsed candidate so during the question period he asked Nixon to substantiate his charge. To Voorhis's amazement, Nixon stood and, taking a piece of paper from his pocket, walked over to Voorhis and handed it to him. Here was the proof—a mimeographed bulletin in which a political committee of NCPAC recommended that Voorhis be endorsed. Voorhis was shocked. Glancing at the paper, he mumbled that this was apparently a National Citizen's committee document and not a CIO one. But once again Nixon was prepared. He read to the audience a list of members who belonged to committees or boards of both groups (omitting, of course, those who were members of only one) and took the position that an endorsement from one group (NCPAC) was the same as an endorsement from the other (CIO-PAC). Voorhis had a PAC endorsement.[22]

The debate for Voorhis was downhill the rest of the evening. Unused to answering questions within a short time limit, Voorhis often failed to get to the heart of a question before his time had expired. He sounded as though he would need an hour to answer any question fully. Nixon, on the other hand, was succinct, aggressive, and confident. He was able to condense every issue into a few telling phrases and he seemed prepared to answer questions on any subject.[23]

Following the first encounter, the Nixon forces were jubilant and Nixon immediately demanded a series of joint appearances. Voorhis, still not sure what he was in for, agreed. He was concerned that since Nixon seemed to be getting all the newspaper support in the district he needed a way to get his message to a considerable number of voters, and a series of debates might stir up enough public interest to allow him to do so. The formats for the debates varied, but they generally called for each speaker to have twenty minutes to present his position followed by an opportunity for the debaters to question each other and for the audience to ask questions, with each speaker concluding with a ten minute rebuttal.[24]

To get further mileage out of the PAC issue, Nixon supporters issued the following ad: "The truth comes out, Voorhis admits PAC Endorsement," asserting that during the Pasadena debate, Voorhis had admitted that he in fact had a PAC endorsement.  The May 31 issue of the *People's World* was offered as further support of Voorhis PAC endorsement.  The ad continued: "Forty bills backed by the political action committee have been considered by Congress during the last four years. Voorhis voted against the PAC only four times." Clearly, the reader was supposed to infer that Voorhis was supported by CIO-PAC, but the evidence pointed to a possible NCPAC endorsement and the article in the *People's World* listing endorsements by five liberal groups pointedly said of Voorhis, "No CIO endorsement." Nevertheless, in a speech to his supporters in mid-September, Nixon concluded: "Today the American people are faced with the choice of two philosophies of government.  One of these, supported by the radical PAC and its adherents, would deprive the people through regimentation; the other would return the government to the people under constitutional guarantees, and needless to say that is the philosophy for which I will fight with all my power in Congress."[25]

Voorhis continued his series of mistakes.  He wired the national headquarters of NCPAC and asked that any "qualified endorsement" of his candidacy be withdrawn.  He then sent copies of the wire to the district press.  Nixon supporters saw this as an admission that Voorhis had an endorsement that he had previously denied having. When Nixon once again held high his copy of the endorsement during the second debate, Voorhis could only reply that he could not be responsible for what other groups did.  Republicans added to Voorhis discomfort by giving away 40,000 plastic thimbles bearing the slogan "Vote for Nixon—Put the needle in the PAC."[26]

The Nixon-Voorhis debates captured the popular imagination. The two candidates were compared to Lincoln and Douglas and large crowds appeared at each location to cheer for their favorite.  A band would offer a stirring march as each of the debaters entered the crowded hall.  Voorhis got the large audiences he was hoping for, but they generally turned out to be highly partisan rather than voters in search of information.[27]

The second debate was held on September 20 in Patriotic Hall in Whittier.  The Whittier Ex-Servicemen's Association sponsored the event and restricted the audience to veterans.  Not surprisingly, housing for returning war veterans became one of the main issues. Voorhis supported limitations on commercial buildings so that the materials would be available for veterans' housing.  Nixon termed this class legislation and demanded a policy that would benefit all the people.  He proposed the removal of all restrictions on housing construction to give private enterprise an opportunity to produce the needed housing.  The topic of OPA restrictions allowed him to pitch his favorite issues: he decried the ceiling on beef prices, which he claimed was responsible for the meat shortages consumers were suffering, and he called for the elimination of the OPA.[28]

In discussing shortages, particularly meat shortages, Nixon put himself squarely on the side of the consumer and forced Voorhis to take responsibility for a situation over which he had little control. Earlier that day, the manager of the Southern California Meat Dealers Association had reported that twenty-five hundred of the four thousand retail meat markets in the Los Angeles area were closed for lack of meat. Open stores had only twenty percent of their normal supply. Butchers favoring the Nixon campaign put signs on their counters advising, "No meat today? Ask your Congressman." Nixon billboards across the district asked, "Where's the meat?"[29]

Nixon tried to identify with his audience as a fellow veteran, while Voorhis claimed their allegiance based on his service for them in Congress. He claimed that one-third of the bills he introduced were at the behest of the American Legion, the Veterans of Foreign Wars, or the Disabled American Veterans. When he deliberately tried to take advantage of any resentment enlisted men might have toward an officer by continually referring to his opponent as "Commander Nixon," Nixon drew the biggest laugh of the evening by patiently explaining to the nonveteran that in the Navy a lieutenant commander like himself was always addressed as "Mister."[30]

Jointly sponsored by the Claremont Kiwanis and the League of Women voters, the third debate was held on October 11 at Pomona College before a crowd of 1,850. Once again Nixon attacked the OPA and Voorhis had to defend controls. Nixon continued his attack on big labor: "I see no difference whatever between the dictatorial practices of labor and those of Hitler and Mussolini." Voorhis discussed monetary reform. He wanted to nationalize the federal reserve banks and he warned against the growth of business monopolies, two topics that generated little interest in the district and that many found difficult to understand. Republicans often referred to Voorhis's monetary proposals as "funny money."[31]

Between the third and fourth debates, Nixon initiated two issues that dominated the later discussions. He charged that Voorhis had voted against the PAC line only three times out of forty-six and that in the previous four years Congress had passed only one of the more than one hundred bills he had introduced. When during the fourth debate at the Monrovia High School, Voorhis demanded to know what votes Nixon was referring to, Nixon again was ready. This time he produced three lists of what he called CIO test votes and claimed that Voorhis nearly always followed the CIO line. Whether he had actually been endorsed by them was irrelevant. He deserved their support. The lists Nixon provided and the votes he seemingly criticized included such noncontroversial issues as Voorhis's support for the school lunch program, for aid to Great Britain, and his vote against the poll tax. It was not until Voorhis had spent a sleepless night reviewing the votes that he discovered that many of the them appeared on more than one of the lists. The total number of votes was 27 rather than 46. More importantly, the lists were not CIO test votes at all. They had been compiled by the *New Republic* staff and the

Union for Democratic action, a strongly anticommunist group.  The votes may have been acceptable to the PAC, but in many cases they were also acceptable to the majority of the House.  Voorhis prepared a detailed explanation of each of his votes, but even he doubted that many voters took the time to read it.[32]

Also in October Nixon asked the voters in newspaper advertisements, "*DO YOU* know that your present Congressman introduced 132 public bills in the last four years?  That *only one* of them was passed?   That the one bill adopted transferred activities concerning *rabbits* from one federal department [Department of the Interior] to another [Department of Agriculture]?  A vote for NIXON is a vote for A CHANGE."  To keep this issue before the voters, a Nixon supporter was planted in the Monrovia audience on October 23 to ask: "Mr. Voorhis, would you tell us how many of your public bills were enacted into law in the last four years?"  Instead of asking why the questioner limited himself to the war years and ignored his first six years in office when, for example, the Voorhis Act to register all agents of a foreign government was passed, Voorhis attempted a long explanation of how Congressmen get their names attached to bills.  He remarked candidly that it was pure accident that his name appeared on the rabbit bill at all.  He had merely offered an amendment to someone else's bill.  Aha, Nixon rejoined.  He does not even deserve credit for the one bill we granted to him.  When Voorhis claimed credit for a bill authorizing an "Employ the Handicapped Week," Nixon was ready.  Again he waved a document.  This one, he asserted, was a copy of the bill and and it was not a law at all, it was a joint resolution.  Since joint resolutions have the force of law, a fact that he was sure Nixon was aware of, Voorhis became incensed and stood up in his place while Nixon continued to speak.  This action drew the wrath of Nixon supporters and they booed loudly.  Voorhis never had an opportunity to explain the effect of a joint resolution.[33]

Also in the Monrovia debate, Nixon put himself on the popular side of an important issue.  There was little unionized activity in the district and Nixon spoke out strongly against strikes calling for labor and management to live up to their contracts.  Voorhis bore the burden of having voted against the Case bill designed to control labor activities.  More importantly, however, Voorhis had voted to include farm workers under the provisions of the National Labor Relations Act.  Most district farm and ranch owners did not want farm laborers to organize, and Nixon paraded Voorhis's record in front of every rural voter.  A group of two hundred farm owners formed their own committee to oppose Voorhis because of his stand on farm labor so Nixon was on solid ground in attacking Voorhis's labor record.[34]

The final debate attracted the largest crowd of the series.  Two thousand spectators filled the San Gabriel Civic Auditorium and more than two hundred stood outside to hear the debate over loudspeakers.  Roy Day later claimed that at the start, many listeners had refused to accept any Nixon literature, but at the end, most of the audience was on Nixon's side.  The Republican candidate received the most sustained applause of the night when he declared: "If we send back to Congress the same men who have failed this country ever since V-J Day, in matters of industrial relations, price controls, lack of production, and others of the present Administration's notable failures, we will only get another helping of the same." Again Nixon brought up the rabbit issue, gaining howls of laughter with his observation that "I assume you have to be a rabbit to have representation from the Twelfth District in Washington." In his own words, Voorhis "just came apart at the seems." Instead of discussing in depth the issue of his representation of the district, noting, for example, that he had recently been voted one of the hardest working Congressmen by the Washington press corps, he concentrated on attacking those "interests" that he claimed were holding back goods and materials to obtain a higher price for them. He called for rigorous enforcement of the antitrust laws and for government control of public utilities.[35]

In addition to the success Nixon was scoring on the debate platform, he had the overwhelming support of the district's newspapers. Bullock claimed that twenty-six of the thirty papers supported Nixon editorially, with three neutral and only one in Voorhis's camp. Editorial comments had a way of creeping into news stories as well. For example, the Monrovia *News-Post* ran this story on October 3: "Campaign statements that Jerry Voorhis, California's congressman, is not pro-Russian were placed in serious doubt today by a check of the official Congressional Record by the Republican National Committee. Sympathy for Russia and for left-wing programs in the United States is revealed in six votes by Voorhis, the record shows." The news article went on to describe the bills that included pro-lend lease votes that showed Voorhis's "decided bias for Russia."[36]

The week before the election, Herb Klein, editor of the Alhambra *Post-Advocate,* compared in his editorial column the voting records of Voorhis and Democratic Congressman, Vito Marcantonio, a communist sympathizer from New York. Earlier, Klein had written that Voorhis was not a communist, but in Klein's mind, because Voorhis had voted against bills that communists had opposed, Voorhis was certainly sympathetic to their cause. This same guilt by association tactic would be used by Nixon with even greater effectiveness in the Douglas campaign of 1950.[37]

To say that the Nixon campaign concentrated on "rabbits and radicals" or that "communism" was the biggest issue is to ignore the issue that most vitally affected the voters of the Twelfth District and that Nixon masterfully exploited. Shortages of meat and consumer goods confronted the voter every day and Nixon recognized this. In person, in a radio address, in press releases, and through billboards, he hammered away at the "bureaucratic restrictions" that "have created shortages and boosted prices." A Voorhis supporter was frustrated by another Nixon tactic that took advantage of the situation. She recalled: "[T]hat was when it was awfully hard to get electric utensils—electric irons, electric toasters—but if you answered your phone and said 'Nixon for Congress,' and it was the Republican headquarters calling, you could immediately come up there and take your choice and buy an electric toaster, an electric fan, they had their window just filled. Why, I would call my friends that were good Democrats and . . . they would pick up their phones and say 'Nixon for Congress' instead of saying hello. And people were doing that all over. . . . Well, you can get conditioned that way, and I guess that was their gimmick that absolutely worked." As Voorhis wrote immediately after the election: "The most important single factor in the campaign of 1946 was the difference in general attitude between the 'outs' and the 'ins.' Anyone seeking to unseat an incumbent needed only to point out all the things that had gone wrong and all the trouble of the war period and its aftermath."[38]

Republican billboards across the district asked: "Had enough? A vote for Nixon is a vote for a change." Voorhis had no billboards and fewer volunteer supporters to get out his message. Zealous Nixon campaign workers serving as community chest volunteers carried Nixon literature with them and distributed it to every house they visited. After it became clear that Nixon had a chance to defeat Voorhis, campaign contributions increased tremendously and by the end of the campaign Nixon had spent about $32,000 while Voorhis spent less than $10,000. Nevertheless, Republican leaders consistently badmouthed their chances before the election and even Voorhis felt he had a fair chance of winning up to election night.[39]

When the voters of the Twelfth District went to the polls on November 5, there was no doubt that they had had enough. Nixon received 65,586 votes to Voorhis's 49,994 and he became one of seven Republicans in California to unseat an incumbent Democrat that election. Nixon and his wife were thrilled: "Pat and I were happier on November 6, 1946, than we were ever to be again in my political career."[40]

Voorhis wrote Nixon on December 7, wishing him well. Pointedly he refrained from discussing the campaign for that would have "spoiled the letter." When he did not hear from Nixon he wondered if the letter had been received. He reported: "Then one day when I came back from lunch he was standing there in the outer office. He smiled and so did I. . . . We talked for more than an hour and parted, I hope and believe, as personal friends. Mr. Nixon will be a Republican congressman. He will, I imagine, be a conservative one. But I believe he will be a conscientious one."[41]

An unknown Naval officer, Richard Nixon returned to his home district and with hard work and thorough preparation defeated a five-term congressman. Using rhetorical stratergies that appealed to an audience tired of postwar shortages and kept his opponent constantly on the defensive, volunteer support, and media backing that he orchestrated from the start, Nixon had learned quickly how to win an election.

# 2
# The Douglas Campaign: Using the Communist Menace

When Roy Day advised Richard Nixon in the summer of 1949, "When your star is up, that's when you have to move," he was only confirming what Nixon had already decided.  The favorable publicity Nixon had received as a result of the Hiss case was something other congressmen could only dream of and there was only one place for a "comer" like Nixon to go—the United States Senate.  As luck would have it, the term of Democrat Sheridan Downey expired in 1950 and little opposition from fellow Republicans would be expected if the now nationally known Nixon decided to go after it.  Thus on November 3, 1949, Nixon announced his decision to seek the Republican nomination for the Senate.[1]

On the Democratic side, the stars were working for Nixon as well. Helen Gahagan Douglas, Broadway actress and operatic singer, wife of actor Melvyn Douglas and representative of California's Fourteenth District, decided to oppose Downey in the Democratic primary.  A New Deal Democrat, a member of the House Foreign Affairs Committee, and a close friend of Eleanor Roosevelt, Douglas believed that the most important single issue facing Californians was the protection of the 160-acre limitation on land qualified to receive cheap government-supplied irrigation water, a policy that Downey opposed. To protect the interest of the small farmer, Douglas announced that she would run against Downey, thus causing a bitter split in the Democratic ranks between conservatives who supported Downey and liberals who encouraged Douglas.[2]

Remembering what had worked in his campaign against Voorhis in 1946, Nixon decided to wage another "rocking, socking" campaign based on hard work, surprise, and keeping his opponent on the defensive.  As in his previous effort, his major public appeals contained half-truths about his opponent's voting record and innuendo about her patriotism.   To fully understand Nixon's rhetorical strategy during the senatorial contest of 1950, however, the Democratic primary must be considered first; for the Democrats provided the inspiration, the ammunition, and many of the tactics that Nixon would later apply to his own campaign.

A poll taken after a radio debate between Douglas and Downey over the 160-acre limitation showed Californians two to one in favor of Douglas's position.   Furthermore, Downey seemed vulnerable to Douglas's charges that he was controlled by the oil industry in California and that he had done little for most of the state's residents.  On March 22, 1950, Downey withdrew from the race claiming that his health prevented him from "waging a personal and militant campaign against the vicious and unethical propaganda" of his opponent. But Douglas had not wrapped up the Democratic nomination yet.[3]

With Downey out of the election, conservative Democrats sought a new champion, and they enlisted Manchester Boddy, publisher of the Los Angeles *Daily News* who had supported Douglas in her previous campaigns.  Boddy, however, wasted no time in attacking her: "There is indisputable evidence of a statewide conspiracy on the part of this small subversive clique of red hots to capture, through stealth and cunning, the nerve centers of our Democratic party."  Boddy added that Douglas had a consistent pattern of voting "with the notorious radical, Vito Marcantonio."  Downey, out of the race but still no fan of Douglas, declared in a statewide radio broadcast: "Mrs. Douglas does not have the fundamental ability and qualifications for a United States Senator. . . . She gave comfort to the Soviet tyranny by voting against aid to Greece and Turkey."  He also argued that Douglas should be defeated because she wanted to eliminate the House Un-American Activities Committee (HUAC).[4]

Douglas, who was commuting from Washington to campaign, suddenly found her congressional attendance record under attack. Using the campaign period for his analysis, Boddy claimed that Douglas had the worst attendance record of any member of the California delegation. Pamphlets by the hundreds of thousands were distributed throughout California picturing Douglas as a traitor to the Democratic party and a disloyal American.  On April 28, Boddy's *Daily News* referred to Douglas as "the pink lady" a tag that stuck with her throughout the primary and general elections.[5]

With Boddy accusing Douglas of treason to her party, questioning her patriotism, and comparing her voting record to that of the only member of Congress generally recognized as a communist, Nixon had no reason to say anything about Douglas in his own campaign.  In fact, Murray Chotiner, the Los Angeles attorney who had written press releases for Nixon's first campaign and who had been selected by Nixon as his campaign manager because of his winning efforts for William Knowland and Earl Warren, admitted that Nixon was deliberately silent about Douglas: "Quite frankly, we wanted her to be the Democratic nominee on the basis it would be easier to defeat her than a conservative Democrat.  So nothing was ever said pertaining to Helen Gahagan Douglas in the primary."[6]

Nixon, facing little opposition on the Republican side, nevertheless toured California in a secondhand Mercury station wagon with

"Nixon for Senate" signs attached to the sides. At busy street corners, in front of factories and businesses, the car was parked, a record played over a portable loud speaker system to attract a crowd, and then Nixon, standing on the tailgate, spoke for five or ten minutes and answered questions. Then it was on to the next stop where he repeated the procedure. Pat usually accompanied her husband and distributed campaign literature. Ambrose has identified five purposes of Nixon's primary campaign: (1) through more than six hundred speeches he made himself known to large numbers of voters; (2) he clearly identified himself as a supporter of nationalist China and blamed the loss of mainland China on the Truman Administration. He often called for the resignation of Secretary of State Dean Acheson; (3) he sought the labor vote, admitting that Taft-Hartley could use revision; (4) he supported California in the dispute with Arizona over Colorado River water. He accused Truman of discrimination against California; (5) he retained his base of support among small businessmen by advocating tax incentives for them and by defending the basic provisions of the Taft-Hartley Act. In short, he prepared himself for the fall campaign with his fingers crossed that he would get to oppose the liberal Douglas instead of the conservative Boddy.[7]

The results of the June 7 primary were all that Nixon could reasonably expect. Douglas received 890,000 votes to Boddy's 535,000 and became the Democratic nominee. Nixon swept to victory on the Republican ticket, and even picked up 22 percent of the Democratic votes (cross-filing was allowed).[8]

And Nixon's friendly star was still ascending. On June 25, 1950, communist North Korea invaded South Korea, and Nixon looked like a prophet. He had warned about communist aggression in the Far East, claiming that Truman was more concerned about Europe than he was about Asia. Although Nixon supported Truman's immediate response to the military challenge, he claimed that it was too little, too late. Secretary of State Dean Acheson had reportedly declared that Korea and Formosa were outside the American defense perimeter in Asia and now that the communists had responded, the partial mobilization favored by Truman was not enough. According to Nixon, only total mobilization could meet the worldwide communist threat.[9]

The communist attack on South Korea was merely the latest step in what Nixon saw as a series of foreign and domestic setbacks for the United States. First the red Chinese had taken over mainland China and forced Chiang Kai-shek and the remainder of his army to flee to Formosa. At the same time the American public learned that Russia had exploded an atomic bomb. On the domestic front, Alger Hiss was convicted of perjury and less than a month later Klaus Fuchs admitted that he had passed on atomic secrets to Russia. Nine Americans, including Julius and Ethel Rosenberg were charged with membership in an atomic spy ring. Senator Joseph McCarthy declared in a speech in Wheeling, West Virginia, that communists in the State Department were responsible for the loss of China and that he could name them. The FBI said there were twelve thousand dangerous communists at large in the United States, half of them citizens. J. Edgar Hoover knew somehow that there were exactly 6,977 communists in California, many of them in the movie industry. In short, domestic communists were everywhere and Nixon claimed that they were "well briefed on the finer points of how to sabotage our war efforts." Even President Truman asked the public to report any suspicious behavior of their friends and neighbors to the FBI.[10]

The United Nations forces that went to Korea to defend the south were defeated in most of the early battles. "They beat the hell out of us," one angry general reported. California's newspapers, like those across the country, listed the number of American casualties daily. It looked as though the democratic Korean government might be pushed into the sea, and Helen Douglas had long said that America could rely on the United Nations. Communism seemed to pose a clear and present danger to the United States, and Helen Douglas had been quoted as saying that "communism is no real threat to the institutions of this country."[11]

Into this picture of fear and confusion strode Richard Nixon, the man who had uncovered Alger Hiss, and Nixon's chief advisor, Murray Chotiner, whose first rule for success in a political campaign was "You must destroy your opponent." Inspired by the Boddy campaign, Nixon set out to destroy Helen Douglas by adopting and expanding the conservative Democrat's argument that Douglas did not appreciate the Communist challenge. His major weapon was a pink handout that accused Douglas of voting the same way as communist representative Vito Marcantonio 354 times, that she had opposed the creation of HUAC, and that she failed to recognize the communist menace abroad when she voted against aid to Greece and Turkey.[12]

Headlined "Douglas-Marcantonio Voting Record" the pink broadside claimed to be offered because, "Many persons have requested a comparison of the voting record of Congresswoman Helen Douglas and the notorious Communist party-liner Vito Marcantonio of New York." The sheet noted that since the time both members had entered the House, they had voted the same way 354 times. More importantly, according to the sheet, the two had voted the same way on 24 issues related to national security. Among these issues, they had both voted against the establishment of HUAC, against contempt proceedings for certain HUAC witnesses who refused to testify, against Greek-Turkish aid, against the Selective Service Act of 1948, and against bills requiring security checks of federal employees.

The leaflet was quick to point out that Nixon "has voted exactly opposite to the Douglas-Marcantonio axis." Also noted was the fact that the communist press had labeled Nixon "the man to beat" in 1950 while in 1947 both Douglas and Marcantonio had been labeled "Heroes of the 80th Congress." The last line of the pink sheet asked the rhetorical question, "Would California send Marcantonio to the United States Senate?"[13]

There was some truth in each of Nixon's charges, b
accusation omitted a number of relevant details. For ex
Douglas favored aid to Turkey if it were given through the U
Nations. Although she had voted against most of HUAC's conte
citations, she had supported those she thought justified. 1 e
cumulative effect of all the charges was an attack on Douglas's
patriotism and for Douglas to refute any specific charge was not
enough. The voter was left with the impression that she was soft on
communism. Nixon presented the truth, but not the whole truth.[14]

The leaflet and, especially, its pink color caused quite a stir. To
some the color implied that Douglas was, if not a communist, at least
a communist sympathizer; to others it was a reminder that Douglas
was a woman playing the man's game of politics. Another line
Nixon used throughout the campaign to remind his listeners that
Douglas was a woman who did not appreciate the communist menace was to describe her as "pink right down to her underwear."
Originally planning to issue 50,000 of the leaflets, when Chotiner
realized their value, he ordered 500,000 more and spread them across
the state. Hecklers attending Douglas's rallies waved them at her
and asked questions like "Why did you vote for this communist bill?"[15]

Throughout the campaign, Nixon used a guilt by association
technique to brand Douglas a communist sympathizer: "If she had
her way, the Communist conspiracy in the United States would never
have been exposed, and instead of being a convicted perjurer, Alger
Hiss would still be influencing the foreign policy of the United States."
Hiss, of course, had not had a policy making role in the State Department for some time before he ever ran into Nixon, but Nixon used the
line repeatedly to associate Douglas with Hiss. He also repeated the
statistics about Douglas and Marcantonio voting together to associate
her with communism.[16]

Like Jerry Voorhis in 1946, Douglas never knew what hit her.
She later wrote that Nixon's attacks "made me feel I was standing in
the path of tanks." Contrary to popular belief, however, she did not
decide to take the high road. She answered Nixon's charges with
personal attacks of her own. As early as the primary she referred to
Nixon as a "peewee" and to Nixon and McCarthy as "pipsqueeks." An
editorial writer for the *Independent Review* provided her with more
ammunition when he referred to the Republican candidate as "Tricky
Dick." Douglas used the appellation throughout the campaign.[17]

In a misguided attempt to show that Nixon also voted with
Marcantonio, Douglas issued her own leaflet charging that Nixon
had "voted with Representative Marcantonio against aid to Korea"
and that he and Marcantonio had acted together to cut aid to Europe
in half. Douglas's research, however, was faulty and Nixon had little
trouble disproving her charges. Nixon voted against a bill to send aid
to Korea, but only until aid to Formosa was added to it. Then he supported it. He had voted against a European aid bill, but only until it
was limited to a year instead of to two years. Naturally, the one year
bill he voted for carried half the appropriation of the two-year bill.

Nixon's record of support for European aid was so well known that Douglas's charge worked against her and helped him.[18]

Nevertheless, Douglas kept trying. She issued a yellow flyer: "THE BIG LIE. Hitler invented it. Stalin perfected it. Nixon uses it. YOU chose the Congressman the Kremlin loves!" She claimed that on five important votes Nixon and Marcantonio had voted together. If she could be accused of being soft on communism because of her votes, so too could Nixon. But Nixon had built a reputation as the leading opponent of communism in the House, and all the leaflets in the world were not about to change that reputation. Douglas could be hurt by association with Marcantonio, but Nixon could not. He had a ready answer for the particular votes Douglas was concerned about anyway.[19]

Unable to tar Nixon with the Communist brush, a few of Douglas's supporters tried to picture Nixon as a bigot. They asked questions like: "How can you be for Nixon? Don't you know he's anti-Semitic?" Or "Don't you know he's Jim Crow?" Nixon's stand against the poll tax and for fair employment practices were dismissed with, "He just did that to look good." Since Nixon was endorsed by the largest Negro newspaper in Los Angeles, the *Sentinel*, and since the Anti-Defamation League of B'nai B'rith issued a denial of any anti-Semitism, these charges carried little weight with the electorate but they added greatly to the bitterness of the campaign.[20]

While attempting to indict Nixon as a coconspirator with Marcantonio, Douglas also tried to level the charge of McCarthyism at him. She asked one reporter to investigate the story that McCarthy was campaigning across the state for Nixon but the Republican press was too embarrassed to print the story. He looked into the allegation, found that McCarthy had delivered only one speech, to the Order of the Purple Heart, and had left immediately. Twenty years later, Douglas was still convinced that Nixon had asked McCarthy to come to California to campaign for him.[21]

Nixon and Douglas did not debate, probably because Douglas had learned from a source she respected that Nixon was "the cleverest speaker" he had ever heard. The one time they both appeared on the same platform, before the Press Club of San Francisco, Nixon's effective use of surprise and humor carried the day. After Douglas had reported her difficulty in raising funds, Nixon sympathized with her, but added that he was making progress. Drawing a letter from his pocket, he read the following: "I am enclosing a small contribution to your campaign for the Senate. I only wish it could be ten times as much. Best wishes to you and Mrs. Nixon." The letter was signed, "Eleanor Roosevelt." Douglas admitted she was stunned and could not believe that Nixon would tell so obviously a lie about her friend Eleanor. As the commotion died down, Nixon continued: "I, too, was amazed with this contribution—amazed, that is, until I saw the postmark: "Oyster Bay, New York." The contribution came from the wife of Theodore Roosevelt, Jr., a Republican Eleanor Roosevelt.[22]

Another contribution that Nixon received might have surprised Douglas's supporters. In his memoirs Nixon reported that he was in his Washington office when he was approached by John F. Kennedy who gave him a check for $1000 from his father Joseph P. Kennedy. Kennedy said that he could not endorse Nixon publicly, but "It isn't going to break my heart if you can turn the Senate's loss into Hollywood's gain."[23]

Many groups tried to bring Nixon and Douglas together for a debate. The Fresno *Guide* reported: "More than a month ago, the [Junior Chamber of Commerce] invited senatorial [candidates] to debate the campaign issues at one of our meetings. Richard Nixon, the GOP nominee accepted by return mail. But today, three registered letters later, the Jaycees haven't heard a line from Mrs. Douglas." When the League of Women Voters offered to sponsor a joint appearance, Nixon refused, hoping that Douglas would accept. When she did, Nixon appeared at the meeting while she was speaking. Upon seeing Nixon, Douglas concluded her remarks quickly and left the auditorium, forcing Nixon to debate the issues without her.[24]

Both candidates had spokesmen to carry their messages to the public. The biggest names in the Truman administration appeared on Douglas's behalf. Averell Harriman, Vice-President Alban Barkley, Secretary of Labor Maurice Tobin, Attorney General Howard McGrath, Secretary of Agriculture Charles Brannan, and Eleanor Roosevelt (FDR's wife) toured the state for Douglas and for James Roosevelt who was running for governor against Earl Warren. Nixon referred to the many Democrats from outside the state as "carpetbaggers"; but not all of the outsiders proved helpful to Douglas. Under questioning by reporters, Democratic Senator Dennis Chavez of New Mexico, in Los Angeles to campaign for his party's ticket, called Nixon "a grand person—loyal, sincere, patriotic."[25]

"Democrats for Nixon" spoke on Nixon's behalf. Led by George Creel, Woodrow Wilson's propaganda director in World War I, the Democratic group echoed Nixon's attacks on Douglas. Ruth Turner, a former president of the League of Women Voters in San Francisco, issued an open letter to Douglas: "You, and you can't deny it, have earned the praise of Communist and pro-Communist newspapers for opposing the very things Nixon has stood for. And you have done this, as I and so many of my Democratic friends are aware, against the judgments and the votes of the majority of Democrats in Congress. I am a Democrat and I am an American, and I believe on the critical issues before the Congress where you went one way and the majority of Democrats and Mr. Nixon the other, they were right and you were wrong."[26]

Nixon had another influential ally. Archbishop J. Francis McIntyre of Los Angeles sent a letter to all the priests in his diocese asking that for four successive Sundays in October their sermons deal with the dangers of communism, especially the danger of communists in government. Douglas claimed that each priest received a list of candidates the Archbishop wanted to see defeated and that her name was at the top of the list.[27]

Nixon saved his best speech and his clearest statement of the issues for the conclusion of the campaign. A week before the November 7 election, he addressed a statewide radio audience. Although the "one issue that is more important than all the others combined" was how to deal with the world communist movement at home and abroad, Nixon never mentioned Douglas's voting record or her alleged alliance with Marcantonio. He called, as he had throughout the campaign, for the removal from office of those who were responsible for adopting "the policy of appeasing Communism in Asia."[28]

Nixon declared that the major difference between himself and Douglas was over one fundamental issue: "She says that the way to wealth and prosperity is for the government to take various institutions and enterprises in the nation and either operate them directly or control them from Washington. I say that we already have too much government ownership and control and the way to increase our productive capacity and our wealth is to adopt a program which will encourage to the fullest extent possible individual opportunity and cooperative effort."

Tidelands oil, farm policy, and small-business regulations exemplified the difference between the two candidates. Nixon favored state ownership of tidelands oil. He compared the "fine record" of Governor Warren's administration of the state's funds with the "wasteful spending of the federal government" and concluded that the people of California would get more for their money by leaving the income from the tidelands with the state than by turning it over to the federal government as Douglas was prepared to do. On farm legislation, Nixon opposed the Brannan plan favored by Douglas because he claimed it would result in higher prices to the consumer. He called for a policy of providing tax incentives to new businesses and for the elimination of red tape that, he claimed, was "virtually choking the small businessman to death."

Toward the end of his thirty-minute address, Nixon confronted the racial bias issue: "The men who fought and died in Korea were not selected on the basis of their race, their color, or their creed. Their only qualification was that they were Americans. It is for that reason that we must rededicate ourselves to the task of combatting at every point those elements in our nation who would create race, class, and religious hatred. . . . Every time there is an instance of discrimination in the United States, it gives the Communists a weapon which they can use against us."

After asking for votes not because "you are a member of my political party," but because you "believe as I believe," Nixon called for the election of individuals who have "proven by their records" that they would stand "against the forces which would weaken and destroy our democracy. . . ."

When Californians went to the polls on November 7, they cast 2,183,454 votes for Nixon and 1,502,507 for Douglas. It was the largest margin of victory received by any senator that election. As Nixon and his wife went from victory party to victory party that night, he always looked for a piano and played "Happy Days are Here Again" to the delight of his jubilant supporters.[29]

Earl Mazo wrote that "the autumn of 1950 was ready-made for mean electioneering." The economy was faltering and congressional investigations were depicting Washington as a haven for subversives. Fear was especially rampant in California—fear of communist military aggression and fear of communist subversion. Books on how to build a bomb shelter were popular as were attempts to guess how many casualties would result from the dropping of an atomic bomb on Los Angeles or San Francisco. But atomic attack was not the biggest fear. Governor Earl Warren, a moderate on most issues, warned that communist subversion was the threat to be feared the most. Communists lurked everywhere in California and even liberal Democrats took credit for the state's new antisabotage program. James Roosevelt, running against Warren, claimed its appropriation should have been higher.[30]

Richard Nixon's rhetorical strategy was to exaggerate the communist menace and to offer himself as the best solution to the problem of subversion. He exploited voters' fears by declaring that Moscow-trained agents were being taught "how to contaminate food supplies, wreck trains, seize arsenals and cities, dismantle rifles and small artillery, sabotage defense plants, and deprive major industrial cities of lights, power, and gas." Carrying arguments against Douglas first heard in the Democratic primary to their extreme, he tied her to Hiss and to Marcantonio and made her a part of the conspiracy. He was careful, however, not to call her a communist. He simply put her voting record, or what he claimed was her record, before the public. As campaign manager Chotiner put it: "We only stated the facts. The interpretation of the facts was the prerogative of the electorate." Fearful California voters turned to Nixon and Democratic Senator Downey resigned his seat early so that Nixon could be appointed to fill his position and get a head start toward seniority. Nixon's lucky star was still ascending and he would spend only two years as California's junior senator.[31]

# 3
# The Fund Speech:
# The Best Defense
# is a Good Offense

> The broadcast will be a half-hour. In line with my conviction that the truth is the best answer, both to smear and to honest misunderstanding, I intend to lay before the American people all the facts concerning the fund which was used for political purposes, and in an unprecedented action, I am going to present to the American people my entire financial history from the time I entered political life.[1]

With these words, Richard Nixon made the first formal announcement of a speech to be delivered on September 23, 1952, which was to attract the largest radio and television audience to that time, greatly influence Nixon's career and the outcome of the 1952 presidential election, and play the central role in what Stewart Alsop has called "one of the most extraordinary episodes in American political history."[2]

This chapter will discuss the circumstances that called forth the fund speech, show how Nixon's background influenced what he said, evaluate the speech on both argumentative and narrative criteria, and examine the immediate and subsequent effects of the speech on the audience and on Nixon himself.

A Gallup poll taken before the presidential campaign of 1952 had begun in earnest reported that only 45 per cent of the electorate could name the Republican candidate for vice-president. Within a week of the beginning of his first whistle-stop tour, however, "Nixon became the most talked-about, most controversial, and, as it developed, the most politically fortunate vice-presidential candidate in history."[3]

The reason for the public's sudden awareness of the Republican vice-presidential candidate was the exposure of a political fund that collected and disbursed more than $18,000 between 1950 and 1952. The fund had been set up by Nixon's supporters in California after his election to the Senate in 1950.  Dana Smith, Nixon's financial chairman in the 1950 campaign, was trustee of the fund that was used to pay for Nixon's travel expenses between Washington and California, the printing and mailing of Nixon's speeches to his supporters, extra clerical help for the senator's correspondence, and for other partisan political purposes.  Although open solicitation for money was made to Republican groups in California, the fund was not well-known nationally and rumors about its purpose, unfavorable to Nixon, had first surfaced during the Republican convention in July.[4]

That some people were still interested in the fund became apparent on September 14, after Nixon had finished an appearance on the "Meet the Press" television program, when Peter Edson, a syndicated columnist, asked him about an alleged supplementary salary of $20,000 a year provided by two hundred supporters: "Without a moment's hesitation, he told me that the rumor as I had it was all wrong.  But there was a story there and it would be all right for me to use it."  Nixon suggested that Edson telephone Dana Smith in Pasadena, California, and get the details of the fund from him.  The next day, Smith reviewed the fund's history with Edson and later the same day with three other reporters including Leo Katcher of the New York *Post*.  Nixon wrote that when he was warned by some newspaper friends that a story about his fund was about to break, he assumed they were referring to Edson's story and that nothing unfavorable about the fund could be written.  He was very much mistaken.[5]

The New York *Post* of September 18, 1952, carried the headline "Secret Nixon Fund" and the accompanying story by Katcher was headed "Secret Rich Men's Trust Fund Keeps Nixon in Style Far Beyond His Salary."  The story began: "The existence of a 'millionaies' club' devoted exclusively to the financial support of Senator Nixon, GOP Vice-Presidential candidate, was revealed today.  So far Nixon has received $16,000 through a trust fund set up by the 'club' after his election to the Senate in November, 1950.  The total amount of the fund and how much still remains to be expended during the current year was not disclosed."[6]

A number of other papers printed Edson's column, but because it was written as a straight news story it lacked the speculative flamboyance that made the "exclusive" New York *Post* article seem more sensational.  The wire services relayed both stories across the country.[7]

One of the main issues Republicans of 1952 campaigned on was that they should be elected to clean up the "corruption in Washington."  Thus Democrats were quick to jump at an opportunity to point out that the Republican vice-presidential candidate's hands might not be clean. Democratic National Chairman Stephen Mitchell demanded in press interviews and in radio and television appearances that Eisenhower throw Nixon off the ticket or eat his fulsome observations on "public morals."[8]

With the Democrats pressing the attack, another factor contributed to Nixon's discomfort over the situation—his physical remoteness both from Eisenhower and from the main sources of attack on the East Coast. At the time the fund story broke, Nixon was on a campaign train in central California heading north for appearances in northern California and Oregon. Eisenhower's train was touring Iowa and Nebraska. Only during stops, when the candidates themselves were usually busy, could there be any contact between the two groups. Thus while Nixon was out "to meet the people" he was cut off from Eisenhower and the rest of the world. Furthermore, while Nixon assumed that Eisenhower would issue a statement defending him soon after the *Post* story broke on Thursday morning, Eisenhower said nothing about the situation until Friday. This delay helped spread rumors about the fund. Nixon discovered later that Eisenhower's strategists had not mentioned the fund stories to him until late Friday, after his major speeches, so they would not risk upsetting him.[9]

As Nixon's train pulled slowly northward, the stories about the fund began to hold implications of tax evasion, bribery, and graft; and at each stop more and more hecklers began to appear. Some carried signs such as "Pat, what are you going to do with the bribe money?" Friday afternoon, Eisenhower finally issued a statement that "the facts will show that Nixon would not compromise with what is right." He said that Nixon was "an honest man" and that he would put "all the facts before the people," but privately he sent word to Nixon that he "wanted to get to the bottom of this thing."[10]

Democrats everywhere, and even a few Republicans, joined in the attack. Saturday morning the New York *Herald Tribune*, an early supporter of Eisenhower and a paper that had been friendly to Nixon, suggested that Nixon make an offer of withdrawal from the ticket. Since Eisenhower was close to the *Tribune*'s publisher, Nixon felt the paper could well be speaking for Eisenhower. Less worrisome was the same advice from the Washington *Post* which supported Stevenson. But Nixon's discomfort continued to grow. Eisenhower invited reporters into his private train compartment for beer and off-the-record conversation. He had heard that a great majority of the reporters traveling with him felt he should dump Nixon, but he was not ready to do that: "I don't care if you fellows are forty to two. I am taking my time on this." Then he added in confidential words that soon flashed across the country, "Of what avail is it for us to carry on this crusade against this business of what has been going on in Washington if we, ourselves, aren't clean as a hound's tooth?"[11]

On Sunday, Harold Stassen, a longtime friend and supporter of Nixon, wired him that he thought that Nixon should withdraw in favor of Earl Warren. He even included the wording of the message he thought Nixon should send to Eisenhower. Advice was pouring in from all over the country to the Nixon and Eisenhower trains. For the most part the messages Nixon received were encouraging, but an unofficial count on the Eisenhower train showed that the messages were three to one in favor of dropping Nixon from the Republican ticket. Sunday afternoon Nixon heard from Thomas Dewey in New York. He had been in touch with the Eisenhower train and learned that most of Ike's advisors wanted Nixon to resign.  He suggested that Nixon go on television to explain the fund (a suggestion Chotiner had been pushing) and to ask the American people to tell him whether he should continue on the ticket or not.  Such a move would take Eisenhower off the hook and give Nixon a chance to tell his side of the story.[12]

At 10:05 p.m. Sunday, Nixon received a long-awaited telephone call from Eisenhower.  "I'm at your disposal," Nixon told him; but Eisenhower was unsure of what to do and unwilling to make a final decision about Nixon's future.  Even though Nixon reminded him that "a time comes in politics when you have to shit or get off the pot," Eisenhower would not be rushed into a decision about Nixon's status. He did, however, support Dewey's suggestion to use television to go to the people with the fund story.  He advised Nixon "to tell them everything there is to tell, everything you can remember since the day you entered public life.  Tell them about any money you have ever received."  This, Nixon decided to do.[13]

Arthur Summerfield, chair of the Republican National Committee, arranged a national hook-up of 64 NBC television stations, 194 CBS radio stations, and the entire 560 station Mutual Broadcasting System, at a cost of $75,000.  The time for the broadcast was chosen with an eye toward capturing the largest possible audience.  Monday night following "I Love Lucy" was considered but had to be rejected as too soon.  Tuesday night, September 23, following the "Milton Berle Show" was selected.  To further insure a large audience, Nixon refused to tell newspapermen what he was going to say.  Instead, he told them to watch the show.  Rumors about the fund, about Nixon's decision, and even about his physical condition were spread in the press and over the air waves.  At the direction of Paul Hoffman, chair of Citizens for Eisenhower, fifty lawyers from the Los Angeles law firm of Gibson, Dunn and Crutcher and a team of accountants from Price, Waterhouse, Inc. worked throughout the weekend investigating the fund.  Their findings, that everything had been legal and exactly as Smith had told the reporters earlier in the week, were presented to Summerfield in an eighteen-page single-spaced report on Monday and Nixon would quote directly from their report in his speech.[14]

Alsop wrote: "You can find in Nixon's background the genesis of much of the content of the famous speech," and this is true.  There are two elements in Nixon's background that especially deserve notice—his fighting spirit and his economic circumstances.[15]

Nixon has often said that "When somebody launches an attack, your instinct is to strike back."  When he was attacked because of the fund, he knew immediately that he had to counterattack: "You cannot win a battle in any arena of life merely by defending yourself."  It would have been completely against Nixon's nature for him to offer his resignation, as many were urging that he do, or even for him to be satisfied with a defense of his conduct.  Perhaps, as Alsop suggested, it is because Nixon is "Black Irish" (the Irish whose Iberian bloodlines are seen in their black hair and dark coloring, and who have the

reputation of being the most aggressive of all the Irish) that Nixon is a
fighter.  Nixon felt that his own "competitive characteristic" came
from his father.  Frank Nixon liked nothing better than an argument,
and his spirit was inherited by his sons.[16]

There are numerous instances of Nixon's competitive character
being displayed throughout his high school and college years.  One of
the best examples is his football career.  He sat on the bench at Whittier College for four years: "He was used chiefly as a kind of tireless,
indestructible, animated ninepin for the better players to knock
down."  But Nixon kept coming back for more.  "He sure had guts," a
fellow player recalled.[17]

A second element in Nixon's background that influenced what
he said was his family's financial situation.  Frank Nixon had limited
success as a wage earner.  After futile attempts at farming and at
growing lemons, he became the owner of a grocery store in Whittier.
His wife and five sons worked in the store and helped make it
profitable.  Richard's job was to visit the Los Angeles produce markets
every morning at 4 a.m., bring his purchases back to Whittier, and
clean and display them at the store before attending classes at
Whittier College.  At Duke University Law School he took a number of
odd jobs to stay solvent.  Under such conditions, Nixon learned the
value of a dollar and worked hard for what little money he had.[18]

Nixon was thirty-nine at the time of the fund speech.  He had
been in politics only six years.  He had come about as far in his chosen
career as a man his age could expect, when suddenly he found himself fighting for his political life.  As William Rogers said, "It was not
just that his integrity was challenged; it was the possible
consequences generally."[19]

Nixon wrote that the speech had to meet three
requirements:

> First, I must meet the immediate attack that was being
> made on me be explaining and defending the fund.
> Second, I must ward off future attacks along the same
> lines so that any further allegations that I had profited
> financially from my public service would fall on deaf
> ears.  Finally, I felt I had to launch a political
> counterattack to rally the millions of voters in my
> television audience to the support of the Eisenhower
> ticket.[20]

The first requirement Nixon mentioned had to be met not only
with the voting audience, but with Eisenhower as well.  He still had to
show Eisenhower he was "clean as a hound's tooth."  Thus Nixon
addressed two target audiences.  The first group consisted of
Eisenhower and about thirty of his top aides who were watching a
television in the offices of the manager of the Cleveland Public
Auditorium where Eisenhower was scheduled to address a crowd of
fifteen thousand immediately after the broadcast. This group had been

discussing Nixon's role on the Republican ticket for four days and they were almost unanimously agreed that Nixon should offer to resign. Less than an hour before the broadcast they had made their views known to Nixon through a telephone call from Dewey. Nixon was shocked when Dewey also suggested that he resign his seat in the Senate so that he could run for reelection and seek vindication at the polls. When Dewey asked what he could tell Eisenhower and his advisors that Nixon was going to do, Nixon responded that he did not have the slightest idea; if Eisenhower's strategists wanted to find out, they would have to listen to the broadcast.[21]

The second audience has been numbered at between 58 million and 60 million. Most were seated in groups of twos and threes in their own homes; some were crowded into bars and other public gathering places. The Republicans in the auditorium heard the broadcast over radio.[22]

The nature and source of the arguments used and the emotional language and tone with which they were delivered are the two most striking characteristics of the fund speech. Nixon usually took a week to write his major addresses, but he had less than three days to prepare for the most important speech of his career. In these circumstances it is not surprising that most of the speech is simply a rephrasing of arguments that he had used and found successful in quieting hecklers in California and Oregon.

It had been in Marysville, outside of Sacramento, shortly after the fund story had become public that Nixon had first said, "rather than charging [the American taxpayer] with the expenses of my office, which were in excess of the amounts which were allowed under law . . . what I did was have those expenses paid by the people back home." Of course none of the fund expenses could have been charged to the taxpayers. The report that Nixon had from Price, Waterhouse stated that all the expenses were partisan political ones, above the limit of Nixon's Senate allowance, and could not be paid by any public funds. The argument was specious, but it had drawn cheers for Nixon in California and he offered it again in the fund speech.[23]

In one of the first public statements Nixon issued about the fund he declared, "I might have put my wife on the federal payroll as did the Democratic nominee for Vice President . . . nor have I been accepting law fees on the side while serving as a member of the Congress." This shift of emphasis from his fund to his opponent's conduct is an attempt to meet an attack not with a defense, but with a counterattack. He offered it again in the national broadcast. It fits what has been written about Nixon's "competitive character" and reflects his ability to shift a discussion from the point at issue to another consideration. This had long been a favorite tactic of Nixon. As one of his high school debate coaches recalled, "He was so good it kind of disturbed me. He had this ability to kind of slide round an argument, instead of meeting it head on." Whether Nixon did not put his own wife on the payroll because "there are so many deserving stenographers and secretaries in Washington that needed the work" or because he was afraid that some day someone might attack him as he was attacking Sparkman, we will never know. It is interesting to note that both in California and on television Nixon did not mention Sparkman by name in this portion of the speech. Nixon simply referred to "the Democratic nominee" or "my opposite number." Perhaps this is explained by the fact that before the campaign started the name of the Democratic nominee for vice-president was known by less than 33 percent of the electorate, and Nixon was not going to give his opponent any more exposure that was absolutely necessary.[24]

In Eugene, Oregon, on September 20, Nixon had been greeted by signs that read "No mink coats for Nixon, just cold cash." Nixon immediately responded, "That's absolutely right—there are no mink coats for the Nixons. I'm proud to say my wife, Pat, wears a good Republican cloth coat." The mink coat signs were torn to shreds and Nixon used the same lines in his telecast. He added on television, however, "and I would always tell her that she would look good in anything." Somehow this line seems to ring true and gives a picture of Nixon as the proud husband talking about the wife who always campaigned beside him.[25]

The cloth coat, Sparkman's wife, and savings for taxpayers were only some of the arguments Nixon found successful in California and carried over into his television address. Others include his suggesting that the attacks on himself were a result of his involvement in the Hiss case and the references to the three big issues of the Republican campaign—corruption, communism, and Korea. Arguments found to quiet hecklers on the stump were repeated in the broadcast whether they were sound or not. Nixon also developed a number of arguments that came to him as he was on the plane returning to Los Angeles for the broadcast. He jotted them down on post cards from the seat pocket in front of him.[26]

In one of many statements Mitchell issued after the fund story broke he said, "If a fellow can't afford to be a Senator, he shouldn't seek the office." Nixon saw this as a perfect spot for an attack of his own. After verifying the source with his former history professor, Nixon countered with the Lincoln quotation about God loving the "common people" and at the same time reminded his audience about Stevenson's "inherited wealth." Again Nixon parried an attack with one of his own.[27]

Nixon's argument that no contributor to the fund had ever received special favors has never been successfully refuted, though many attempts to do so have been made. Even William Costello, the author of an "unfriendly biography" of Nixon wrote, "This much is certain. Nixon was not bribed. The fund did not in any conscious way compromise his integrity or independence."[28]

Nixon also argued that he needed the fund to get his political message to the American people, a message that would expose "this Administration, the communism in it, the corruption in it." Those who accused him of misconduct were obviously trying to stop this message from being heard. Having denied any moral wrong doing because of the fund, Nixon turned to the legal question. He quoted the report of the law firm, and the statement of Price, Waterhouse to support his contention that there was no illegality involved in the fund. In selecting a leading Los Angeles law firm and a nationally respected accounting agency to audit the fund, Hoffman had selected firms whose reputations would impress the average voter and would be well-received by the business and financial interests backing Eisenhower's campaign.[29]

We can now turn to the second characteristic of the fund speech—the emotion filled content, language, and delivery that opponents called "all the schmaltz of and human interest of the 'Just Plain Bill'-'Our Gal Sunday' genre of weepers" and that supporters called "eloquent and manly." It is impossible to say that Nixon meant every word he said and that the emotion shown was genuine or that the entire speech was just a performance and that nothing said was genuine. We can come close to the truth, however, as far as certain specific topics are concerned.[30]

Nixon had to be emotionally involved with what was happening. Here was an ambitious man nearing the top of his career only to find that he had to fight for his political life. Here was a man, who had always been hard working, and who no doubt believed he had earned everything he owned, suddenly accused of wrongdoing. Here was a man who had an aggressive nature and who would never willingly give up in adversity being told just thirty minutes before he went on the air that Eisenhower's advisors and probably Eisenhower himself thought he should resign from the ticket. Here was a man who admitted that just before the broadcast he had his worst moment: "I turned to Pat and said, 'I just don't think I can go through with this one.' " Pat, however, reassured him, took him by the hand and led him out to the stage of the El Capitan Theatre where he faced 750 empty seats and the television cameras. A salesman with Nixon's coloring had participated in what little rehearsal the technical crew was able to have. When asked if he would stay seated at the desk that had been provided for him, Nixon said he did not know, but to keep the cameras on him. Under these circumstances, Nixon must have been deeply emotionally involved with what he was saying, but did he express his emotions genuinely? In some cases he did, but in others he overdramatized or expressed sentiments that he really did not feel.[31]

To show that he had never feathered his own nest with contributed funds, Nixon offered "a complete financial history" from his boyhood to the time of the speech. The entire picture was drawn to elicit the sympathy of the audience toward his situation and to prevent future attacks on his honesty. The fund which caused the uproar did not come into existence until 1950. No charge had been made that Nixon had benefitted from public office before that time. He did not have to go back to the beginning to discuss his finances, but he did so in order that any new charges would not be taken seriously. Although we can accuse Nixon of overdramatizing in some spots and showing false modesty in others (for example, "I guess I'm entitled to a couple of battle stars"), the story itself even in a colorless narrative is a dramatic one, and for someone deeply involved in it, telling it to 60 million people, the chance to "ham it up" a bit was probably irresistible. Nevertheless, the emotions shown have some basis in reality, but this was not always the case.

The most often remembered section of Nixon's speech is that portion that deals with Checkers, "a little cocker spaniel dog." Some time after the speech Nixon was asked, "Did you have Fala [FDR's dog] in mind?" His reply, which indicates Nixon's true feelings about this point, was "Of course I did. I got a kind of malicious pleasure out of it. I'll needle them on this one, I said to myself." Nixon used Checkers as a device to get sympathy for himself. (As it turned out he also got a year's supply of dog food and hundreds of assorted collars, leashes, toys, etc.).[32]

Nixon's call for Stevenson and Sparkman to make public their financial records as he had done is yet another example of changing a defense to an attack, but it was something more. It was a complete surprise to Eisenhower. Though Nixon did not mention it in his speech, if three of the major candidates had to make their finances public, the fourth would have to also. Eisenhower was seen to stab his pad with his pencil sharply as Nixon made his suggestion. Intentionally or otherwise, if Nixon was going to have to open his records to everyone so was Eisenhower.[33]

The second surprise of the speech hit Eisenhower even harder. In his first phone call, Dewey had suggested that Nixon end his speech by asking the audience to offer suggestions on what course of action he should follow. The audience would decide if he should stay on the ticket or not. But the question arose, where should the advice be sent? In the speech Nixon named the Republican National Committee as the ones who should be advised on "the decision that is theirs to make." Eisenhower broke his pencil at this point as he jabbed it completely through the pad of paper. Technically, the national committee did decide on the candidates, but every Republican understood that Eisenhower would name his running mate. Perhaps Eisenhower saw in Nixon's remarks a veiled threat that if Eisenhower tried to dump Nixon he could fight the decision in the national committee. Nixon certainly was "not a quitter" as his fellow football players at Whittier would attest and as Eisenhower realized as he listened to the speech.[34]

The emotion of the speech was heightened by the language that was used and the tone with which it was delivered. Nixon was direct and conversational. He used short sentences and a number of parenthetical remarks to bring himself closer to his audience. The dramatic quality of his delivery was enhanced by his practice of refusing to read a manuscript. At the same time he did not memorize what he was going to say. Only when he could deliver a speech extemporaneously did it have the "spark of spontaneity" he felt was "essential for a television audience."[35]

Nixon went before the cameras with five handwritten sheets of yellow legal pad paper, but soon he was speaking directly at the camera without using the notes until he quoted directly from the auditors' report. He remained seated behind a desk until he finished the part of the speech calling for financial statements from Stevenson and Sparkman. Then he rose, stood in front of the desk, and spoke directly to the camera. Only five times did the camera stray from Nixon—to pick up Pat Nixon, who was seated to the right of the desk, whenever she was mentioned by her husband. With ten minutes left in the speech, Ted Rogers crouched under a camera and began to give time signals. But Nixon, involved in what he was saying, missed the final minute warning and was still speaking as time ran out. Because he had failed to give the address of the Republican National Committee, where he wanted the audience to send their opinions about his future, he feared that the speech might not be successful. He had no reason to worry.[36]

Nixon was speaking to two audiences and with both he succeeded beyond his expectations. Before he had finished, many of those in the room with Eisenhower, including Mrs. Eisenhower, were weeping and "the tears of those who had urged Nixon's withdrawal were particularly conspicuous." Immediately after Nixon concluded, the crowd in the auditorium began chanting, "We want Dick! We want Dick!" Hearing the roar of the crowd, Eisenhower turned to Summerfield and said, "Well Arthur, you surely got your $75,000 worth." Instead of addressing his supporters in the auditorium on inflation, Eisenhower talked to them about decisionmaking and about Nixon: "I have seen brave men in tough situations. I have never seen anyone come through in better fashion than Senator Nixon did tonight." He added, however, "It is obvious that I have to have something more than one single presentation, necessarily limited to thirty minutes," before making a decision about Nixon's future. In a telegram to Nixon, he wrote, "Whatever personal affection and admiration I had for you—and they are very great—are undiminished." Nixon did not receive the message until days later; but when he heard through a wire service report that Eisenhower was insisting on a personal meeting before deciding his future, Nixon became angry. He would not subject himself to further humiliation; he would resign. He dictated a resignation telegram to Rose Mary Woods and told her to send it immediately. Instead Woods showed the resignation to Chotiner and he destroyed it. A defiant Nixon telegraphed Eisenhower that he was going to continue to his next scheduled campaign stop in Missoula, Montana, that he would be in Washington, D.C., in five days, and that Eisenhower could meet with him anytime after that. Eisenhower's advisors were shocked, but when they convinced Nixon that he would receive Eisenhower's blessing when he arrived in Wheeling, Nixon agreed to fly there from Montana. When Nixon's plane landed, Eisenhower climbed the stairs into the plane and told a surprised Nixon, "You're my boy!" In the meantime, those members of the national committee who could be contacted (107 out of 138) unanimously agreed that Nixon should stay on the ticket.[37]

The reaction of the second audience to Nixon's speech was mixed but overwhelmingly favorable.  People stood in long lines to send telegrams urging that Nixon remain on the ticket.  More than three hundred thousand telegrams and letters, signed by more than one million people, poured into the national Republican headquarters. Additional hundreds of thousands of messages were directed to state and local headquarters, the candidates' offices, and to people connected in any way with the candidates.  Those received by the Republican National Committee supported Nixon 350 to 1. Respondents represented the forty-eight states, the territories of Alaska and Hawaii, Puerto Rico, and even Canada.  A content analysis of the responses showed that writers tended to ignore issues and to comment instead on personal qualities, such as honesty, courage, sincerity, patriotism, and devotion to family, they saw in Nixon—exactly those qualities he attempted to enhance in his speech. The *Herald Tribune* announced that "The air is cleared," and the Denver *Post* declared, "Senator Nixon talked his way into the hearts of millions . . . by speaking plainly about the dilemma of a poor man and the rich sweepstakes of politics."  Nixon established himself as a national figure and, according to Earl Mazo, became "the best-known, largest-crowd drawing vice-presidential candidate in history."[38]

The public response Nixon received contrasts with that offered by some rhetorical critics.  Barnet Baskerville found in the speech "the illusion of proof" rather than proof itself.  He argued that fully "two-thirds of this dramatic speech . . . had nothing at all to do with the case."  Lawrence Rosenfield concluded: "Nixon's response to attack, though emotionally appealing, was not fully appropriate to the public man."  Others have noted that, contrary to Nixon's denials, he benefitted financially from the fund since his standard of living would have been reduced by whatever amount he would otherwise have spent out of his own pocket.[39]

But too much attention can be paid to whether Nixon's arguments stand up to logical tests or not.  In large part Nixon succeeded because of his successful use of narrative.  From "I was born in 1913" to "That's what we have and that's what we owe," Nixon's defense of himself was the story of a poor boy making good in the best Horatio Alger tradition.  Walter Fisher has suggested that for any narrative to be successful, it must have "coherence" and "fidelity."  By coherence he meant that the story must hold together structural, materially, and with what the audience already knows about the characters.  At the same time the story must have fidelity or truthfulness.  The American public found that Nixon's life story met both of these criteria.  They could identify with the materials of the story—the low-cost apartment, the struggle with the mortgage payment, the parental loans, the lack of life insurance on the wife and children, and even the wife's cloth coat.  By reputation Nixon was a political fighter and also a family man, and the public admired the father who cared so much for his children that he would not give back the family dog "regardless of what they say about it."  The reports from the accounting firm and from the attorneys supported the truthfulness of what the earnest young man was saying. As Henry McGuckin pointed out, the values Nixon portrayed in his life story were values millions of Americans held dear.[40]

The long-term result is much harder to assess. Those who remember the speech best are those who thought the whole production was terrible. Earl Mazo suggested that much of the "I don't like Nixon, but I don't know why" talk in the 1960 election can be traced back to the speech. Some commentators have claimed that if it were not for the broadcast, Nixon might have won the election of 1960. Nixon, however, had the perfect rejoinder to that remark, "If it hadn't been for that broadcast, I would never have been around to run for the presidency."[41]

When Richard Nixon was attacked for being the beneficiary of a secret political fund, his instinct and background called for the attack to be met by a counterattack which he launched through a televised speech. The speech utilized arguments chosen for their previous acceptance rather than for their logical soundness. Throughout the speech, instead of defending himself against Democratic attacks, Nixon launched his own attacks—on Sparkman for putting his own wife on his payroll, on Stevenson for having funds of his own, and on the Truman Administration for losing countries and men to communism and for internal graft and corruption. The speech was highly emotional because of the man, the situation, the language chosen, and the manner of delivery. Its immediate effect was completely pleasing to Nixon, but the effect of the broadcast on Nixon's later career is a somewhat different story.

# 4
# The Kennedy-Nixon Debates: Important but not Decisive

The election of 1960 was one of the closest presidential elections in American history. When all the votes were counted (in some cases in Chicago they were counted twice), John F. Kennedy became president with 34,226,731 popular votes (303 electoral votes) and Richard Nixon returned to life as a private citizen with 34,108,157 votes (219 electoral). Theodore White has noted that if 28,000 voters in Texas and 4,500 voters in Illinois had changed their votes from Kennedy to Nixon, Nixon would have won the election. Because the vote was so close, many have asked of the Nixon campaign, "What if . . . ? In fact, Nixon himself listed sixteen possible changes in his campaign tactics or strategy that might have resulted in victory for him. Two of the possibilities he mentioned are of special interest: (1) "I should have refused to debate Kennedy;" (2) "My campaign was 'me too'—I had not attacked Kennedy hard enough." Nixon went on to claim that the first possibility was removed from his hands and that the second complaint was not true. A close examination of the background of the debates, the issues discussed, the images that prevailed, and the research findings about the effect of the debates, shows that Nixon was correct on the first count, but wrong about the second.[1]

In February, 1959, the Federal Communications Commission ruled that under law, all candidates for a particular office must be granted free and equal time on television, even if their opponent had appeared during a news broadcast. At first, Congress amended Section 315 of the Communications Act to exclude news programs, but the amended act still did not allow for debates limited to the candidates of the major parties. On June 27, 1960, however, Congress passed a joint resolution suspending the "equal time" provision for the duration of the 1960 campaign, at least as it applied to candidates for president and vice-president. Joint appearances of the major parties' candidates were now possible.[2]

Immediately following the congressional action, the national chairmen of the two major parties appeared on "Meet the Press" and agreed that their candidates, not yet selected, would be willing to debate.  Thus before he was ever nominated, Nixon was put in the position of having to debate or appear to be welshing on the agreement made by Republican chairman, Thurston Morton.   Eisenhower thought Nixon should not give the lesser-known Kennedy the exposure such debates would bring; but Nixon believed that had he refused the challenge, he would have been attacked for being afraid to defend the administration's and his own record.  Besides, because of his earlier campaign victories and the response to the fund speech, he was well regarded both as a debater and as a television speaker. He should have little trouble with his inexperienced opponent.  The issue facing Nixon was not whether to debate but how to arrange the debates to give Kennedy the least possible advantage.[3]

Once Kennedy and Nixon had received the nomination of their parties, they sent representatives to New York's Waldorf-Astoria Hotel to discuss in a series of meetings the format and number of debates.  Kennedy preferred five debates; Nixon wanted only one. Eventually they agreed on four.  The first and last debates permitted opening and closing statements by the candidates.  In the second and third encounters, they would answer questions and comment on each other's answers.  The debaters had two-and-a-half minutes to answer any question; no notes could be used; comments on each other's answers were limited to one-and-a-half minutes.  Questions in the middle two debates could be on any topic, but it was agreed that one debate would concern foreign policy and one debate would be limited to domestic issues.  Nixon was given the choice of when each topic should be discussed.  He felt that foreign policy would be his strongest issue, but should it be the subject of the first or the fourth debate? Assuming that the first debate would attract the largest audience because of its novelty, Nixon wanted it to be the foreign policy debate. His advisors argued, however, that the audience would build and that foreign policy should be saved for the climactic fourth debate.  In "one of my biggest mistakes" of the campaign Nixon reluctantly went along with his advisors and agreed that domestic issues would be the subject of the first debate.[4]

To understand what happened to Nixon in the first debate, two significant factors must be noted.  In mid-August while campaigning in Greensboro, North Carolina, Nixon bumped his knee on the edge of a car door.  Although he noticed pain immediately, it disappeared until a week later when it became so severe he had to notify a doctor. The doctor examined him, found the knee badly infected, and sent Nixon to Walter Reed Hospital for massive doses of penicillin that were injected directly behind the kneecap.  For two weeks Nixon lay in bed instead of visiting the seven states on his agenda.  He admitted that the physical pain, bad as it was, was nothing compared to the psychological pain of knowing that Kennedy was out on the stump gathering votes as he lay in his hospital bed.[5]

The second factor was a result of Nixon's acceptance speech at the Republican nominating convention.  In it, Nixon declared: "I personally will carry this campaign into every one of the fifty states of this nation between now and November 8." To keep this pledge in spite of his hospital stay, Nixon had to cover in eight weeks what he had planned to do in ten. Jim Bassett, in charge of scheduling, argued that Nixon's hospitalization was all the excuse he needed to rescind his pledge. It would be better to skip those states that were safely in his column and those that were hopelessly lost. But Nixon refused. He would keep his commitment. Nixon later admitted: "In retrospect, this decision is open to serious question."[6]

The second week of campaigning after Nixon was released from the hospital gives some indication of the pace he maintained. From Monday through Friday he visited Pennsylvania, Michigan, Illinois, Missouri, Kentucky, South Dakota, Wisconsin, and Kansas. On Saturday he flew to Lafayette, Louisiana, and Jackson, Mississippi and returned to Washington at midnight. In each of these states there were a number of press conferences, airport and downtown rallies in a number of cities, motorcades, and often stadium or auditorium rallies as well. At the end of the first two weeks Nixon had traveled fifteen thousand miles and spoken to two million people. He had reached even more through local radio and television broadcasts. The effect of this intense campaigning would soon be visible to all. The first ever televised debate between two presidential candidates was scheduled for Monday, September 26, from Chicago.[7]

When Nixon arrived in Chicago from Washington at 10:30 p.m. on Sunday, in plenty of time for a good night's sleep before the next day's debate, he discovered that local Republicans had planned a rally in each of the five precincts the Nixon party would pass through on their way to his downtown hotel. Thus it was after 1 a.m. when Nixon arrived at the Pick-Congress Hotel. Nixon's preparation for the debate was further interrupted by a speech he made Monday morning at the annual convention of the Carpenters Union. The generally hostile reaction he received from a group that favored Kennedy did not put him in a good frame of mind when he finally got to work that afternoon on the evening's debate. He spent five hours going over one hundred questions his staff had felt could be raised on domestic issues during the debate. He continued studying his notes in the car enroute to the CBS studio. He reported later that he felt he was as thoroughly prepared for this appearance as he had ever been in his political life.[8]

As Nixon was getting out of the car to enter the studio he once again banged his knee against the car door and a reporter observed that his face went all "white and pasty." Nixon was in pain and the entire country would soon be aware of it.[9]

While Kennedy and Nixon posed for still photographers, Don Hewitt, who produced the show for CBS, asked both men if they wanted make-up. Kennedy, who had been campaigning in an open car in California and who had spent part of the afternoon sunning on the hotel rooftop, quickly declined. When Nixon heard Kennedy decline, he too refused, fearing that stories would appear the next day that he had used makeup but Kennedy had not.  Instead, his advisors covered his always present five o'clock shadow with Instant Shave, a type of pancake makeup.  When Nixon returned with the white substance on his face, Hewitt, watching him on the control room monitor, thought he "looked like death warmed over."  He immediately summoned Frank Stanton, the president of CBS who was in the studio, to take a look at what the camera was showing.  "I think we're heading for trouble," he said.  Stanton agreed and asked Ted Rogers, Nixon's television advisor, to come into the booth to see if he was satisfied with the way his candidate looked.  Rogers glanced at the screen and responded, "He looks fine to me," and left.  Stanton told Hewitt, "If that's what they want, I don't think we should impose ourselves."  Thus a limping, white-faced Nixon went before the largest television audience ever assembled for a political broadcast.  But still another factor was working against him.[10]

Nixon's advisors had based their decision on the color suit he should wear, a light grey one, on the information that the background would be dark grey.  They figured that the light suit would offer a nice contrast to the dark backdrop.  That morning at 8:30 a.m. when they had arrived at the WBBM studios to check everything out, they found the backdrop was light grey and they asked that it be repainted.  This was done, but again the paint dried lighter than expected.  Yet another coat of paint was added and the background was, in fact, still wet to the touch when the debate started; but it was still a medium grey color and offered little contrast to Nixon's grey suit.  Kennedy, on the other hand, had elected to wear a dark blue suit and it offered a crisp contrast to the background.  When the white shirt Kennedy was wearing did not photograph well, he sent back to his hotel for a blue shirt and changed just in time for the broadcast.  Nixon wore a white shirt that looked too big in the collar since he had lost ten pounds because of his illness and the two strenuous weeks of unrelenting campaigning.  Nixon looked so bad that his mother called Rose Mary Woods, his private secretary, immediately after the debate to find out if her son were ill.  Nixon refused to use the excuse that he was sick, but admitted that he did not look well.  Kennedy, in contrast, looked better than Nixon had ever seen him and he "sounded more vigorous."[11]

When Nixon closeted himself in his hotel room, preparing for the debate, one of the few telephone calls he accepted was from his running-mate, Henry Cabot Lodge, who reportedly urged him to use the televised debate to erase his image as an "assassin."  Nixon apparently took this advice seriously, for when the hour-long debate began, Nixon was not the aggressive attacker who had demolished Voorhis and Douglas.  The candidate, who had made his reputation by attacking his opponent, appeared to be too agreeable.  After Kennedy had delivered an eight-minute attack on America's loss of leadership in the world, Nixon's first words were: "The things that Senator Kennedy has said many of us can agree with."  Five more times in his opening statement, when he had an uninterrupted opportunity to draw a clear distinction between himself and Kennedy on whatever issues he chose, Nixon offered such statements as "Here, again, may I indicate that Senator Kennedy and I are not in disagreement as to aims. We both want to help the old people. . . . Let us understand throughout the campaign that his motives and mine are sincere. . . . I know Senator Kennedy feels as deeply as I do. . . ." And six additional times during the course of the debate, instead of offering reasons why his views should prevail, Nixon offered comments like: "I agree with Senator Kennedy completely on that score. . . . I agree with Senator Kennedy's appraisal generally in this respect. . . ."[12]

Republicans and others who supported Nixon were looking for much more than this. Not only was their champion agreeing with the challenger, but when he had an opportunity to attack, he was silent. When Kennedy was asked by Bob Fleming of ABC News: "Senator, the Vice President in his campaign has said that you were naive and at times immature. He has raised the question of leadership. On this issue, why do you think people should vote for you rather than the Vice President?" Kennedy mentioned briefly his fourteen years in government. "Our experience in government is comparable," he declared. He then pointed out that the Democratic Party that he represented had produced Woodrow Wilson, FDR, and Harry Truman. He contrasted the Democratic record with that of Republicans who "opposed federal aid for education, medical care for the aged, development of the Tennessee Valley, development of our natural resources. . . ." When Nixon had his chance to object to what Kennedy had said, on what he claimed was a major issue in the campaign, all the expectant audience heard from the vice-president was: "I have no comment."

The question of "experience" was renewed when panelist Sander Vanocur brought up President Eisenhower's off-the-cuff remark at the end of a press conference when he was pressed for an example of a major idea of Nixon's that he had adopted. Eisenhower said, "If you give me a week I might think of one. I don't remember." Nixon tried to put Eisenhower's remark in perspective: "The President has asked me for my advice. I have given it. Sometimes my advice has been taken. Sometimes it has not. I do not say that I have made the decisions." But, then, instead of comparing his access to the president and to the decision-making process with Kennedy's, he said: "His experience has been different from mine. Mine has been in the executive branch. His has been in the legislative branch." Anyone judging the debate would be hard pressed to conclude that Nixon's experiences had been shown to be any more impressive than Kennedy's.

Many commentators have noted that just seeing Nixon and Kennedy together helped the lesser-known Kennedy and showed that he was as capable as Nixon to handle the presidency. But the text of the debate demonstrates Nixon's failure to document his charges of inexperience and thus he gave the issue to Kennedy both visually and verbally.  Samuel Lubell summarized the effect of the debate on the "experience" issue: "At the outset of the campaign the 'images' of the two men held by most voters were not too favorable for Kennedy. During the early summer typical comments being voiced about Kennedy ran, 'He's so good-looking I'm afraid to vote for him' or 'He's so new and inexperienced you wonder what he would do.' Nixon's strategy, of course, was framed around the idea that with war a constant threat, the public would decide it was unwise to choose someone new and uncertain over 'the man with experience.' The first debate almost completely demolished this 'experience against youth' argument."[13]

Nixon answered the argument that he was too defensive during the debate by claiming that it was not the substance of his remarks that worked against him but his physical appearance and that those who heard the debate on the radio thought that he had won.  Even Pierre Salinger, Kennedy's press secretary, supported Nixon's position.  In a 1984 television interview Salinger said: "while the overwhelming number of people who saw the debates . . . believed that Kennedy had won them, an equally overwhelming number of people who heard the debates—didn't have a television set—thought Richard Nixon won them."[14]

In spite of such strong statements, poll data do not support Nixon's or Salinger's conclusion.  A study by David Vancil and Sue Pendell traced all the statements made by historians and participants about Nixon's alleged superior effect on the radio.  They observed several problems with the only poll that attempted to characterize the effect of the debate on the radio audience: "The Sindlinger data reported in *Broadcasting*, therefore, has serious flaws in every dimension examined: (1) the sample size of the audience (282, with 178 opinions on the debate winner) is too small; (2) the national radio audience was not specifically targeted; (3) the unknown partisan characteristics and location of the sample weaken its credibility; (4) the survey results are inconsistent with known partisan characteristics of the debate audience; and (5) there is no evidence to support a mass defection of Kennedy partisans."  A reading of the text of the debate offers support for why some of Nixon's followers were unhappy with his approach to the debate and no evidence for why Kennedy partisans would think that their candidate had been defeated.[15]

An estimated 80 million to 85 million viewers watched the first debate.  Choosing to listen to the debate, however, was related to the viewer's strength of commitment to a particular candidate or party rather than to a desire to gain information.  So called "independent" voters were far less likely to watch the debates; and if they did see one, they probably saw only the first one.  These viewers observed Kennedy at his best and Nixon at his worst.  Kennedy's performance elated his advisors.  Salinger reported that everywhere Kennedy campaigned from then on, his crowds were larger and more enthusiastic than they had been before the debate.  Volunteers enlisted in record numbers. Democratic governors of the southern states moved from apathy to enthusiastic support. With the "experience" question answered, Kennedy was a viable candidate and more people than ever were willing to work for his election.[16]

The second debate, scheduled for Friday, October 7, in Cleveland had to be moved to Washington when the Cleveland studio proved to be too small to handle the press who accompanied the candidates. Nixon, although he said he learned a lot about image from what happened in the first debate, did not allow himself much time to relax before the telecast. He spent all day Thursday campaigning in Ohio and did not return to Washington until midnight. Up early on Friday morning, he spent the day preparing for the second encounter. This time, however, he was determined to be more aggressive. He remembered the words of Louis Selzer, editor of the Cleveland *Press*, who told him just before leaving Ohio, that "you are most effective when you are on the attack. Tomorrow night with Kennedy on TV, take him on. Take the offensive from the first, with the gloves off."[17]

Kennedy faced a different Nixon in the second debate. Thanks to four milkshakes a day, Nixon had regained five pounds and looked healthier; his knee no longer hurt; his television advisor made sure his makeup improved his appearance; by his own account he was ready to project knowledge, sincerity, and confidence.[18]

With no opening or closing statements by the candidates, the second debate was a joint press conference with each speaker allowed to comment on his opponent's answer. The first words Nixon spoke showed his more aggressive attitude: "Well, first of all, I don't agree with Senator Kennedy that Cuba is lost and certainly China was lost when this Administration came to power in 1953. . . . Now I'm very surprised that Senator Kennedy, who is on the Foreign Relations Committee, would make such a statement. . . . I don't think this kind of defeatist talk by Senator Kennedy helps the situation one bit."[19]

With any topic fair game in this debate, the questioners asked about the U-2 incident, civil rights, the cold war and American prestige, unemployment, Eisenhower, a possible summit meeting, possible tax incentives, and the islands of Quemoy and Matsu. Nixon spelled out his differences with Kennedy in most of these areas. For example, on the U-2 incident, Nixon said: "I think Senator Kennedy is wrong on three counts" and he went on to enumerate them. On civil rights, referring to Kennedy's choice of Lyndon Johnson as vice-president, Nixon said, "When he selected his vice presidential running mate, he selected a man who had voted against most of these proposals and a man who opposes them at the present time. . . I selected a man who stands with me in this field and who will talk with me and work with me on it." Nixon saved some of his toughest comments for his disagreement with Kennedy over whether the United States should defend the islands of Quemoy and Matsu if they were attacked by China. Nixon wanted to defend them: "[T]he question is not these two little pieces of real estate—they are unimportant. It isn't the few people who live on them—they are not too important. It is the principle involved. These two islands are in the area of freedom." Kennedy's position would give the islands to the Chinese and eventually lead to the take over of Formosa. It was "the same kind of woolly thinking that led to disaster for America in Korea. I am against it. I would never tolerate it as president of the United States, and I will hope that Senator Kennedy will change his mind if he should be elected."

The difference in response Nixon received after this debate was as "night from day." The *New York Times* reported that Nixon had clearly made a "comeback" and the New York *Herald Tribune* gave the "second round" to Nixon. Most other polls rated the debate even, but clearly the more aggressive Nixon had done better than the nice one. The only problem for Nixon was that twenty million fewer viewers witnessed the second debate.[20]

The third debate, on October 13, found Nixon in Los Angeles and Kennedy in New York speaking from identical studios. The press conference format was again used and the first question dealt with a change Kennedy had made the previous day. Referring to Nixon's pledge to defend Quemoy and Matsu, Kennedy called Nixon "trigger-happy." Nixon said he "resented" the comment and added, "I would remind Senator Kennedy of the past fifty years. I would ask him to name one Republican president who led this nation into war. There were three Democratic presidents who led us into war . . . any statement to the effect that the Republican party is trigger-happy is belied by the record." Nixon's private polls indicated that his position on Quemoy and Matsu had much support and Nixon kept Kennedy on the defensive throughout. He claimed that Kennedy "is only encouraging the aggressors. . . . We're not going to have peace by giving in." When the topic changed to disarmament, Nixon remained aggressive: "When Senator Kennedy suggests that we haven't been making an effort, he simply doesn't know what he is talking about."[21]

The subject of President Truman's use of strong language came up (he had suggested that southerners who voted Republican "could go to hell"), and Kennedy dismissed it with the joke that he could do nothing about it, but "perhaps Mrs. Truman can." Nixon became sanctimonious. A former president should not lose his temper in public, Nixon asserted. Especially since there were often children in the crowds: "and I can only say that I'm very proud that President Eisenhower restored dignity and decency, and, frankly, good language to the conduct of the presidency of the United States."

Nixon made up for this less than candid remark in answer to another question about keeping religion out of the campaign: "The worst thing I can think that can happen in this campaign would be for it to be decided on religious issues. I obviously repudiate the Klan; I repudiate anybody who uses the religious issue; I will not tolerate it. . . . We cannot have religious or racial prejudice. We cannot have it in our hearts. But we certainly cannot have it in a presidential campaign."

The Houston *Chronicle* called the third debate the "hardest hitting of the three" and the national polls indicated that it was Nixon's finest hour. The Opinion Research Corporation reported that Nixon had been more effective with the viewers in the third debate than Kennedy had been in the first. The audience, however, while still at 60 million, did not approach the size of the audience that heard the first debate. Pollsters suggested that after all the campaigning and speaking that both candidates had done to this point, the race was still too close to call.[22]

The fourth debate, on foreign policy, with opening and closing statements by the candidates, provided Nixon with an opportunity to showcase brilliantly a debate technique he may not have used since his college days. He argued strongly and eloquently for a position in which he did not believe. The question was what to do about Cuba and Nixon had argued with the Eisenhower administration for stronger action against Castro who had nationalized millions of dollars worth of American businesses. The CIA was training Cuban exiles for an assault on Cuba and Nixon pressed for quick action. He hoped it would occur before the election for it would show how a Republican administration would deal with a communist dictator in the Western Hemisphere. Eisenhower, however, refused to act. On October 20, Kennedy, who may have known it was already being done, advocated U.S. intervention in Cuba and aid to rebel forces. Instead of explicitly telling Kennedy that the U.S. was undertaking just such action and that public debate on the issue was not in the national interest, Nixon decided that the covert operation had to be protected "at all costs." He must not even suggest by implication that the United States was extending aid to rebel forces in and out of Cuba. In fact, he decided that he had to go to the other extreme. He would attack the Kennedy proposal to provide such aid as "wrong and irresponsible" because it would violate American treaty commitments.[23]

This Nixon did on the night of October 21 in the debate from New York. When asked about Kennedy's views on Cuba, Nixon responded: "I think that Senator Kennedy's policies and recommendations for the handling of the Castro regime are probably the most dangerously irresponsible recommendations that he's made during the course of this campaign. . . . We have five treaties with Latin America, including the one setting up the Organization of American States in Bogota in 1948, in which we have agreed not to intervene in the internal affairs of any other American country." He added: "The Charter of the United Nations . . . also provides that there shall be no intervention by one nation in the internal affairs of another. . . . If we were to follow [Kennedy's] recommendation . . . we would lose all of our friends in Latin America, we would probably be condemned in the United Nations, and we would not accomplish our objective."[24]

Not surprisingly, Nixon's position won him the applause of the usually critical liberal columnists. James Reston congratulated Nixon and wrote that Kennedy's call to aid the rebels was "probably the worst blunder of the campaign." As Nixon put it: "This was the only occasion in the campaign where I won the eggheads (and at the same time lost among the voters)." Poll results about the debate were about equally divided. There was no clear winner, although some gave a slight edge to Kennedy. Following the debate, however, both candidates started to reverse themselves about the best way to handle Cuba. Nixon spoke of the Eisenhower Administration's quarantine as something that would allow the Cuban people to see what kind of a man Castro was. He predicted that sooner than you think "they will get rid of him in their own way." He hinted that what had happened in 1954 to Guatemala's leftist leader, Jacobo Arbenz, could happen to Castro. Kennedy expressed his opposition to the use of naked force and said he would never violate existing treaties. On October 23, Nixon challenged Kennedy to a fifth televised debate devoted solely to Cuba, but Kennedy refused and the campaign marched on to its well-known conclusion. After spending an entire night watching Kennedy's early popular lead drop from more than two million to less than half a million, Nixon sent the customary telegram wishing Kennedy well.[25]

The overall effect on the four debates on the voting public is not clear. Estimates ranged from little or none to claims that it was the most important factor. Those who stressed the importance of the debates turned to the results of pollster Elmo Roper. Six percent of his respondents said that the debates "made them decide" for whom they were going to vote. If his sample was accurate, four million voters decided on the basis of the debates which candidate they would support. Twenty-six percent (one million) voted for Nixon and seventy-two percent (three million) voted for Kennedy. Since Kennedy's margin of victory was only 119,000 votes, the debates had a determining effect on the election result. Kennedy himself declared, "It was TV more than anything that turned the tide."[26]

But a number of factors outside the debates almost certainly played a more important role. Robert Kennedy's call to the judge in Georgia who subsequently allowed Martin Luther King to be placed on bail rather than be sentenced to a work farm in Reedsville, from which his supporters feared he might never return, gained Kennedy thousands of additional black votes. The Kennedy organization distributed pamphlets outside Negro churches across the country that compared what Kennedy had done for King to Nixon's perceived lack of interest in his case. Although Eisenhower carried 40 percent of the black vote against Stevenson in 1956, Nixon received about 22 percent against Kennedy.[27]

To an even greater extent, Nixon was hurt by the Catholic vote. Normally Democratic anyway, Catholic voters gave almost 80 percent of their votes to their fellow Catholic; Eisenhower had received 50 percent four years earlier. Nixon received the lowest percentage of the Catholic vote of any Republican presidential candidate in history. The Catholic vote was particularly important to both candidates because it was concentrated in the states with the largest electoral votes.[28]

A third factor influencing the outcome of the election was the economy.  In generally good shape in 1960, the economy suffered rising unemployment during the political campaign, and Nixon tried unsuccessfully to get Eisenhower to do something about it.  From 3.38 million unemployed in September, the figure grew to 4.03 million in November.  Since the election started with 47 percent of the eligible voters calling themselves Democrats and only 30 percent Republicans, Nixon had to have a tremendous number of breaks in order to win.  Most of them went against him, yet he still almost won. One explanation is the sheer determination he showed.  During the campaign Nixon traveled 65,000 miles, gave 180 major speeches and hundreds of minor ones, and was seen "in the flesh" by 10 million Americans throughout all fifty states.  At his best in the give and take of stump oratory, Nixon almost succeeded.

A pale, nervous, perspiring Nixon lost the first presidential debate because of his appearance and because he agreed too often with his opponent.  A more aggressive Nixon more than held his own in the three subsequent debates; but many people saw or remembered only the first.  The lesson Nixon learned about appearance versus substance strongly affected the way he would use television in presidential campaigns to come.[29]

# 5
# The Vietnam Speeches: Successful but Divisive

President Richard Nixon faced strong opposition in the fall of 1969. In office less than a year, he found himself subject to many of the forces and pressures that had caused his predecessor, Lyndon Johnson, to decline to seek a second term. The return of students to the nation's college campuses instilled new life in the antiwar movement. Protest leaders planned a series of monthly demonstrations across the counry, beginning with the October 15 moratorium, to show the president that the war in Vietnam must be ended immediately. Nixon had promised to end the war but only on terms that assured the safety of the South Vietnamese and of their government, what he called "peace with honor." His plan to end the war contained three elements: direct diplomatic negotiations with the North Vietnamese in Paris; indirect diplomatic pressure on the North Vietnamese through our allies and, he hoped, through the Soviet Union, to force them to accept a negotiated settlement; and continued military pressure on the battlefield so that the North Vietnamese would believe they were involved in a war they could not win.[1]

In order to mitigate domestic antiwar pressure, Nixon, with the strong encouragement of Secretary of Defense Melvin Laird, adopted a policy of Vietnamization of the war. South Vietnamese troops would be responsible for as much of the fighting as possible and American troops would be withdrawn as the Vietnamese proved they were capable of handling the fighting themselves. To encourage the North Vietnamese to negotiate a peace settlement, Nixon warned Hanoi on August 4, 1969, that unless progress had been made at the peace talks in Paris by November 1, the first anniversary of the bombing halt, "measures of the greatest consequences" would be taken. Nixon feared, however, that such an ultimatum would have little effect if Hanoi believed that antiwar demonstrations in the United States would force him to reduce American troop commitments or even to withdraw unilaterally.[2]

Nixon took three steps to counter any impression that his re-solve would be moved by antiwar protest. At a press conference on September 26 the president said that "under no circumstances" would he be affected by demonstrators. On October 13, press secretary Ron Zeigler announced that the president would make a major address on Vietnam on November 3. So early an announcement of a presidential speech was unprecedented, and Nixon hoped it might take some of the wind out of the October 15 protest since the demonstrators would want to hear what the president had to say It would also put Hanoi on notice that following the deadline in the ultimatum Nixon had given them, an important announcement about his military policy would be made. As antiwar protesters circled the White House on October 15, Nixon watched a football game on television, a fact he wanted both the protestors and Hanoi to know. Even a demonstration the size of the moratorium was not going to affect his Vietnam policy.[3]

Nixon prepared for the promised address by having Henry Kissinger solicit position papers from the State and Defense Departments. Kissinger, Laird, and Secretary of State William Rogers offered their personal recommendations as did Ellsworth Bunker in Saigon and Henry Cabot Lodge in Paris. Nixon wrote the speech himself, working twelve to fourteen hours a day beginning at Camp David on the weekend of October 24. The following week he went through twelve drafts, and after an all-night session on Friday, he informed H. R. Haldeman early Saturday morning, "The baby's just been born." No one but Kissinger and Rose Mary Woods, who typed the final manuscript, knew exactly what he planned to say. Speculation in the media about the speech predicted some form of accelerated troop withdrawals or, perhaps, a unilateral ceasefire. No doubt remembering how rumors had helped build the audience for the Checkers speech, the president refused to comment on what he would say.[4]

Nixon's plan worked. Seventy-two million listeners were in his television and radio audience the night of Monday, November 3, when Nixon offered what has been called "the most effective speech of his presidency." Aiming directly at the large segment of the American populace who neither favored increased participation in the war nor immediate unconditional withdrawal, Nixon based his persuasive appeals on principles and values they would readily accept. He identified his position with truth, morality, dedication to duty, and patriotism. The most important was truth, especially in light of the "credibility gap" that had plagued the last years of the Johnson administration. Nixon said: "The American people cannot and should not be asked to support a policy which involves the overriding issues of war and peace unless they know the truth about that policy." The answers to five questions would yield the truth: "How and why did America get involved in Vietnam in the first place? How has this administration changed the policy of the previous administration? What has really happened in the negotiations in Paris and on the battlefield of Vietnam? What choices do we have if we are to end the war? What are the prospects for peace?"[5]

Before answering these questions, however, Nixon enhanced his ethos with the audience. That is, he attempted to demonstrate competence, goodwill, and good moral character in order to make himself and his policies more credible to his listeners. He began by pointing out what he considered to be mistakes in Johnson's handling of the war, implying that he had greater competence than the former president. When he took office, Nixon found that the South Vietnamese were not getting proper training; no Americans were scheduled to leave Vietnam; and the United States had not yet offered "a comprehensive peace proposal" at the Paris talks. Clearly, the previous Administration had not done all that it could to end the war, and Nixon, acting more competently than Johnson, had recognized and remedied these problems.[6]

To show good moral character, Nixon asserted that he did not take the politically easy way out of the Vietnam problem. He could have ordered the immediate withdrawal of American forces and blamed the defeat on Johnson; but Nixon claimed, "I had a greater obligation than to think only of the years of my administration and of the next election. I had to think of the effect of my decision on the next generation and on the future of peace and freedom in America and in the world." Although he said that ordering an immediate withdrawal and not allowing "Johnson's war" to become "Nixon's war" would have been a popular and easy course to follow, Nixon suggested later in the speech that only a minority in the country supported such an action. If this was so, then the course Nixon described would not have been as "popular" as he asserted, and his decision was not so difficult as he tried to make it seem. But his introductory statements, his promise to tell the truth, his superior competence in handling the war, and his refusal to take the easy way out, all served to strengthen Nixon's credibility before he began to answer the questions he posed.

Why and how did the U.S. get involved in Vietnam? Nixon reported: "Fifteen years ago North Vietnam, with the logistical support of Communist China and the Soviet Union, launched a campaign to impose a Communist government on South Vietnam by instigating and supporting a revolution." Although some critics have disputed the truthfulness of this explanation, Nixon repeated the justification offered by previous presidents and, thus, answered the why of the question without commenting on its accuracy. By his silence, Nixon supported this justification, but he again distanced himself from the unpopular Johnson by adding: "Many others—I among them—have been strongly critical of the way the war has been conducted."

Returning to the possibility of "precipitate withdrawal" Nixon rejected it as a potential solution, basing his arguments on morality and patriotism. Noting what the communists had done in the North and the tragic results of their successful takeover in Hue the previous year, Nixon claimed that immediate withdrawal would lead to a massacre of innocent civilians. Moreover it would result in a "collapse of confidence in American leadership" around the world. He quoted President John Kennedy to support this assertion, thus enabling Nixon to support his point and to associate himself with a popular hero. Nixon showed that he stood in a long line of presidents from both political parties who supported the South Vietnamese and followed the same ethical course they had set. As a patriot, he sought to avoid the "first defeat in our Nation's history."

Furthermore, Nixon pictured himself as a dedicated and shrewd negotiator. He had used secret couriers and had written directly to Ho Chi Minh. Negotiations, however, had not been easy: "Hanoi has refused even to discuss our proposals," but Nixon would not give up. Even though his attempts to deal directly with the leaders of North Vietnam and indirectly with them through the Soviet Union had proven fruitless, Nixon felt there were "channels of communication which may still prove to be productive." Nixon put the failure of negotiations in blunt terms: "No progress whatever has been made except agreement on the shape of the bargaining table." By discussing previously secret messages with Hanoi and by admitting the lack of progress in negotiations, Nixon reinforced the idea that he was telling the American people "the truth."

Blame for the failure of negotiations was placed squarely on Hanoi whose policy was to "wait for our next concession, and our next one after that one, until it gets everything it wants." While Nixon did not use the term, he implied that Hanoi was not playing fairly. Even a skilled negotiator cannot succeed if the opposition refuses to bargain.

If negotiations failed to bring peace, however, the president had a second plan, and this marked another difference between him and his predecessor: "In the previous administration we Americanized the war in Vietnam. In this administration we are Vietnamizing the search for peace." From this time on, America's primary mission was "to enable the South Vietnamese forces to assume the responsibility for the security of South Vietnam." The United States would have withdrawn sixty thousand troops by December 15 and "the South Vietnamese have continued to gain in strength." Nixon reported that American casualties had declined to the lowest level in three years and he promised that as the South Vietnamese forces became stronger, the rate of American withdrawal would continue to increase.

Nixon spent little time arguing against a withdrawal by a set date. Supported by advice he had received from Dean Acheson while he was working on the speech, Nixon refused to set a timetable for withdrawal. Such a timetable would "completely remove any incentive for the enemy to negotiate an agreement. They would simply wait until our forces had withdrawn and then move in." Speaking to the leaders of the North Vietnamese as well as to his American audience, Nixon cautioned that if the level of enemy activity increased, the rate of American withdrawal would have to decrease: "If I conclude that increased enemy action jeopardizes our remaining forces in Vietnam, I shall not hesitate to take strong and effective measures to deal with that situation."[7]

Karlyn Campbell objected to Nixon's summary statement that: "We have only two choices open to us if we want to end the war. I can order an immediate precipitate withdrawal of all Americans from Vietnam without regard to the effect of that action. Or we can persist in our search for a just peace through a negotiated settlement if possible, or through continued implementation of our plan for Vietnamization if necessary." She argued that other policy options, particularly Senator Charles Goodell's plan for a fixed termination date combined with economic and military aid, were possible and were supported by more Americans than favored immediate withdrawal. But Nixon had already ruled out any plan that limited the potential of fruitful negotiations and thus he did not consider it a viable option. With his choices limited to the two he mentioned, Nixon refuted the immediate withdrawal option with an argument based on the Puritan work ethic. Although it would be the "easy" way, its results would be devastating since "inevitable remorse and divisive recrimination would scar our spirit as a people." The easy way was not the correct way. Nixon may have had another reason for not wanting to compare his proposal specifically with the Goodell plan for, as Forbes Hill has noted, Nixon's Vietnamization plan called for the removal of "all the United States combat ground forces" while Goodell's plan involved all United States military forces.[8]

Turning directly to the antiwar demonstrators, Nixon recalled a sign he had seen held by a protester in San Francisco which said "Lose in Vietnam, bring the boys home." But Nixon refused to be moved by "the minority who hold that view and who try to impose it on the Nation by mounting demonstrations in the street." Only elected officials should determine governmental policy. In attacking antiwar protesters, Nixon picked an easy target. Even among those who thought the war was a mistake, sixty-three percent viewed protesters negatively. Nevertheless, Nixon offered a special plea "to the young people of this Nation who are particularly concerned." He claimed that he shared their idealism and that he desired peace as much as they did. This section of the speech was very conciliatory and attempted to bridge the gap between Nixon and America's youth. Nixon softened considerably the hard line he had considered using in an earlier draft where he had written: "If you want defeat, let me know."[9]

The most memorable phrase in the speech came in the conclusion when Nixon said, "And so tonight—to you, the great silent majority of my fellow Americans—I ask for your support." To redeem his pledge to end the war, Nixon needed the support of those Americans who had not vocalized their position before. Although the term "silent majority" had been used previously, by Vice-President Spiro Agnew in May, it had attracted little notice. Within a few weeks of Nixon's use of the term, however, a number of sub-groups within the United States were eagerly identifying themselves as members of the now not-so-silent majority. In Safire's words, Nixon "dispelled pluralistic ignorance and gave the majority both its identity and a new confidence."[10]

When Nixon asked the "silent majority" to speak out he could only hope that they would support his policies, and support them they did. A Gallup telephone poll taken immediately after the broadcast indicated that 77 percent of those who listened to the speech supported Nixon's position. Fewer that 14 percent opposed it. Letters, telegrams, and phone calls flooded the White House. Within a few days fifty thousand telegrams and thirty thousand letters, most of them favorable, reached the White House. A very happy Nixon called reporters into the Oval Office to show them the response, the largest mail response to a presidential speech ever, according to Nixon. More importantly, the public reaction had the desired effect on Congress. Both the House and Senate passed resolutions expressing confidence in Nixon's handling of the war. The president was so pleased he went up to Capitol Hill to address both groups individually. The speech gave Nixon time to negotiate with Hanoi and to try to persuade them that holding out for American opinion to support unconditional withdrawal would not be an effective policy.[11]

The antiwar forces were shaken. They had been led to believe that Nixon's speech would offer something new, something more in line with what they wanted, and they were terribly disappointed. New impetus was given to the November 15 moratorium, but it would be the last major demonstration for six months. Congressional doves made their displeasure with Nixon's policies known, but now it was clear that they held a minority view. In December Richard Starnes of Scripps-Howard headlined his story "Peace Marchers Give Round to Nixon."[12]

Nixon's success was predictable. Throughout the speech the audience was asked to support a truthful man who showed himself to be more competent than his predecessor, working hard to fulfill a moral commitment expressed by a long line of presidents, a dedicated and shrewd negotiator, a lover of peace, a patriot who would not be swayed by demonstrators who wanted to impose their will on the nation, a man who chose the right way instead of the easy way. As Hill concluded, "The message is crowded with these overt cues from which we infer the good *ethos* of political figures in situations like this." While some critics have lamented the lack of supporting materials for the Vietnamization plan and the small attention paid to alternative plans for limiting American involvement in the war, Nixon's apparent concern was with how the speech would affect the audience's opinion of him. If he could sell himself, Vietnamization and continued negotiations would be accepted as well. Robert Vartabedian observed correctly that Nixon so personalized the presidency and his policies that he viewed the speech as an opportunity to justify himself rather than to defend a position. Much as he did in the Checkers speech, Nixon appealed to his listeners' values of truth, morality, and patriotism and won their overwhelming support.   This support, however, would not last forever.[13]

Six months later, military events in Southeast Asia forced Nixon to go again before the American people to talk about Vietnam. This speech, described by William Safire as "harsh, self-pitying, and superpatriotic," succeeded with his friends but brought down on Nixon the wrath of his enemies. Polarization rather than support resulted.[14]

Nixon recognized that the major result of his November 3 speech was "time," but by the spring of 1970 it was running out. The North Vietnamese negotiators remained intransigent and Nixon had to do something to shore up his support at home.  The American people wanted action; and on April 20, Nixon announced that 150 thousand American troops would be returned from Vietnam by the end of the year.  An unexpected event in Cambodia, however, presented a new problem for the president.  A pro-Western leader, Lon Nol, had overthrown Prince Sihanouk, the cagey ruler of neutral Cambodia.  As Safire pointed out, Sihanouk had been a master opportunist.  He allowed the North Vietnamese to use Cambodian territory for logistical support within easy striking distance of Saigon. At the same time he allowed Americans to bomb the North Vietnamese troops within his territory.  All he demanded was secrecy. He would protest his nation's neutrality being broken "by the side that blabbed."[15]

Both sides played Sihanouk's game until Lon Nol entered the picture, leading a coup against Sihanouk while the head of state was visiting Moscow.  The North Vietnamese feared that Lon Nol would change the rules of engagement to their detriment and tried to take over Cambodia.  When Lon Nol asked for American military aid, Nixon had to decide how to respond.  He eventually determined to send a South Vietnamese force against the North Vietnamese in that part of Cambodia known as the "Parrot's Beak" and to send a combined American and South Vietnamese force against the North Vietnamese in the area called the "Fishhook" where, it was thought, the central command of the North Vietnamese was headquartered.  This second operation raised considerable opposition from Nixon's chief advisors.  Both Rogers and Laird opposed the use of American ground troops in Cambodia.  Some members of the White House staff thought the use of American troops was a repudiation of the Nixon doctrine that declared that the United States would no longer send troops to help a country defend itself.  But Nixon decided that American forces were needed to make the operation successful.  He would "go for broke."[16]

Patrick Buchanan, Nixon's most conservative speechwriter and the author of some of Spiro Agnew's best known phrases, was selected to draft the justification for Nixon's decision, though the president himself took an active part in composing the speech that went through eight drafts.  On the evening of April 30, 1970, Nixon went before a radio and television audience of 60 million to "describe the actions of the enemy, the actions I have ordered to deal with the situation, and the reasons for my decision."[17]

Using a map of Southeast Asia to show the relationship of Cambodia to South Vietnam and to illustrate how close the North Vietnamese forces in the Parrot's Beak were to Saigon, Nixon argued that the protection of American forces demanded "cleaning out major North Vietnamese and Vietcong occupied territories—these sanctuaries which serve as bases for attacks on both Cambodia and American and South Vietnamese forces in South Vietnam."   He promised that "once enemy forces are driven out of these sanctuaries and once their military supplies are destroyed, we will withdraw." He reviewed the course of Vietnamization (announced withdrawals of 250 thousand men, air operations down 20 percent, etc.) and claimed that the actions he had taken in Cambodia were "indispensable" to the successful completion of the Vietnamization program.

Directly contrary to the advice he had received that afternoon from Defense Secretary Laird, Nixon listed as a major target of the incursion the "headquarters of the entire Communist military operation in South Vietnam."   As Rowland Evans and Robert Novak reported, that headquarters "was no fortified bastion, no single entity, but a floating, amorphous command that slithered from one place to another in Cambodian jungles near the border of South Vietnam." Laird and Henry Kissinger warned Nixon that the chances of capturing such a command were remote and that the entire operation might be considered a failure if it were not found, but they were ignored. Nixon apparently felt that mentioning the headquarters dramatized his rationale for the operation and he refused to omit it from his text.[18]

Laird and Kissinger also warned Nixon about the political reaction the incursion would have, but Nixon pointedly ignored the feelings of those listeners who would see his move as an enlargement of the war, an increase in the fighting and its casualties, and an indication that he was still intent on seeking a military victory instead of a negotiated settlement.  On the contrary, the president seemed to go out of his way to attack his critics. He implied that antiwar demonstrators were responsible for destroying America's great universities and that Americans were witnessing "mindless attacks on all the great institutions which have been created by free civilizations in the last 500 years." Using the strongest language of the speech, he transcended the immediate Cambodian question to describe the global results of the situation: "If, when the chips are down, the world's most powerful nation, the United States of America, acts like a pitiful, helpless giant, the forces of totalitarianism and anarchy will threaten free nations and free institutions throughout the world. It is not our power but our will and character that is being tested tonight."

One portion of the speech was filled with self-pity as Nixon discussed his personal problems with critics.  In spite of the fact that he was making decisions in the same room that Wilson, Roosevelt, Eisenhower and Kennedy had used when they made their most fateful decisions, his policies, unlike theirs, were immediately assailed by "counsels of doubt and defeat from some of the most widely known opinion leaders of the Nation." The idea that the location where a decision was made should count for more than its quality probably did not appeal to many of Nixon's listeners, but Nixon's presentation had a more significant flaw.

In a thoughtful analysis of "expectations" of the American public in their president, James David Barber noted three important presidential duties. The president should provide reassurance, a feeling that things will be all right; he should provide a sense of progress and action; and the president should be a master politician who is above politics. Clearly Nixon was active and reassuring. Unfortunately for him, he also appeared to be politically motivated. Attempting to show that his decision was not political, Nixon made clear that he had studied the political aspects of the question and had considered the political results of his policy: "I have noted, for example, that a Republican Senator has said that this action I have taken means that my party has lost all chance of winning the November election. And others are saying today that this move against enemy sanctuaries will make me a one-term President. No one is more aware than I am of the political consequences of the action I have taken. . . . I would rather be a one-term President and do what I believe is right than to be a two-term President at the cost of seeing America become a second-rate power and to see this Nation accept the first defeat in its proud 190-year history." As Ruth Gonchar and Dan Hahn have observed, "There is nothing more political than a President's pretense of being above politics."[19]

As in the November 3 speech, Nixon refused to take the "easy political path." He repeated the assertion that he could "blame this war on previous administrations and to bring all of our men home immediately regardless of the consequences." Besides showing that Nixon considered the political ramifications of his actions, this argument carried considerably less weight than when he used it previously for the immediate withdrawal option he suggested was no longer available to him. Early in his administration he might have blamed the war on Johnson and brought the troops home, but by April 1970 he was as much responsible for the war as Johnson and he could hardly repudiate everything he had done for the past sixteen months. Furthermore, it had been clear since November 3 that a large segment of the populace opposed immediate withdrawal. Nixon would not gain politically by trading the leadership of the "silent majority" for the support of those he had shown to be a vocal minority.

The effect of this speech was mixed but those Nixon antagonized had the louder voices. The *New York Times* noted that the speech "appeared to harden previous convictions." Editorially, it found "astonishing . . . the intrusion of Presidential politics into a speech of this nature." The Cleveland *Plain Dealer* thought that Nixon's "maudlin appeal to patriotism" was offensive, but the Phoenix *Gazette* saw the Cambodian invasion as the "kind of thing we should have been doing all along." Editorial criticism of Nixon's position reached the front cover of the *New Republic*. On the floor of the Senate, Mike Mansfield of Montana denounced the president's conduct and Hugh Scott of Pennsylvania defended it. Antiwar activists saw the speech as a rallying point and as an impetus to renewed protest.[20]

A CBS telephone survey taken immediately after the broadcast found the respondents two to one in favor of Nixon's position. Two related Gallup polls suggested that most Americans were willing to support the president. A poll taken between March 18 and March 25 (before the invasion) showed 53 percent approving the way Nixon was handling his job as president and 30 percent disapproving. In the poll taken between April 29 and May 3, 57 percent approved and 31 percent disapproved, a slight gain over the previous poll. By late May, after the president's speech, the number favoring Vietnamization had decreased slightly, but the number favoring increased American military involvement had nearly doubled. On the other hand, more than half of those who responded wanted an immediate withdrawal from Vietnam or one with a set time of one year.[21]

Antiwar sentiment filled the mass media. Much of this was due to two events that occurred immediately after the speech rather than because of the speech itself. Nixon was responsible for the first. He failed to follow his own advice that the time immediately after a crisis is the most dangerous for the person involved because his guard is down then and he is not mentally prepared for challenges. The president found himself in such a situation the morning after his speech when he visited the Pentagon to be briefed on the Cambodian operation by the Joint Chiefs of Staff. Cheered by Pentagon employees, Nixon reacted with an impromptu speech much as Andrew Johnson responded to the serenaders in 1866. Caught up in the crowd's enthusiasm Nixon compared the soldiers in Vietnam, "the greatest," with "these bums, you know, blowing up the campuses. . . . The boys that are on the college campuses today . . . are burning up the books, storming around about this issue." Within a few days it was widely believed, especially on college campuses, that Nixon had called all college protesters "bums" and the estrangement between campus dissidents and the president increased tremendously. The editors of eleven major Eastern college newspapers ran a joint editorial calling for a nationwide strike by the academic community.[22]

The second event that flamed antiwar protest occurred on the campus of Kent State University. On May 4 two student demonstrators and two onlookers were killed by bullets fired by Ohio National Guardsmen. The grieving father of one of the dead students told the press, "My child was not a bum." Antiwar sentiment grew tremendously. By the second week in May, almost 450 colleges and universities were on strike or closed. But on May 30 Nixon reported to the nation that the Cambodian incursion had met its objectives and on June 30 he announced that the last American troops had left Cambodia. Safire concluded that the incursion was "daring, surprising, successful in the short run and successful in the long run. But Nixon acting as a leader came across to all too many people as a belligerent con man."23

On November 3, 1969, President Nixon successfully persuaded a majority of Americans that his Vietnamization policy would work if only he had their support. Having built his ethos by demonstrating his competence and trustworthiness, Nixon identified his policy with morality and patriotism. He also attempted to find common ground in the search for peace with those with whom he disagreed. Nixon's speech was overwhelmingly successful. But when the war dragged on and Nixon decided that he should send American ground troops into Cambodia, he once again had to seek support for his Vietnam program. To a limited degree he succeeded, but his language and tone alienated rather than quieted his opposition, and the number and fervor of antiwar protests increased dramatically. The results included tragedy on college campuses and a country more divided than ever on the conduct of the war.

# 6
# The Watergate and Resignation Speeches: Rhetoric Versus Fact

Following the announcement that a peace settlement had been negotiated in Vietnam in January 1973, President Richard Nixon's
popularity reached its zenith. Gallup reported that 68 percent of the
American people approved of the way he was handling his job; 25
percent disapproved, and 7 percent had no opinion. Eighty percent
expressed satisfaction with the Vietnam agreement; only 7 percent
were dissatisfied. From that moment on, however, Nixon's approval
rating declined sharply. By August 1974 only 24 percent of the public
approved of the way he was handling his office and 65 percent
thought he should be impeached. The main reason for this pre-
cipitous decline can be found in the response to a question Gallup
began asking in September 1972: "Have you heard or read about
Watergate?" Within nine months, 97 percent of the respondents answered "Yes."[1]

Throughout 1973 and 1974, Nixon sought to improve his standing with the public by issuing statements, holding press conferences,
and by delivering three major radio and television addresses. With
few exceptions he failed to convince the American people of his
innocence in the Watergate matter. The televised Watergate
investigation chaired by Senator Sam Ervin of North Carolina, the
confessions resulting from the sentencing tactics of Judge John
Sirica, the House Judiciary Committee's televised hearings, and
Nixon's own words transcribed from tapes made in his offices and
over his telephone proved to be far more persuasive than Nixon's
rhetorical strategy of denial, and ultimately led to his resignation.

The Watergate story began on June 17, 1972, when five men
were arrested in the ninth floor office of the Democratic party national chairman, Lawrence O'Brien, in the Watergate Office
Building. One of the culprits carried a notebook with the name "E.
Howard Hunt" and the initials "W. H." next to it. When asked at a
press conference for his reaction to the attempted burglary and
alleged wiretapping, White House press secretary Ron Zeigler

refused to comment on "a third-rate burglary."   Although George McGovern attempted to use the Watergate incident in his presidential campaign against Nixon as an example of "corruption" in the White House, the Watergate matter had little effect on voters who returned Nixon to the White House by an overwhelming majority in the November election.[2]

Hush money to the defendants in the burglary trial and per-jured testimony by those who had directed them kept Watergate out of the public consciousness until February 3, 1973, when the Ervin committee was set up by the senate to investigate irregularities in the 1972 election.  At the same time, Judge Sirica, convinced that there was more to the Watergate affair than those convicted of the burglary were telling, threatened the defendants with extremely harsh sen-tences that he promised to reduce if they would cooperate with the senate investigators.  As rumors about the involvement of a number of White House personnel began to circulate in the press, they sought to protect themselves and to protect the president.

Presidential counsel John Dean was the first to recognize that a conspiracy of silence could not be maintained and he began talking to the federal prosecutors during the week of April 9.  Attorney General Richard Kleindienst quickly reported to Nixon that John Ehrlichman, Bob Haldeman, and John Mitchell were indictable for various offenses leading up to or attempting to cover up the Watergate burglary.  Nixon had no choice if his administration were to have "even a chance at survival."  He had to act before further develop-ments involved him personally in the affair.  Regretfully he agreed to "cut off one arm and then the other" by summoning Haldeman and Ehrlichman to Camp David and asking them to resign.[3]

Speechwriter Ray Price was also invited to Camp David that weekend to write the speech explaining to the public what had hap-pened.  Through Ron Zeigler, Nixon told Price what he wanted to say: that he had been given assurances that none of those close to him had been involved, that since March, when he had heard from Dean that there was potential wrongdoing at a higher level, he had tried to investigate "this bizarre, senseless, wrong activity," and that the man at the top must assume responsibility for what happens in his organization.  He informed Price that he was not going to "pound the gavel of justice" because the judicial system was going to handle the culprits.  He added that whatever had happened had to be looked at "against the background of the violence, the disruptions, and the radical threats to the lives of public officials which had marked the 1972 political season."  He wanted Price to point out that although it was important to investigate and punish the guilty, it was equally important to "get on with the nation's business."[4]

Thinking the president had nothing to hide, Price went to work on the speech.  Nixon, however, was so distraught over losing his two top advisors, he could not work face-to-face with his speechwriter. Though they were both at Camp David they discussed the speech over the telephone.  Only on Monday afternoon did they get together.  Price described the scene: "Neither before or since, not even during the bitter ordeal of resignation week, did I ever see him so unraveled or so distraught as he was that afternoon. At one point he dropped the pages he was working on, and they simply lay on the floor beside him." Nixon's mind kept drifting away from the speech he hated to give. Finally, his voice "flat, distant, defeated," he turned to Price and asked: "Maybe I should resign. Do you think so? You've always been the voice of my conscience. If you think I should resign, just write it into the next draft, and I'll do it." By mentioning the unfinished business Nixon wanted to accomplish and the probable inability of Vice-President Agnew to see it through, Price encouraged Nixon to remain in office, though twice more that afternoon Nixon repeated his question.[5]

Both Zeigler and Price had grave reservations about Nixon's ability to pull himself together for the Monday evening broadcast. Shortly before Nixon went on the air, Zeigler attempted to bolster his confidence by telling him that the press statement that announced the staff resignations had been well received by the media. Nixon arrived in the Oval Office only ninety seconds before the scheduled start of the speech. Still nervous, but with his emotions under control, and flanked by a picture of his family and a bust of Abraham Lincoln, Nixon spoke "from my heart" to the American people and through a specially arranged hookup to a live audience in Great Britain where it was 2 a.m.[6]

William Benoit has analyzed a number of rhetorical strategies used by Nixon in his Watergate speeches and press statements. Three important strategies he noted in this first address on Watergate were "emphasizing investigations," "shifting blame," and "refocusing attention."[7]

Nixon first portrayed himself as a tireless investigator, attempting to find out what really happened: "I immediately ordered an investigation. . . . I personally assumed the responsibility. . . . I personally ordered those conducting the investigations to get all the facts and to report them directly to me. . . ." The number of investigations and the determination shown by Nixon were summed up in his statement: "I was determined that we should get to the bottom of the matter and that the truth should be fully brought out—no matter who was involved." By describing all that he had done to bring out the facts, Nixon implied that he personally has nothing to hide. He was seeking the evidence that would convict the guilty.

Nixon attempted to shift the blame for the burglary and the coverup to others both directly and indirectly. Directly, he claimed that he relied on repeated assurances that members of his Administration were not involved: "Because of these continuing reassurances, because I believed the reports I was getting, because I had faith in the persons from whom I was getting them, I discounted the stories in the press that appeared to implicate members of my Administration or other officials of the campaign committee." Indirectly, Nixon implied that his closest advisors were involved in the coverup by accepting their resignations. Although he protested that he wanted to avoid "any action that would appear to reflect on innocent people," he announced the resignations of Haldeman, Ehrlichman, Kleindienst, and Dean. The juxtaposition of the announcement of their resignations immediately following the statements that he had recently learned that facts had been concealed "from the public, from you, and from me," suggested that the perpetrators had been asked to resign.

Nixon attempted to excuse any misbehavior on his own part by blaming his busy schedule for his lack of attention: "1972 was a year of crucially important decisions, of intense negotiations, of vital new directions." Nixon recalled that he even "severely limited the number of my own campaign appearances." Important foreign policy matters took precedence over election campaigning and the Watergate affair.

Finally, Nixon tried to focus attention on other presidential activities. He claimed that it was essential "that we not be so distracted by events such as this that we neglect the vital work before us." He listed a number of events that demanded attention—the "Year of Europe," the next Soviet-American summit, a reduction of arms in Europe, a potential nuclear arms agreement, and peace in Southeast Asia and in the Middle East. Domestic programs required the president's attention as well and Nixon listed a number of goals that he hoped to accomplish in his second term.

Nixon's strategy did not work. The statements about his attempted investigations were not persuasive because the public did not trust those under suspicion to investigate themselves. Even Elliot Richardson, the newly named Attorney General, was not thought capable of investigating an administration he was now a part of. Before the Senate would consent to his nomination, he was forced to promise that he would name an independent prosecutor to get to the roots of Watergate. Eventually he named Archibald Cox.[8]

The attempt to shift blame onto others failed for two reasons. First, Nixon's reputation as the man in charge, most recently enhanced in the speech when he talked about how he was taking over the investigations, proved far stronger than his denials. Many listening to him thought he might have directed the Watergate burglary himself. The public also found it hard to believe that Nixon could be deceived by his own advisors. He was not considered gullible and a number of his aides would have had to lie to him to keep him from understanding the coverup. This, too, seemed highly unlikely. As Hugh Sidey wrote: "The fraternity of ex-White House aides believes that it would be impossible for a President to remain as ignorant of events as the White House indicates. 'You don't lie to a President' said one former White House aide. 'I can't imagine any man working with the President who would keep such facts from him,' said another."[9]

Making it even more difficult for Nixon to disassociate himself from his resigned aides were the words he used to describe Haldeman and Ehrlichman, "two of the finest public servants it has been my privilege to know." Price had attempted to talk Nixon out of praising his departing aides, but Nixon believed it and was determined to say it. He also attempted to justify their conduct. Those responsible for the Watergate affair were "people whose zeal exceeded their judgment, and who may have done wrong in a cause they deeply believed to be right." Later in the speech he said, "I know that it can be very easy, under the intensive pressures of a campaign, for even well-intentioned people to fall into shady tactics." Nixon claimed that what his aides did had been done before. He asserted that "inexcusable campaign tactics" have been "too often practiced and too readily accepted in the past" and that "both of our great parties have been guilty of such tactics in the past." Rather than condemn wrongdoing, Nixon offered as justification the idea that everyone was doing it. The public might accept this argument. Fifty percent believed that Watergate was not unusual and was the kind of activity both parties engaged in. But such a tactic did nothing to prove Nixon's own innocence.[10]

In attempting to focus public attention elsewhere, Nixon used his most persuasive argument. Many Americans felt the media had provided too much coverage of Watergate and related matters. Nixon's statement that the Watergate affair "has claimed far too much of my time and my attention" was persuasive, but he needed to spend more effort comparing what could be gained from such attention to what would be learned about Watergate.[11]

The basic problem with Nixon's speech, with its contradictory notion of fine public servants misleading the president, was that Nixon was not telling the truth. As he wrote later, he had known "some of the details" of the coverup before March 21, and when he became aware of their implications, he "embarked upon an increasingly desperate search for ways to limit the damage to my friends, to my administration, and to myself." Nixon recognized that his talk of bearing responsibility because he was the man at the top was "an abstraction" that people saw through. Instead of accounting for his role, he offered excuses: "They were not explanations of how a President of the United States could so incompetently allow himself to get in such a situation. That was what the people really wanted to know, and that was what my April 30 speech and all the other public statements I made about Watergate while I was President failed to tell them."[12]

Nixon would never again have an opportunity to extricate himself from the Watergate incident. The news media were filled with stories that seemed to confirm the fact that the president had something to hide. From the time John Dean began to testify before the Senate Committee investigating Watergate on Monday, June 25, until the hearings closed on August 7, on the average, twenty-two hours per week were devoted to Watergate-related televised news shows, specials, and the hearings themselves. White House use of wiretaps, potential misuse of the Internal Revenue Service, misappropriation of campaign funds, and the shocking discovery that Nixon had secretly recorded his conversations in the Oval Office and the Executive Office Building added to the public's distrust of the president and his popularity plummeted. By August 1973, Gallup reported that only 31 percent of the public thought he was handling his job well, the lowest rating any president had received in twenty years.[13]

Resolved to fight back, Nixon began at 2 a.m., August 7, a six-page outline of the main points he would cover in a television address designed to put Watergate behind him once and for all. The next day he asked Alexander Haig, who had taken Haldeman's position in the White House, to poll his staff on what he should say in his speech. Their suggestions ranged from "*mea culpas*" to a "two-fisted hard-line approach." On August 9, Nixon went to Camp David where he continued working on the speech with Ray Price and Patrick Buchanan. Not until August 14, when the speech had gone through eleven drafts, was Nixon satisfied.[14]

Nixon attracted a large television audience on the evening of August 15, but he almost immediately disappointed his listeners by saying, "I shall not attempt to deal tonight with the various changes in detail." He provided instead a "perspective from the standpoint of the Presidency." Barry Brummett has pointed out the difficulty Nixon faced by approaching the topic as a problem faced by the presidency. The office of president was not in trouble with the public. The holder of the office merited their distrust. Nixon would have to defend himself rather than his office and he would need to supply facts in support of his position. His word was no longer enough.[15]

Nixon, however, added little to his earlier statements. He claimed: "I had no prior knowledge of the Watergate break-in; I neither took part in nor knew about any of the subsequent coverup activities; I neither authorized nor encouraged subordinates to engage in illegal or improper campaign tactics." As in his April presentation, Nixon asserted that he had been misled by those around him: "Because I trusted the agencies conducting the investigations, because I believed the reports I was getting, I did not believe the newspaper accounts that suggested a coverup."

Turning to the tapes Nixon explained why he was unwilling to turn them over to the Special Prosecutor or to the Senate Investigating Committee "to help prove the truth of what I have said." He articulated clearly the need for confidentiality: ". . . frank discussion is only possible when those who take part in it know that what they say is in strictest confidence." Without assurance that their remarks would remain secret: "No one would want to advance tentative ideas that might later seem unsound. No diplomat would want to speak candidly in those sensitive negotiations which could bring peace or avoid war. No Senator or Congressman would want to talk frankly about the Congressional horsetrading that might get a vital bill passed."

However accurate Nixon's view of the need for confidentiality in the office of the president was, two factors worked against him. Many thought he did not want to surrender the tapes because they would disprove what he had claimed. His motives were not considered pure. Thus the Scripps-Howard papers that usually supported Nixon editorialized: ". . . people with nothing to hide do not hide things." Secondly, if confidentiality was so highly valued by the president, why did he tape the conversations in the first place? Seventy-five percent of the American public thought he should never have done it. Because Nixon seemed to be the first one to sacrifice the principle of confidentiality, he had little moral authority behind his argument. He had a similar problem with his pledge to "ensure that one of the results of Watergate is a new level of political decency and integrity in America." Everyone could approve of his goal, but the news of break-ins and "enemies lists" and "dirty tricks" in political campaigns, caused many to believe that Nixon was not the best person to accomplish such a goal. One could give weight to such a pledge only if he had no doubts about the integrity of the person giving it. Nixon's problem was that he had not resolved such doubts. As in the previous speech, Nixon listed "matters that cannot wait." Inflation, the cost of living, military strength, peace with honor in Southeast Asia, bringing home our prisoners of war, all these matters demanded his attention. Nixon promised that "those who would exploit Watergate in order to keep us from doing what we were elected to do will not succeed."16

Since Nixon was guilty of many of the offenses he denied, he could not hope to offer proof of innocence. What he might have done was admit what had happened, apologize, promise he would do better in the future, and ask the public's forgiveness. This was the route suggested by some supporters who, admittedly, did not know how much Nixon would have to confess. But Nixon's assertions of innocence when compared to the hours of testimony the public had already heard, did little to exonerate him. The most common complaint about Nixon's presentation was that he offered nothing new. Sixty-one percent of those who heard the broadcast were "dissatisfied" with his explanation. Nixon's rating in the Gallup poll showed an increase of seven percentage points immediately after the speech, but within six weeks, the additional points had disappeared.17

A number of unpleasant events and revelations kept Nixon from doing what he was elected to do. Vice-President Spiro Agnew was forced to resign in October, pleading "no contest" to a charge of evading income taxes. On October 12, the Court of Appeals ruled that Nixon had to turn over to Judge Sirica the nine tapes that Special Prosecutor Archibald Cox had requested. Still attempting to preserve the principle of confidentiality, however, Nixon offered a compromise. He would release edited transcripts of the relevant materials to Cox and Senator John Stennis, a well respected Democrat. They could listen to the tapes to verify the accuracy of the material Nixon turned over. Cox rejected the compromise and Nixon felt he had no option but to fire him. When Elliot Richardson and his deputy, William Ruckelshaus, resigned rather than carry out the order to fire Cox, Solicitor General Robert Bork accepted the responsibility and dismissed

Cox on October 20. What quickly became known as the "Saturday Night Massacre" was described by Theodore White: "The reaction that evening was as near instantaneous as it had been at Pearl Harbor, or the day of John F. Kennedy's assassination—an explosion as unpredictable and as sweeping as mass hysteria." A total of 450 thousand telegrams reached Congress, most calling for Nixon's impeachment. *Time* offered the first editorial in its fifty-year history: "The President Should Resign." Talk of impeachment became serious and Nixon's position became more and more untenable.[18]

In November, the White House disclosed, but could not explain, an eighteen-and-a-half minute gap in a subpoenaed tape of a meeting between Haldeman and Nixon in June 1972, shortly after the Watergate burglary. On February 6, 1974, the House of Representatives voted 410 to 4 to begin impeachment proceedings against Nixon and gave its Judiciary Committee, headed by Peter Rodino, broad subpoena powers. On March 1, several key Nixon aides, including Mitchell, Haldeman, Ehrlichman, and Charles Colson were indicted by a federal grand jury for conspiracy to cover up the Watergate incident.[19]

The pressure on Nixon to release the tapes grew throughout the spring of 1974. On April 11, 1974, the House Judiciary Committee subpoenaed forty-two tapes relating to Nixon's role in Watergate. On April 16, Special Prosecutor Leon Jaworski asked a federal district court to subpoena sixty-three White House conversations to use as evidence against accused Watergate coverup conspirators. By the end of April, five different subpoenas for tapes had been served on the president. Nixon searched for a dramatic way to end the requests for tapes and to dispose of the Watergate issue. The route he chose proved disastrous.[20]

On April 29, 1974, Nixon offered a televised address in which he announced that he was making public more than 1200 pages of transcribed tape recordings of his personal conversations about Watergate with his White House aides. The transcripts included most of the conversations requested by the Judiciary Committee; eleven of the subpoenaed tapes, he later reported, did not exist. Nixon claimed that "everything that is relevant is included—the rough as well as the smooth." Chairman Rodino and the ranking Republican member of the House Judiciary Committee, Edward Hutchinson, were invited to come to the White House and listen to the tapes in their entirety to verify that all portions related to the Watergate issue had been given to the Committee.[21]

Nixon described his situation accurately when he noted: "I have been well aware that my effort to protect the confidentiality of Presidential conversations has heightened the sense of mystery about Watergate and, in fact, has caused increased suspicions of the President. Many people assume that the tapes must incriminate the President, or that otherwise, he would not insist on their privacy." To prepare the audience for what they would read in the transcripts, Nixon noted that different readers would emphasize different things:

"From the beginning, I have said that in many places on the tapes there were ambiguities—a statement and comments that different people with different perspectives might interpret in drastically different ways—but although the words may be ambiguous, though the discussions may have explored many alternatives, the record of my actions is totally clear now, and I still believe I was totally correct then."

Nixon offered his conversation with John Dean on March 21, 1973, to show how he reacted when he first learned of the coverup. Howard Hunt was seeking to blackmail the president and Nixon concluded: "But by the end of the meeting, as the tape shows, my decision was to convene a new grand jury and to send everyone before the grand jury with instructions to testify." After quoting himself in a number of different conversations to show that he was not part of a coverup effort, Nixon declared: "To anyone who reads his way through this mass of materials I have provided, it will be totally, abundantly clear that as far as the President's role with regard to Watergate is concerned, the entire story is there."

Initial reactions to the speech were mixed, but reaction to the published transcripts was devastating. At first many Republicans welcomed the transcripts. On the day after the broadcast, a few Republicans took the House floor to praise Nixon's initiative. The Los Angeles *Times* said in an editorial that Nixon had "taken a giant step toward resolving the controversy over his relationship to the Watergate crimes and the subsequent coverup conspiracy."[22]

The House Judiciary Committee took a different view. They wanted tapes, not edited transcripts, so they voted twenty to eighteen to renew their subpoena for the tapes. Those who listened to the speech or heard or read excerpts from the transcripts were polled by Gallup who found 17 percent had a more favorable view of the president, but 42 percent had a less favorable one.[23]

As the transcripts were read in their entirety, more and more newspapers turned against Nixon. A number of editors who had supported Nixon throughout the Watergate crisis changed their minds when they read the transcripts. The Chicago *Tribune* spoke for many when it found: "The evidence against Mr. Nixon is in his own words, made public at his own direction. . . . It is saddening and hard to believe that for the first time in our history it is better that the President leave office than fight to keep it." The editor of the Omaha *World-Herald*, long a heartland supporter of the president, wrote: "The thrust of the 1308 pages of the transcript is that the President was trying to save his own skin and would consider almost any option, however bizarre, if it would help him do that." Even the Los Angeles *Times* had a change of heart: "Justice for the President and for the nation now requires his impeachment."[24]

Republicans in Congress quickly retreated from their previous statements of support. John Ashbrook spoke for many of his congressional colleagues when he said, "I listened to him on television last Monday night and for the first time in a year I believed him.

Then I read the March 21st transcript and it was incredible, unbelievable." Republican Minority Leader, John Rhodes, thought the president should consider resigning.[25]

The congressional leaders reflected their constituents.  A Gallup poll taken between May 31 and June 3, 1974, found 44 percent in favor of Nixon's removal from office, 41 percent opposed, and 15 percent with no opinion.  The published transcripts were selling as fast as they could be printed.  Bookstores reported that they were the hottest selling item since *The Exorcist*.  Clearly, Nixon's transcribed words had more impact than his televised attempts to explain them.  And, unfortunately for him and for his remaining supporters, there were still more tapes to be heard.[26]

The House Judiciary Committee voted twenty-seven to eleven on July 27, 1974, to impeach Nixon for engaging in a course of conduct designed to obstruct the Watergate investigation.  On July 29, by vote of twenty-eight to ten, the committee declared that the president had abused the powers of the presidency, and on July 30, they charged that by defying the committee's requests for tapes and documents, Nixon had committed an impeachable offense.  On two additional articles, one dealing with the bombing of Cambodia and the other with his personal finances, the Committee decided not to impeach.[27]

In the early morning hours of July 31, 1974, Nixon weighed the unhappy political choices before him: he could resign immediately; he could wait until the House voted to impeach him and then resign; or he could fight the impeachment charges in the Senate and hope for acquittal.  The major argument against resigning was, in his own words, that he "was not and never had been a quitter."  The idea that he would be forced from his job and end his career in disgrace was "repugnant."  On the other side of the ledger, he realized that once he was impeached by the House, he would be "crippled politically."  Further, if he stayed and fought, he would probably end "defeated and dishonored."  The 1974 Congressional elections would surely become a referendum on his administration and Republicans would probably lose a large number of House and Senate seats.  Nevertheless, Nixon turned over the yellow sheets on which he was making notes and wrote, "End career as a fighter."[28]

Nixon's resolve lasted less than a week.  Once again, his own words, this time those recorded at a series of three meetings with H. R. Haldeman on June 23, 1972, a week after the Watergate break-in, returned to haunt him and cost him the support of those staff members who had been encouraging him to continue the fight.  What Ronald Zeigler heard and what Alexander Haig read in transcript form, was a conversation in which Haldeman told the president that John Mitchell had probably been aware of the Watergate operation from the beginning and that the FBI was about to trace presidential campaign funds through a Mexican back to the Watergate burglars.  Nixon agreed with Haldeman that the CIA should be used to tell the FBI to drop their investigation and "don't go any further into this case period!"  The tape showed Nixon guilty of obstructing justice and proved that he had lied about his efforts to get to the bottom of the affair.[29]

That these words of the president were heard at all resulted from a unanimous Supreme Court decision in *United States v. Nixon* that held that Nixon would have to turn over to Special Prosecutor Leon Jaworski, the sixty-four tapes he had subpoenaed. In preparing the tapes for submission to Jaworski, Fred Buzhardt, assistant to James St. Clair, who was handling Nixon's defense, heard the conversation between Nixon and Haldeman and reported to St. Clair and to Alexander Haig that it was the "smoking pistol" that Nixon supporters had dreaded and Nixon opponents had been searching for. Nixon had not only lied to the public about his involvement in the coverup, he had lied to his attorneys.[30]

St. Clair, immediately recognizing the significance of the June 23 tape, told Nixon he would have to make it public immediately. It contained evidence of a crime and it could not be concealed. Nixon agreed reluctantly and the tape was released on Monday, August 5, together with a statement by Nixon that the tape was "at variance with certain of my previous statements." Nixon admitted that "those arguing my case, as well as those passing judgment on the case, did so with information that was incomplete and in some respects erroneous. This was a serious act of omission for which I take full responsibility and which I deeply regret." Nixon concluded that the record "in its entirety, does not justify the extreme step of impeachment and removal of a President." Nixon's press support did not agree. Those few newspapers that had remained on Nixon's side throughout the revelations of the past two years immediately called for his resignation or impeachment in the light of the most recent disclosure. Even the *Wall Street Journal* concluded that Nixon's resignation would be "fitting."[31]

On Tuesday, John Rhodes, the Republican minority leader in the House, announced that unless the president resigned, he would vote on the House floor for Article I of the Impeachment Articles, that Nixon had acted to obstruct justice. That afternoon, Nixon decided that resignation was the only realistic course of action left to him and he told Haig to notify Ray Price to begin work on a statement: "Not a breast-beating *mea culpa*, not a speech proclaiming a guilt that he did not feel—but a healing speech, one that would help rally the country to his successor."[32]

Price received a draft back from Nixon on Wednesday with the scribbled notation that he had met with congressional leaders of both parties and they had unanimously advised him that he did not have the support of Congress "for difficult decisions affecting peace abroad, and our fight against inflation at home so essential to the lives of every family in America." Nixon had written these lines before the meeting had actually taken place, but he knew what the leadership was going to tell him. No more than a dozen representatives would support him in the House and, probably, a like number in the Senate.[33]

Also in the margin of the Price draft Nixon wrote, "I have never been a quitter.  To leave office is abhorrent to every instinct in my body."  These words with the addition of "before my term is completed" after "office" were placed in the speech.  Nixon also asked Price to look up a favorite quotation by Theodore Roosevelt that Nixon had given copies of to friends after his 1962 defeat for the governorship of California.  In a speech delivered at the Sorbonne in 1910, Theodore Roosevelt had said:

> It is not the critic who counts; not the man who points out how the strong man stumbles, or where the doer of deeds could have done them better.  The credit belongs to the man who is actually in the arena, whose face is marred by dust and sweat and blood; who strives valiantly; who errs, and comes short again and again, because there is not effort without error and shortcoming; but who does actually strive to do the deeds; who knows the great enthusiasms, the great devotions; who spends himself in a worthy cause; who at the best knows in the end the triumph of high achievement and who at the worst, if he fails, at least fails while daring greatly, so that his place shall never be with those cold and timid souls who know neither victory nor defeat.[34]

Not wanting Nixon's critics to have any more reason for attacking him than they already had, Price omitted the first sentence and the last part of the paragraph beginning with "so that . . ." from the speech.  He thus placed the emphasis of the quotation on the "man in the arena" and not on the "critic" or the "timid souls" and Nixon agreed to the change.[35]

Throughout Wednesday evening and well into Thursday morning, Nixon called Price at his home to offer further suggestions that Price incorporated into the speech.  He wanted the speech to look to the future.  He suggested words like: "We have ended America's longest war, but the goals ahead are ultimately greater and more important.  We've started to limit nuclear arms between the U.S. and the U.S.S.R.  But our goal must be not just limitation of nuclear arms, but these terrible weapons that could destroy civilization as we know it must be destroyed."[36]

In his final telephone call on Thursday morning, Nixon instructed Price not to consult with Haig or with the National Security Council on the content of the speech because, "On this one, I just want to say the things that are in my heart.  I want to make this *my* speech."[37]

Nixon's opening, "This is the 37th time I have spoken to you from this office, where so many decisions have been made that shaped the history of this Nation," was suggested by him at an 11 a.m. meeting with Price.  The exact number had to be checked by staff members and they found that the speech marked the 37th time, the

Nation's 37th president spoke from the Oval Office.   By Thursday afternoon, the speech was ready for delivery.[38]

Following a farewell meeting with the leadership of the House and Senate and a very emotional session with forty to fifty of Nixon's strongest congressional supporters, Nixon went before an audience of 110 million at 9 p.m. to become the first president ever to resign his office.   Gerald Wilson has noted that one-third of the speech was a recounting of Nixon's accomplishments and his promise to continue working for peace "as long as I have a breath of life in my body."   A second significant segment of the speech dealt with Nixon's assertions that he was resigning for the good of the country and against his own personal predilection.   He was attempting to do "what was best for the nation."[39]

Fewer than twenty-four seconds were spent on regret.   Nixon simply stated: "I regret deeply any injuries that may have been done in the course of the events that led to this decision.   I would say only that if some of my judgments were wrong—and some were wrong— they were made in what I believed at the time to be the best interest of the Nation."   Given that criminal prosecution was still a distinct possibility at the time Nixon spoke, it was not surprising that Nixon never specified which of his judgments were wrong and never admitted that any deeds were unlawful.   Nixon had told Price to avoid any groveling mea culpas and those who expected such remarks were disappointed.[40]

Nixon refused to accept any moral blame for what had happened and some critics have complained that Nixon failed to offer the real reason for his resignation.   Roger Mudd, for example, criticized the speech because "it did not deal with the realities of why he was leaving.   There was no accounting in the speech of how he got there, why he was leaving that oval room."   In Nixon's mind, however, he was leaving because he had lost his political base.   If his supporters in Congress had remained steadfast in spite of the obstruction of justice heard in the Nixon-Haldeman tape, he would not have resigned.   Other presidents, he was convinced, had done the same or worse.   His fault had been that he had taped himself talking about it.   He was not ashamed of the acts he had done; he was not resigning because he had committed a crime.   He was resigning because he did not have enough support in Congress to continue.[41]

Nixon's final attempt to justify his actions on the basis of national security fell on deaf ears.   Not once in the many speeches or statements related to Watergate had he been able to offer support for his assertion.   To most of his listeners, Nixon's assertion of "national security" translated into "saving my own skin" and at this late date, Nixon could do nothing to change that perception.[42]

Except for those who felt the president had not gone far enough in explaining his downfall, reaction to the speech and to the resignation was generally favorable.   *Newsweek* reported that Nixon left office "with as much grace as he could muster and as much face as he could save."   Perhaps because of his muted delivery, Nixon's "voice did not display the aloofness and superiority characteristic of his 'I am the President' posture."  Both Dan Rather and Walter Cronkite observed a genuineness in Nixon's remarks attributable to what Gerald Wilson called a "non-verbal tone of dignity and conciliation."  Gallup reported that 79 percent thought that Nixon had done the right thing by resigning; only 13 percent thought he should have remained in office.  By a majority of 55 percent to 37 percent, the public thought he should not be pursued to answer criminal charges.[43]

Nixon's Thursday evening speech should have been his last public address as president, but it was not.  Against the strong protests of his wife and daughters, Nixon invited the American public to watch his farewell statement to his cabinet and staff assembled in the East Room of the White House on Friday morning, shortly before his departure for California.  For reasons that are not clear, even to a reader of Nixon's memoirs, Nixon allowed television cameras to record a very private moment: "That's the way it has to be.  We owe it to our supporters.  We owe it to the people."[44]

Nixon's impromptu remarks were directed toward the immediate audience, revealed some of the best and some of the worst sides of his character, and presented onlookers with an insider's view of the president most had not witnessed before.  Adding great impact to the moment were Nixon's hesitant delivery and the emotional nonverbal cues that made some listeners feel he would be unable to finish.  Missing from the remarks was any organizational thread as Nixon voiced the thoughts that came to him as he looked around the room at friends and associates he felt he had let down.  Many of them would be forced to seek new positions when the Ford administration took over.  Nixon wanted to thank them for their service to him and to inspire them to continue working for the government if asked.[45]

That Nixon was more concerned with the people in front of him than with the television audience can be seen in the way he spoke to the "you" in his audience, and in the type of praise and encouragement he offered them.  He noted that "many of you have been here for many years. . . . We want you to continue to serve in government if that is your wish."  He asked them "to serve our next President as you have served me."  He praised them for their commitment and thanked them for the services they had rendered, for "this great office, great as it is, can only be as great as the men and women who work for and with the President."  The people he was addressing were "indispensable to this Government."[46]

Both the dark and light sides of Nixon's character were displayed in these impromptu remarks.  On the dark side there was the distrust of the media, the belief that the media would not accurately portray the reception his supporters had given him.  He was sure that the four-minute ovation he received upon entering the East Room would be misinterpreted as staged and he wanted the world to know it was spontaneous.  He attempted to set the record straight with humor: "I think the record should show that this is one of those spontaneous things that we always arrange whenever the President comes in to speak, and it will be so reported in the press, and we don't mind, because they have to call it as they see it.  But on our part, believe me, it is spontaneous."  He clearly did mind, yet he felt the need to say that he did not.

Also on the dark side was the inappropriate preoccupation with wealth and financial gain.  He noted that the White House "isn't the biggest house" and did not contain the paintings "of great, great value" that homes of other heads of state had.  He eventually concluded that the White House was the best house because it had "a great heart."  That Nixon made such comparisons at this time is surprising.  Equally interesting were Nixon's repeated statements about the cost of government service.  He was pleased that "no man or woman ever profited at the public expense or the public till" during his administration.  He wished that he were a wealthy man because "I would like to recompense you for the sacrifices that all of you have made to serve in government."  He was proud that his staff "have been willing to sacrifice, in a pecuniary way, to serve in government." He was worried that young people felt that a public servant was interested only in "feathering his nest."  His comment that "at the present time, I have got to find a way to pay my taxes" was the best use of humor in the speech, but it too showed how many of his thoughts were on financial matters.

Finally, Nixon's basic insecurity showed itself in two additional attempts at humor.  When he introduced a quotation by Theodore Roosevelt, whom he had also cited in his resignation speech, Nixon remarked: "As you know, I kind of like to read books.  I am not educated, but I do read books."  The Whittier College graduate had never forgotten that he could not afford to take the scholarship to Harvard.  Apparently feeling that he had to justify his remark that he had passed the California bar exam on the first try, Nixon offered this reason: "My writing was so poor the bar examiner said, 'We have just got to let the guy through.'"  Even as a joke, the line does not make sense, but an insecure Nixon felt compelled to justify his success on the bar exam he had taken almost forty years earlier.

Price wrote that some portions of the speech seemed to show Nixon's light side lecturing the dark.  This was most notably the case when Nixon, who as president may have been more conscious of "enemies" than any of his predecessors, advised: "Always give your best, never get discouraged, never be petty; always remember, others may hate you, but those who hate you don't win unless you hate them, and then you destroy yourself."[47]

Another lecture from the light side to the dark came early in the speech when Nixon, one of the most secluded of presidents, regretted he was not more open to his staff.  As Nixon looked around the room, he said: "I see so many on this staff that, you know, I should have been by your offices and shaken hands, and I would love to have talked to you and found out how to run the world."  But he never did, "I just haven't had the time."

Nixon's primary purpose was to inspire his listeners to get on with their lives in spite of any difficulties they might face. As he had in numerous campaign speeches, especially stumping across the Middle West, Nixon found examples of successfully overcoming adversity in his own parents. His "old man" had owned "the poorest lemon ranch in California," but he was "a great man, because he did his job, and every job counts up to the hilt, regardless of what happens." His mother, who had witnessed the early deaths of two sons and who had taken care of tubercular patients to support herself and an ill son in Arizona, was a "saint."[48]

Theodore Roosevelt provided a more heroic example of someone who faced a tragedy but did not allow it to prevent him from reaching his goals. Nixon was not thinking of his own problems exclusively when he read from Roosevelt's diary about the sudden death of his young wife. He was concerned about "all of us" and warned his listeners that we think that "when someone dear to us dies, we think when we lose an election, we think that when we suffer a defeat that all is ended. We think, as T. R. said, that the light has left his life forever. Not true. It is only a beginning, always." He had said the previous night that he was "not a quitter" and he wanted to use the example of Roosevelt to inspire his staff not to quit, no matter how disappointed they were. He suggested that only if you "have been in the deepest valley can you ever know how magnificent it is to be on the highest mountain." With gratitude and with the promise that they would always be in his heart and in his prayers, Nixon concluded to a last round of applause and the tears of many in attendance.

One observer commented, "That's probably the real Nixon. It's a shame he couldn't have been like that more often." Barbara Walters, noting that Nixon had made no effort to wipe away the perspiration that always bothered him on previous public occasions and that he had used his reading glasses in public for the first time when he read Roosevelt's words, noted that on this occasion Nixon showed himself to be "a very *human* man, a side he felt a president shouldn't show." Richard Nixon may have revealed more about himself in the last speech of his presidency than he had ever revealed before.[49]

# Conclusion

Those who knew Richard Nixon as a child, as a student in high school and college, and even as a law student described him as "rather quiet—a little shy," "not a hail-fellow-well-met by a long shot," and "the last person in the class one would have picked to become a political headline." Even after he attained the presidency, observers found him a "loner" and his friend Bob Finch reported, "He's still a solitary." Although he was never comfortable with people on an individual basis, Nixon discovered that in a public speaking situation, he could address everyone without speaking to anyone in particular. Longtime associate William Rogers observed about Nixon, "While he is likely to maintain a serious, almost brooding countenance in the company of three or four persons, he lights up like a Christmas tree when confronted with a crowd." It was in the classroom that Nixon first learned that through public speaking he could shed his inhibitions and achieve the admiration of his listeners. He also learned to debate both sides of an issue, to control an encounter through extensive preparation and by surprising his opponent, to value feedback, and to attack his opponent's position rather than to defend his own.[1]

The center of attention at high school assemblies, Nixon spoke not because he had something he wanted to say, but because contest speaking and interscholastic debating offered him an opportunity to gain recognition and applause. Since he had to debate both sides of an issue, Nixon developed no emotional involvement with the truth or the real merits of a position. He spoke to win. When he entered political life, Nixon applied what he had learned in high school and college, but now the rhetorical strategies he used in political debates were often not appropriate. What he said affected people's lives. When he debated against Jerry Voorhis in 1946, his arguments that Voorhis had been endorsed by a political action committee dominated by communists and that Voorhis was an ineffective legislator were not true, and Nixon probably knew it. He successfully put Voorhis on the defensive, but he misled the voters about Voorhis's attitude toward communism and about his ability to get legislation passed.[2]

Stewart Alsop found that 98 percent of the examples used by anti-Nixon writers to support their negative viewpoint toward him were examples of "tricky debating techniques."   Furthermore, as in the Voorhis campaign, these techniques probably had little impact on the outcome of the election.  In 1946, for example, high prices and the shortage of consumer goods influenced voters to seek a change and incumbent Democrats lost elections throughout the country.  But Nixon used questionable debate tactics anyway, Alsop believed, "because he was trained in their use."   Speaking against Helen Douglas in his campaign for the Senate in 1950, Nixon pointed to the number of times she had voted the same way as Vito Marcantonio, a representative from New York thought to be a communist.  He knew that he himself had voted with them on more than one hundred occasions and that a majority of the House had supported many of the issues in question.  The statement about Douglas's voting record was true, but the inferences Nixon wanted his audience to draw about her political philosophy were not.  Nixon told the truth, but certainly not the whole truth.[3]

Perhaps the most revealing example of Nixon's attitude toward the truth in a debate situation took place in the fourth Nixon-Kennedy debate.  He opposed the taking of aggressive action against Castro brilliantly, even though he knew that the Eisenhower administration was planning just such action and that he himself had urged that it be undertaken as soon as possible.  The fact that he was taking a public position on an issue of major importance in the midst of a campaign for the presidency did not stop Nixon from arguing a position he did not believe in.  Apparently, it was just another debate and he wanted to win.

The inner conflict caused by the desire to win an argument at the risk of sacrificing the truth may be the key to understanding a hallmark of Nixon's extemporaneous speaking style—his use of such phrases as "Let me be perfectly clear" or "Let me be candid." Psychiatrist Eli Chesen observed that such statements were not required by the listening audience, but they were "obligatory for Nixon."  Chesen argued that Nixon "*needs* to use these expressions to convince himself of the 'truths' that he is uncertain about."  In other words, such expressions are directed at the speaker himself.  Chesen concluded that Nixon "in his attempts to document his candor . . . is demonstrating a lack of it."[4]

As part of his debate training, Nixon learned the value of extensive preparation, immediate feedback, and the importance of an attack over a defense.  Before the Voorhis campaign started, Nixon studied his opponent's voting record until he knew it better than Voorhis did.  With little time to prepare for the fund speech in 1952, he relied on those arguments he had found successful in quieting hecklers along the campaign trail, but he also contacted the history department at Whittier College to verify the accuracy of a quotation by

Lincoln he wanted to use.  Preparing his first inaugural address in 1969, Nixon reportedly read all the inaugural speeches of all his predecessors.  He especially liked FDR's, Theodore Roosevelt's, John Kennedy's, and Thomas Jefferson's.  Working with Ray Price, he gathered suggestions from such diverse sources as Henry Kissenger, Billy Graham, and Paul Keyes, the gagwriter who created the "Laugh In" television show.  Thus, even for this ceremonial occasion Nixon was well prepared.  Every important televised address called for extensive preparation.  Nixon began writing his November 3, 1969, speech on Vietnam almost three weeks before it was to be delivered.  On the weekend of October 14, he secluded himself at Camp David where he worked twelve to fourteen hours a day on the speech.  He conferred in person with members of his cabinet and with members of Congress.  The speech went through more than twelve revisions before he was satisfied.[5]

A tactic that grew out of Nixon's concern for preparation, a concern that one psychiatrist claimed was a result of a compulsive need to control every situation, was the use of surprise, an unexpected statement or idea for which his opponent would be unprepared.  Nixon surprised Voorhis by producing during a debate a memorandum from a political action committee calling for the election of Voorhis, support even Voorhis was unaware he had.  He shocked Helen Douglas with a letter of support and a contribution to his campaign from the other "Eleanor Roosevelt."  He looked forward to the "surprise" he had in store for the antiwar protestors when he adopted a hard line against them in his November 3, 1969 speech.  The revelation of the incursion into Cambodia was even more shocking to antiwar activists.  The imposition of wage-price controls and the announcement that he would visit China were additional examples of how Nixon used surprise to control the political agenda.  During the Watergate period Nixon tried to keep his opponents off balance with surprise announcements and changes of position.  He accepted the resignations of his top aides.  He provided transcripts of his private conversations after vowing that the tapes were confidential and that he would never surrender them.  He fired the special prosecutor.  He even kept the timing of his resignation a secret from his own cabinet.[6]

Nixon also attempted to control the media.  Convinced that his poor physical appearance on television, rather than anything he said, contributed to his loss to Kennedy in 1960, Nixon resolved that he would not suffer the same fate in his 1968 campaign.  He refused to participate in presidential debates and he appeared on television only when he could control the format.  He held press conferences only when he deemed it absolutely necessary.  Even the newspaper reporters travelling with his campaign had little access to him.  Nevertheless he made sure that his message reached the voters.  More than 40 television spots saturated the country.[7]

To maintain control but to appear spontaneous, Nixon initiated a new type of program—a question and answer format that allowed six to eight ordinary people (almost always including one black, a housewife, a businessman, a liberal, and a workingman) to ask him unrehearsed questions.  The live hour-long shows were broadcast on state or regional networks so that viewers in one part of the country would never see more than one of the broadcasts.  Thus Nixon could repeat the exact same response a number of times or he could change his reply to reflect the interests of the audience he was addressing. The local Republican club provided a studio audience to applaud Nixon's answers and to impress the viewers with the enthusiasm that Nixon's command of the issues stirred in them.  The press was never allowed into the television studio because they were not part of the "show."[8]

The 1968 campaign ended with two two-hour telethons—one live in the eastern half of the country and one live in the West.  Operators in the Los Angeles studio answered 125 telephones, reported the questions they received to a control desk, and the best questions were selected for host Bud Wilkinson to read to Nixon.  What the television audience did not know was that Nixon had certain questions he wanted to answer and when a question on the right issue reached the control desk, a similar question previously written by the Nixon staff was forwarded to Wilkinson for Nixon's prepared answer.  Again a studio audience, including Nixon's family, was present to applaud on cue.  Nixon received the immediate feedback he desired and his management of the program was complete.  He controlled the questions, the answers, and the audience's response.[9]

As president, Nixon continued to limit the access he allowed reporters.  He preferred to go over their heads to present his messages directly to the people.  He used prime-time television to a far greater extent than did his predecessors.  By changing the time of his State of the Union address from 12:30 p.m. to 9:00 p.m., he more than doubled his audience from 22.5 million in 1970 to 54.4 million in 1971.  Instead of holding televised press conferences in the morning as had been the custom, he moved them to the evening hours and doubled the number of people who heard him.[10]

Nixon also used television in a number of less traditional ways. He agreed to be interviewed about football at halftime of the Texas-Arkansas game.   Tricia Nixon's wedding reception received extensive television coverage.  Nixon appeared with Barbara Walters on the "Today" program where he talked about his family.  Joseph Califano, counsel for the Democratic National Committee, charged that such interviews permitted "the President to project a highly favorable image" because the questions used were of a personal nature and were "asked with the utmost deference."  Perhaps the largest television audience in history, 125 million Americans, watched as Nixon placed a "telephone" call to the astronauts who had just landed on the moon.  Nixon's trip to China dominated prime-time television at a time when Democrats hoped to attract interest to their process of selecting a candidate to oppose Nixon in the upcoming election.[11]

During the 1972 presidential election and early in his second term, Nixon turned to a medium little used by presidents since Franklin Roosevelt. He talked to the country over the radio. Such talks offered Nixon a number of advantages. The substance of what he said was immediately reported by the press. He did not have to worry about his physical appearance and his voice was well suited to radio. Finally, he avoided the potential problem of overexposure on television.[12]

Feedback always played an important role in Nixon's approach to public speaking. He used it to improve his performance and to reinforce his self-confidence. As a congressional candidate, he relied on his wife Pat to sit in the audience, to take notes, and to offer suggestions for improvement. Eventually campaign aides and media specialists took over his wife's role, but after every important speech, Nixon continued to check with his family to seek reinforcement. He took great pride in the telegrams and letters of support he received after a major presentation.

Throughout his career, Nixon's speeches reflected a central belief: "You cannot win a battle in any arena of life merely by defending yourself." The Checkers speech is the prime example of this tactic, but he also used it successfully throughout his congressional campaigns and even in his presidential addresses. In two situations where one might have expected to find Nixon attacking, however, he was surprisingly defensive and, as it turned out, ineffective. Against Kennedy in the first presidential debate he muted his attack and he lost. In the major Watergate speeches, he found few villains to attack. The "zeal" of his staff may have "exceeded their judgment" and they "may have done wrong in a cause they deeply believed to be right," but Nixon said he would accept responsibility for their actions. Not until John Dean testified before the Ervin Committee did Nixon begin to question his former aide's credibility. Perhaps Nixon would have been more effective had he challenged his critics harder in the Watergate speeches; Nixon was his most persuasive when he was attacking.[13]

More than most political figures, Nixon was responsible for his own speeches. Throughout his congressional career, he was his own chief speechwriter and devoted many hours to the preparation of his efforts. His notes for the fund speech, for example, were written in longhand on five sheets of yellow legal pad paper and he made corrections up to the time of the broadcast. Even as vice-president he generally wrote his own material based on "a great deal of reading" in the particular field he intended to cover. He then wrote out the various thoughts he wanted to develop, made a rough outline in which he tried to develop "one central theme," refined the outline, and finally dictated a draft. A major presentation took four or five days to prepare, and even then, he reported that he was seldom satisfied.[14]

Upon reaching the presidency in 1968, Nixon worked with a staff of writers, the most important of whom were Raymond Price,

William Safire, and Patrick Buchanan. Nixon felt that each of the three had his own particular strengths, and he would call on that writer for a specific paragraph or for a draft of a complete speech. Nixon did not want the three men to work together, rather he would select for a particular occasion the writer who would give a speech the particular "tilt" he wanted. Safire reported: "On the old political spectrum, Price was the liberal, Buchanan the conservative, Safire the centrist; Price a WASP, Buchanan a Catholic, Safire a Jew. . . . Price is introverted, I'm extraverted, Buchanan in between." Often a Buchanan draft would be given to Price for softening or to Safire to make it more quotable. At various times, all three writers worked on foreign affairs speeches, depending on the mood Nixon wanted to create. Price was considered relatively dovish, Buchanan, especially after his 1970 Cambodian incursion speech, hawkish, and Safire was in the middle.[15]

During his second administration, Nixon put Ray Price in charge of a speechwriting staff that included Aram Bakshian, Lee Huebner, John Andrews, and Noel Koch. Price's assistant, David Gergen, edited drafts but usually did not write them. Buchanan acted as a special advisor to the president and Safire left the White House in March 1973.[16]

Surprising in light of the strong speechwriting staff he assembled to assist him is that Nixon's most successful speech as president was one he wrote entirely by himself. The "silent majority" speech of November 1969 was written in seclusion at Camp David and the day of the speech Price could only report: "I don't know what's in the speech. I contributed nothing—not even a flourish." This speech took the wind out of the antiwar movement and gave Nixon time for his Vietnamization plan to work. Richard Wilson, chief of the Washington bureau for Cowles Publications, claimed, "No more effective single speech ever was made by a president, certainly in this century."[17]

Yet, while Nixon was an effective political orator, perhaps the best of his generation, he was never an eloquent one. His rhetoric seldom soared beyond the commonplace because, throughout his career, Nixon consciously strived for a simple style. His speeches were meant to be heard by an immediate audience not to be read by future generations. In 1959 Vice-President Nixon reported, "I'm a great believer in making my speeches as simple as possible as far as vocabulary and sentence construction are concerned. In fact I am usually criticized for over-simplifying." Analyzing Nixon's style in 1968, Safire balanced five positive comments with five negative ones. Among the positive attributes he noted that Nixon's speeches were well structured; they had an introduction, a body, and a conclusion. The vocabulary "can be understood by most people." He also applauded the "awareness of the people listening and an effort to relate to them." On the other hand, Safire decried the overuse of verbal signals and too much obvious structure; obvious hedging, and "bending over backwards not to seem like it is going for the jugular in personal criticism."   He found that "a holier-than-thou tone creeps into the Nixon style and elicits a 'where-does-he-come-off' reaction."[18]

Based on a computer analysis of a number of Nixon's speeches in different time periods and before different types of audiences, Rod Hart discovered that although Nixon's language was simple and clear, his ideas could best be described as equivocal or ambivalent. What Hart called Nixon's "verbal absolutism" was generally quite low, except at those times when he was addressing a highly favorable audience, such as a Republican national convention.   Hart claimed that Nixon mastered the best of both worlds, offering his listeners "forthright equivocality."   Such a style was very important to Nixon for it allowed him to reach outside Republican ranks to appeal to Democrats and independents without losing his basic Republican support.[19]

One of the most remarkable features of Nixon's political success was that he won so many elections in spite of the fact that he was a member of a minority party and had to capture the votes of Democrats and independents to be elected.   In his first political contest, Democrat Jerry Voorhis received 7,000 more votes than Nixon in the primary, but Nixon won the general election.   In his Senate race, California Democrats outregistered Republicans by 3 million to 2 million, but Nixon beat Douglas by 680,000 votes.   In March 1960, Gallup found that 58 percent of those polled supported Democratic candidates and only 42 percent favored Republicans.   In the previous Congressional election, Democratic candidates collected 25.3 million votes to 19.9 million for Republicans.   Yet Nixon came within 119,000 votes of John Kennedy.[20]

Nixon faced the same odds in his later presidential races.   In June 1968, Gallup reported that 27 percent of those interviewed considered themselves Republicans; 46 percent were Democrats, and 27 percent were independent.   Nixon won the presidency, but both houses of Congress remained in Democratic hands, the first time this had happened to a new president since the election of James Buchanan.   In 1972, even though Nixon received more than 60 percent of the vote, one of the largest margins ever, Republicans picked up only 13 seats in the House, not enough for control, and lost two seats in the Senate.   Across the country, Nixon ran well ahead of his party.   Nixon always had to appeal to large numbers of voters outside his own party to win an election.[21]

Another way that Nixon's style may have won him supporters outside of his party was through his use of narrative.   Nixon's narratives tended to have the coherence and fidelity needed for acceptance.   His defense of himself from the charge that a millionaires' fund allowed him to live beyond his means was the story of how a poor boy made good.   Millions of Americans found that Nixon's struggles with mortgage payments, the repayment of loans from his parents, and even his wife's cloth coat, were materials with which they could identify   Campaigning in America's heartland in 1960, Nixon avoided formal presentations. Instead he talked extemporaneously about his childhood, the sacrifices his parents had made for him, the pony his dying brother wanted but his family could not afford if they were to pay for shoes and clothing.  Reporters travelling with Nixon were unimpressed, calling the day Nixon spoke about the pony "Maudlin Friday."  But Middle America understood Nixon's anecdotes and the values they affirmed.  The farm belt gave Nixon the most decisive victory any region of the country gave either of the candidates that year.[22]

On the Watergate issue, however, Nixon was much less successful.  The story he told did not have coherence; it did not hang together.  That Nixon was too busy to know what his chief advisors were doing was not credible.  That he felt he had to fire his chief advisors while believing at the same time that they were the finest public servants he had known did not make sense.  That Nixon would not release tapes that he knew would show his innocence because of a belief in confidentiality flew in the face of everything the public believed of Nixon as a survivor.  If he did not have anything to hide he would not be trying to hide anything.  At the same time, John Dean was telling the public another story, a story that had greater coherence, and this story implicated Nixon in the coverup.  Polls showed that as many Americans believed the little known Dean as believed the president.  Dean's story had a great deal of truth to it, Nixon's did not and the public recognized this.  On narrative grounds Nixon was not effective and eventually he was forced to resign.[23]

Nixon placed great value on "controlled" emotional responses.  He believed that the only time to lose your temper was when it was deliberate.  He always delivered his presidential speeches in a controlled, businesslike, presidential manner.  The single exception was the farewell speech to his staff the day he left the White House.  In this speech he allowed his emotions to show and the entire country saw more of Richard Nixon than they had ever seen before.[24]

It was fitting that in his farewell to his staff Nixon said, "only if you have been in the deepest valley can you ever know how magnificent it is to be on the highest mountain."  No public figure has seen as many mountains and valleys as Richard Nixon.  He climbed the political ladder with amazing speed.  Elected to Congress for the first time at the age of thirty-three, he won election to the Senate four years later.  Selected by Eisenhower to be his running mate in the 1952 election, Nixon became vice-president at the age of thirty-nine and a candidate for the presidency when he was forty-seven.  But then the slide began.  Defeated by Kennedy in 1960, he was also defeated in the California gubernatorial election two years later.  His political career appeared to be over.  Network news shows broadcast his obituary and even Alger Hiss was invited by ABC to comment on his demise.  But Nixon refused to give up.  As he later wrote about Ted Kennedy: "A man is not finished when he is defeated.  He's finished when he quits."  Nixon crossed the country speaking on behalf of Barry Goldwater and other Republican candidates in 1964.  In 1966 he campaigned for 86 Republican candidates, 58 of whom won.  A grateful party offered him his second presidential nomination in 1968. He defeated Hubert Humphrey in a close election and in 1972 won reelection over George McGovern by a landslide. He was on top of the mountain again, but then came Watergate, the impeachment hearings, and Nixon became the first president to resign from office. In his own words, "I . . . impeached myself."[25]

But Nixon has not disappeared from public life. In addition to publishing his memoirs and a number of books on foreign policy, he has paid triumphant visits to China, advised President Reagan on arms control, and counseled President Bush on how to use television to his best advantage. In 1985, Nixon received 414 invitations for speeches, interviews, or other public appearances. Columnists regularly applaud or decry the return of Richard Nixon.[26]

Nixon owed much of his political success to his willingness to take chances. Risking his savings to take on a popular five-term congressman was a gamble, but Nixon was willing to take a chance to achieve his goal. Risk-taking behavior can be seen in a number of speeches as well. Telling a nationwide radio and television audience to make their opinions known to the Republican National Committee instead of to Eisenhower risked Eisenhower's good will and support. Agreeing to debate against John Kennedy involved the risk of allowing his lesser known opponent to gain an audience. The biggest risk of all, however, was the decision to lie to the American people about his own role in the Watergate coverup. Nixon gambled that those involved would never implicate him and that he would be able to protect forever the tapes that told the true story. This time the gamble failed and he was forced to resign. Speaking after his resignation to Kenneth Clawson, a former member of his White House staff, Nixon revealed how the risk-taking behavior he had engaged in all his life contributed to his ultimate downfall:

> In your own mind you have nothing to lose so you take plenty of chances and if you do your homework many of them pay off. It is then you understand, for the first time, that you have the advantage because your competitors can't risk what they have already. It's a piece of cake until you get to the top. You find you can't stop playing the game the way you've always played it because it is a part of you and you need it as much as an arm or a leg. . . . So you are lean and mean and resourceful and you continue to walk on the edge of the precipice because over the years you have become fascinated by how close to the edge you can walk without losing your balance.

Clawson interrupted, "Only this time there was a difference." Nixon responded softly: "Yes, this time there was a difference. This time we had something to lose."[27]

# Notes

## Introduction

1. Stephen Ambrose, *Nixon: The Education of a Politician, 1913-1962* (New York: Simon and Schuster, 1987), p 39. Nixon told Stewart Alsop that the debate took place in the fifth grade. See Alsop, *Nixon & Rockefeller* (Garden City, NY: Doubleday and Co., 1960), pp. 184-185.

2. Richard Nixon quoted in Alsop, *Nixon and Rockefeller*, p. 184; Mildred Jackson Johns quoted in Fawn M. Brodie, *Richard Nixon: The Shaping of His Character* (New York: W. W. Norton, 1981), p. 44.

3. Alsop, *Nixon and Rockefeller*, p. 184; Alice Walker quoted in Bela Kornitzer, *The Real Nixon: An Intimate Biography* (New York: Rand McNally Co., 1960), p. 52; Ambrose, *Nixon: The Education of a Politician*, p. 38.

4. Kornitzer, *The Real Nixon,* p. 79.

5. Alsop, *Nixon and Rockefeller*, p. 185; Ambrose, *Nixon: The Education of a Politician*, p. 39; Nixon also consulted with his uncle Philip Timberlake. See Philip Timberlake interview, Richard Nixon Oral History Project, California State University, Fullerton.

6. Sheller quoted in Edwin P. Hoyt, *The Nixons: An American Family* (New York: Random House, 1972), p. 190; James Grieves in Renee K. Schulte (ed.), *The Young Nixon: An Oral Inquiry* (Fullerton, CA.: CSUF Oral History Project, 1978), p. 106.

7. Ambrose, *Nixon: The Education of a Politician*, p. 49; Elizabeth Glover in Schulte (ed.), *The Young Nixon*, p. 124.

8. Nixon's speech is reprinted in Schulte (ed.), *The Young Nixon*, pp. 206-207.

9. Nixon quoted in Henry D. Spalding, *The Nixon Nobody Knows* (Middle Village, N.Y.: Jonathan David Publisher, 1972), p. 60; Ambrose, *Nixon: The Education of a Politician*, p. 49.

10. Helen Letts quoted in Ambrose, *Nixon: The Education of a Politician*, p. 50; Alsop, *Nixon and Rockefeller*, p. 134.

11. Ambrose, *Nixon: The Education of a Politician*, p. 68; Richard Nixon, *RN: The Memoirs of Richard Nixon* (New York: Grosset & Dunlap, 1978), p. 17.

12. Bell and Hornaday are quoted in Brodie, *Richard Nixon*, pp. 107-108.

13. Nixon quoted in Kornitzer, *The Real Nixon*, p. 112 and in Spalding, *The Nixon Nobody Knows*, p. 79; Elliott quoted in Brodie, *Richard Nixon*, p. 108.

14. Nixon, *Memoirs*, p. 18; Hoyt, *The Nixons*, p. 207; *Acropolis* (Whittier College yearbook), 1932, p. 97 and 1933, p. 81.

15. Ambrose, *Nixon: The Education of a Politician*, p. 69; Nixon, *Memoirs*, p. 6; Nixon quoted in Alsop, *Nixon and Rockefeller*, p. 134.

16. C. Richard Gardner, "Richard Nixon: The Story of a Fighting Quaker," typescript, Whittier College Library, p. 60.

17. *Campus* quoted in Ambrose, *Nixon: The Education of a Politician*, p. 61.

18. Dick Thomson quoted in Lael Morgan, "Whittier '34: Most Likely to Succeed," *This Week* (Los Angeles *Times*), May 10, 1970, p. 37.

19. Nixon, *Memoirs*, p. 19; Newman quoted in Nixon, *Memoirs*, p. 20.

20. Ambrose, *Nixon: The Education of a Politician*, p. 83; Howard F. Bremer (ed.), *Richard M. Nixon, 1913-* (Dobbs Ferry, N.Y.: Oceana Publications, 1975), pp. 1-2.

21. New York *Post*, September 18, 1952, p. 1; Earl Mazo, *Richard Nixon: A Political and Personal Portrait* (New York: Harper & Brothers, 1959), p. 119.

22. *Television and the Presidency*, ABC special, June 27, 1984.

23. David Abrahamsen, *Nixon vs. Nixon: An Emotional Tragedy* (New York: Farrar, Straus and Giroux, 1977), p. 176; Nixon, *Memoirs*, p. 414.

24. Nixon, *Memoirs*, p. 635.

## Chapter 1: Nixon-Voorhis Debates

1. Jerry Voorhis to Richard M. Nixon, April 16, 1946, Voorhis file, Nixon Pre-presidential papers, National Archives (Los Angeles branch); *Newsweek*, November 18, 1946: 39.

2. Julie Nixon Eisenhower, *Pat Nixon: The Untold Story* (New York: Simon and Schuster, 1986), p. 85.

3. For a sympathetic biography of Voorhis, see Paul Bullock, *Jerry Voorhis: The Idealist as Politician* (New York: Vantage Press, 1978); John T. Balch, "Richard M. Nixon vs. H. Jerry Voorhis For Congress, 1946," typescript, Department of History, CSU, Fresno, pp. 2-8.

4. Bullock, *Jerry Voorhis*, p. 242; Stephen Ambrose, *Nixon: The Education of a Politician, 1913-1962* (New York: Simon and Schuster, 1987), pp. 117-118.

5. Richard Nixon, *RN: The Memoirs of Richard Nixon* (New York: Grosset & Dunlap, 1978), p. 34; Ambrose, *Nixon: The Education of a Politician*, p. 117.

6. Nixon, *Memoirs*, p. 35; Chotiner quoted in Bela Kornitzer, *The Real Nixon: An Intimate Biography* (New York: Rand McNally, 1960), p. 154; Day quoted in Balch, "Richard M. Nixon," p. 17.

7. Roy Day to Richard Nixon, November 12, 1945, in Balch, "Richard M. Nixon," Appendix E.

8. Nixon, *Memoirs*, p. 36; Balch, "Richard M. Nixon," p. 19.

9. Eisenhower, *Pat Nixon*, p. 88; Ambrose, *Nixon: The Education of a Politician*, pp. 121-122.

10. Balch, "Richard M. Nixon," p. 19; Ambrose, *Nixon: The Education of a Politician*, pp. 122-123.

11. Ambrose, *Nixon: The Education of a Politician*, p. 122; Eisenhower, *Pat Nixon*, p. 89.

12. Los Angeles *Times*, February 14, 1946; Whittier *News*, March 3, 1946.

13. Balch, "Richard M. Nixon," pp. 33-34; Patricia R. Nixon, "I Say He's a Wonderful Guy," *Saturday Evening Post*, September 6, 1952: 17, 19; Eisenhower, *Pat Nixon*, p. 90.

14. Balch, "Richard M. Nixon," p. 36; Alhambra *Post Advocate*, February 7 and May 31, 1946.

15. Frank M. Jordan, *Statement of Vote, Primary Election, June 4, 1946* (Sacramento: California State Printing Office, 1946), p. 17; Nixon quoted in Ambrose, *Nixon: The Education of a Politician*, pp. 130-131.

16. Balch, "Richard M. Nixon," pp. 38-39.

17. Whittier *News*, April 24, 1946.

18. U.S. Congress, House of Representatives, 79th Congress, 2d Session, *Campaign Expenditures*, Part 1, pp. 11, 66-67; San Francisco *Daily People's World*, July 3, 1946.

19. *Daily People's World*, May 31, 1946; Nixon, *Memoirs*, pp. 38-39; Whittier *News*, July 29, 1946 and August 30, 1946.

20. Bullock, *Jerry Voorhis*, pp. 253-254.

21. Bullock, *Jerry Voorhis*, pp. 254-258; Ambrose, *Nixon: The Education of a Politician*, p. 132.

22. Ambrose, *Nixon: The Education of a Politician*, p. 132-133; Whittier *News*, September 14, 1946; Bullock, *Jerry Voorhis*, pp. 259-260.

23. Bullock, *Jerry Voorhis*, p. 261.

24. Jerry Voorhis, *Confessions of a Congressman* (Garden City, N.Y.: Doubleday & Co., 1947), p. 341; Balch, "Richard M. Nixon," p. 53.

25. Pomona *Progress-Bulletin*, September 19, 1946 quoted in Bullock, *Jerry Voorhis*, p. 262; *Daily People's World*, May 31, 1946; Whittier *News*, September 17, 1946.

26. Bullock, *Jerry Voorhis*, p. 264; Balch, "Richard M. Nixon," p. 64; William A. Arnold, *Back When It All Began: The Early Nixon Years* (New York: Vantage Press, 1975), p. 2.

27. Patricia Nixon, "I Say He's A Wonderful Guy," p. 93.

28. Whittier *News*, September 21, 1946.

29. *Post Advocate*, September 20, 1946; Bullock, *Jerry Voorhis*, p. 275.

30. *Post Advocate*, October 28, 1946; Arnold, *Back When It All Began*, p. 2.

31. Whittier *News*, October 12, 1946; Nixon, *Memoirs*, p. 38.

32. Balch, "Richard M. Nixon," pp. 46-47; Voorhis, *Confessions*, pp. 339-341.

33. Whittier *News*, October 18, 1946; Balch, "Richard M. Nixon," pp. 60-61; Ambrose, *Nixon: The Education of a Politician*, p. 135.

34. Balch, "Richard M. Nixon," p. 61.

35. Balch, "Richard M. Nixon," pp. 62-63; Whittier *News*, October 29, 1946; *Post Advocate*, October 29, 1946.

36. Bullock, *Jerry Voorhis*, pp. 274, 338.

37. Bullock, *Jerry Voorhis*, p. 274.

38. Compare Bullock, *Jerry Voorhis*, p. 262 with Ambrose, *Nixon: The Education of a Politician*, p. 138; *Post Advocate*, October 15, 1946; Bullock, *Jerry Voorhis*, p. 277; Voorhis, *Confessions*, p. 334.

39. Bullock, *Jerry Voorhis*, p. 277; Balch, "Richard M. Nixon," p. 64; Voorhis, *Confessions*, p. 343.

40. Balch, "Richard M. Nixon," p. 66; Nixon, *Memoirs*, p. 40.

41. Voorhis, *Confessions*, pp. 348-349.

## Chapter 2: Nixon-Douglas Campaign

1. Day quoted in Stephen E. Ambrose, *Nixon: The Education of a Politician, 1913-1962* (New York: Simon & Schuster, 1987), p. 199; see also p. 203.

2. Helen Gahagan Douglas, *A Full Life* (Garden City, N.Y.: Doubleday & Co., 1982), pp. 291-292.

3. Douglas, *A Full Life*, p. 297.

4. Boddy quoted in Ralph de Toledano, *One Man Alone: Richard Nixon* (New York: Funk and Wagnalls, 1969), pp. 104-105; Downey quoted in Ambrose, *Nixon: The Education of a Politician*, p. 210.

5. Douglas, *A Full Life*, pp. 300-301.

6. Chotiner quoted in Earl Mazo, *Richard Nixon: A Political and Personal Portrait* (New York: Harper and Brothers, 1959), p. 76.

7. Richard Nixon, *RN: The Memoirs of Richard Nixon* (New York: Grosset & Dunlap, 1978), p. 73; Ambrose, *Nixon: The Education of a Politician*, pp. 213-214.

8. Ambrose, *Nixon: The Education of a Politician*, p. 214.

9. Ambrose, *Nixon: The Education of a Politician*, p. 214.

10. Ambrose, *Nixon: The Education of a Politician*, p. 212; Douglas, *A Full Life*, p. 302; Los Angeles *Times*, July 13, 1950 and July, 25, 1950.

11. Los Angeles *Times*, August 1, 1950; Douglas, *A Full Life*, pp. 319, 313 (quotation).

12. Chotiner quoted in Bela Kernitzer, *The Real Nixon: An Intimate Biography* (New York: Rand McNally, 1960), p. 184; A copy of the pink sheet can be found in Nixon's Pre-presidential papers (PPP), National Archives (Los Angeles branch).

13. Pink sheet, PPP.

14. Douglas, *A Full Life*, pp. 257, 306.

15. Nixon quoted in Ambrose, *Nixon: The Education of a Politician*, p. 218; Mazo, *Richard Nixon*, p. 81; Douglas, *A Full Life*, p. 316.

16. Nixon quoted in Ambrose, *Nixon: The Education of a Politician*, p. 218.

17. Douglas, *A Full Life*, pp. 312, 297; Nixon, *Memoirs*, p. 77; Ambrose, *Nixon: The Education of a Politician*, p. 689.

18. Ambrose, *Nixon: The Education of a Politician*, p. 215.

19. Los Angeles *Times*, October 31, 1950.

20. de Toledano, *One Man Alone*, pp. 110-111.

21. de Toledano, *One Man Alone*, p. 111; Douglas, *A Full Life*, pp. 326-327.

22. Douglas, *A Full Life*, p. 315; Ambrose, *Nixon: The Education of a Politician*, p. 216.

23. Nixon, *Memoirs*, p. 75; Arnold offered a different version of the incident, writing that Nixon was not present when Kennedy came to his office and presented the check. See William Arnold, *Back When It All Began: The Early Nixon Years* (New York: Vantage Press, 1975), p. 14.

24. de Toledano, *One Man Alone*, p. 112.

25. Ambrose, *Nixon: The Education of a Politician*, p. 219; Los Angeles *Times*, November 1, 1950.

26. Turner quoted in de Toledano, *Nixon* (New York: Duell, Sloan and Pearce, 1960), p. 94.

27. Douglas, *A Full Life*, p. 322.

28. The text of the speech can be found in Nixon's Pre-presidential papers, National Archives (Los Angeles branch).

29. Ambrose, *Nixon: The Education of a Politician*, p. 223.

30. Mazo, *Richard Nixon*, pp. 77-78; Douglas, *A Full Life*, p. 302; Los Angeles *Times*, August 2, 1950.

31. Los Angeles *Times*, July 13, 1950; Chotiner quoted in Kornitzer, *The Real Nixon*, p. 184; Ambrose, *Nixon: The Education of a Politician*, p. 223.

**Chapter 3: The Fund Speech**

1. Nixon quoted in Phillip Andrews, *This Man Nixon* (Philadelphia: John C. Winston Co., 1952), p. 48.

2. Stewart Alsop, *Nixon & Rockefeller: A Double Portrait* (Garden City, N.Y.: Doubleday & Co., 1960), pp. 57-58.

3. Earl Mazo, *Richard Nixon* (New York: Harper & Brothers, 1959), p. 100.

4. Mazo, *Richard Nixon*, pp. 102-107.

5. Edson quoted in Mazo, *Richard Nixon*, p. 107; Richard M. Nixon, *Six Crises* (Garden City, N.Y.: Doubleday & Co., 1962), pp. 74-75, 78.

6. New York *Post*, September 18, 1952.

7. Mazo, *Richard Nixon*, p. 109.

8. Mazo, *Richard Nixon*, p. 110.

9. Nixon, *Six Crises*, p. 85.

10. Fawn M. Brodie, *Richard Nixon: The Shaping of His Character* (New York: Norton, 1981), p. 280; Mazo, *Richard Nixon*, p. 114.

11. Nixon, *Six Crises*, pp. 85-86; Eisenhower quoted in Brodie, *Richard Nixon: The Shaping of His Character*, p. 278.

12. Stassen's telegram is in Richard Nixon Pre-presidential papers, National Archives (Los Angeles branch); Nixon, *Six Crises*, pp. 98-99.

13. Mazo, *Richard Nixon*, p. 121; Nixon, *RN: The Memoirs of Richard Nixon* (New York: Grosset & Dunlap, 1978), p. 98.

14. Mazo, *Richard Nixon*, pp. 115, 122-123.

15. Alsop, *Nixon & Rockefeller*, p. 64.

16. Alsop, *Nixon & Rockefeller*, p. 197; Nixon, *Six Crises*, p. 83; Alsop, *Nixon & Rockefeller*, pp. 124, 126.

17. Alsop, *Nixon & Rockefeller*, p. 130.

18. See Stephen E. Ambrose, *Nixon: The Education of a Politician* (New York: Simon and Shuster, 1987), Chapters 3-5.

19. Rogers quoted in Mazo, *Richard Nixon*, p. 122.

20. Nixon, *Six Crises*, p. 102.

21. Nixon, *Six Crises*, pp. 94-95, 110-111.

22. Richard Wilson, "Is Nixon Fit to be President?" *Look*, February 24, 1953: 40.

23. "The Record of the Nixon Affair," *U.S. News and World Report*, October 3, 1952: 61.

24. "The Record of the Nixon Affair," p. 61; Alsop, *Nixon & Rockefeller*, p. 134. Quotations from the speech are taken from *Vital Speeches*, XIX(October 15, 1952): 11-15; Mazo, *Richard Nixon*, p. 100.

25. Nixon, *Six Crises*, p. 88.

26. Nixon, *Memoirs*, p. 99.

27. Nixon, *Six Crises*, p. 103; Mazo, *Richard Nixon*, p. 124.

28. William Costello, *The Facts About Nixon* (New York: Viking Press, 1960), p. 113.

29. Ambrose, *Nixon: The Education of a Politician*, p. 280..

30. Mazo, *Richard Nixon*, pp. 135-136.

31. Nixon, *Six Crises*, pp. 112-113.

32. Alsop, *Nixon & Rockefeller*, p. 194; Ryan noted that Nixon delivered the speech exactly eight years after FDR had used Fala in his speech to the Teamster's Union (September 23, 1944) to ridicule the charge that he had wasted taxpayers' money by sending a destroyer back to pick up the dog allegedly lost on an inspection trip to a military base in Alaska. Halford Ryan, "Senator Richard M. Nixon's Apology for the 'Fund'" in Halford Ross Ryan (ed.),

*Oratorical Encounters* (Westport, CT.: Greenwood Press, 1988), p. 109.

33. Ambrose, *Nixon: The Education of a Politician*, p. 288.

34. Alsop, *Nixon & Rockefeller*, p. 65.

35. Nixon, *Six Crises*, p. 107.

36. Nixon, *Memoirs*, p. 104.

37. Mazo, Richard Nixon, pp. 132-134; Eisenhower's speech is in "The Record of the Nixon Affair," p. 70.

38. Ambrose, *Nixon: The Education of a Politician*, p. 290; Robert W. O'Brien and Elizabeth Jensen Jones, "The Night Nixon Spoke: A Study in Political Effectiveness," typescript, Whittier College Library; Newspapers are quoted in Mazo, *Richard Nixon*, p. 135.

39. Barnet Baskerville, "The Illusion of Proof," *Western Speech*, 25(Fall 1961): 238-239; L.W. Rosenfield, "A Case Study in Speech Criticism: The Nixon-Truman Analog," *Speech Monographs*, 35(November 1968): 449; see, for example, Brodie, *Richard Nixon: The Shaping of His Character*, p. 280.

40. Walter Fisher, *Human Communication as Narration: Toward a Philosophy of Reason, Value, and Action* (Columbia: University of South Carolina Press, 1987), p. 47; Henry E. McGuckin, Jr., "A Value Analysis of Richard Nixon's 1952 Campaign-Fund Speech," *Southern Speech Journal*, 33(Summer 1968): 259-269.

41. Mazo, *Richard Nixon*, p. 136; Nixon, *Six Crises*, p. 129.

## Chapter 4: The Kennedy-Nixon Debates

1. Richard M. Scammon (ed.), *America at the Polls* (Pittsburgh, PA.: University of Pittsburgh Press, 1965), p. 22; Theodore H. White, *The Making of the President, 1960* (New York: Pocket Books, 1961), p. 420; Richard M. Nixon, *Six Crises* (Garden City, N.Y.: Doubleday & Co., 1962), pp. 418-419.

2. Samuel L. Becker and Elmer W. Lower, "Broadcasting in Presidential Campaigns" in Sidney Kraus (ed.), *The Great Debates* (Bloomington: Indiana University Press, 1977), pp. 48-49; White, *Making of the President*, p. 338.

3. Nixon, *Six Crises*, p. 323; Stephen E. Ambrose, *Nixon: The Education of a Politician, 1913-1962* (New York: Simon and Schuster, 1987), pp. 558-559; Richard M. Nixon, *RN: The Memoirs of Richard Nixon* (New York: Grosset & Dunlap, 1978), p. 217.

4. White, *Making of the President*, p. 339; Nixon, *Six Crises*, p. 324; Nixon, *Memoirs*, p. 217.

5. Nixon, *Six Crises*, pp. 326-327.

6. Nixon, *Six Crises*, pp. 452, 329.

7. Nixon, *Six Crises*, pp. 335-336.

8. Nixon, *Six Crises*, p. 337.

9. White, *Making of the President*, p. 343.

10. *Television and the Presidency*, ABC Special, June 27, 1984.

11. White, *Making of the President*, pp. 344-347; Nixon quoted on *Television and the Presidency*

12. White, *Making of the President*, p. 343; Quotations from the first debate are taken from U. S. Congress, Senate, Committee on Commerce, *Freedom of Communications*, (Washington, DC: Government Printing Office, 1961), III, 73-92.

13. Samuel Lubell, "Personalities vs. Issues" in Kraus (ed.), *The Great Debates*, p. 158.

14. Salinger quoted on *Television and the Presidency*.

15. David L. Vancil and Sue D. Pendell, "The Myth of Viewer-Listener Disagreement in the First Kennedy-Nixon Debate," *Central States Speech Journal*, 38(Spring 1987): 24.

16. Elihu Katz and Jacob J. Feldman, "The Debate in Light of Research," in Kraus (ed.), *The Great Debates*, p. 192; *Television and the Presidency*; White, *Making of the President*, p. 350.

17. Herbert A. Seltz and Richard D. Yoakam, "Production Diary of the Debates" in Kraus (ed.), *The Great Debates*, p. 98; Nixon, *Six Crises*, p. 343.

18. Nixon, *Six Crises*, p. 344.

19. Quotations from the second debate are taken from U.S. Congress, Senate, Committee on Commerce, *Freedom of Communications*, III, 146-165.

20. Nixon, *Six Crises*, pp. 344-346.

21. Quotations from the third debate are taken from U.S. Congress, Senate, Committee on Commerce, *Freedom of Communications*, III, 204-222; Nixon, *Six Crises*, p. 348.

22. *Chronicle* quoted in Nixon, *Six Crises*, p. 347; Katz and Feldman, "The Debate in Light of Research," p. 196; Ambrose, *Nixon: The Making of a Politician*, p. 583.

23. Nixon, *Six Crises*, pp. 352-355.

24. Quotations from the fourth debate are taken from U.S. Congress, Senate, Committee on Commerce, *Freedom of Communications*, III, 260-278.

25. Ambrose, *Nixon: The Making of a Politician*, p. 594-596; RN to Chuck Lichenstein and Agnes Waldron, September 21, 1961, Nixon Pre-presidential papers (PPP), National Archives (Los Angeles Branch); Katz and Feldman, "The Debate in Light of Research," pp. 196-197; White, *Making of the President*, pp. 28-29.

26. Kennedy quoted in White, *Making of the President*, p. 353.

27. Ambrose, *Nixon: The Making of a Politician*, pp. 596-597.

28. Nixon, *Six Crises*, p. 421; White, *Making of the President*, pp. 426-427.

29. Agnes W[aldron] to RN, September 21, 1961, PPP; Nixon, *Six Crises*, p. 302; Nixon, *Memoirs*, p. 223.

## Chapter 5: The Vietnam Speeches

1. Richard M. Nixon, *RN: The Memoirs of Richard Nixon* (New York: Grosset & Dunlap, 1978), pp. 398-405.

2. Nixon, *Memoirs*, p. 396.

3. William Safire, *Before the Fall* (Garden City, N.Y.: Doubleday & Co., 1975), p. 172.

4. Robert B. Semple, Jr., "Nixon's Nov. 3 Speech: Why He Took the Gamble Alone," *New York Times*, January 19, 1970, p. 23; Nixon, *Memoirs*, pp. 407-409.

5. Newton N. Minow, John B. Martin, and Lee M. Mitchell, *Presidential Television* (New York: Basic Books, 1973), p. 60; Raymond Price, *With Nixon* (New York: Viking Press, 1977), p. 160; Quotations from the speech are taken from "Address to the Nation on Vietnam," *Public Papers of the Presidents of the United States: Richard Nixon, 1969*, (Washington, D.C.: Government Printing Office, 1971), pp. 901-909.

6. Aristotle, *Rhetoric*, I. 2. 1356a, 1-20.

7. Nixon, *Memoirs*, p. 408.

8. Karlyn Kohrs Campbell, "An Exercise in the Rhetoric of Mythical America," in *Critiques of Contemporary Rhetoric* (Belmont, CA.: Wadsworth, 1972), p. 51; Forbes Hill, "Conventional Wisdom—Traditional Form—The President's Message of November 3, 1969," *Quarterly Journal of Speech*, 58(December 1972): 377.

9. Philip E. Converse and Howard Schuman, " 'Silent Majorities' and the Vietnam War," *Scientific American*, 222(June 1970): 24; Semple, "Nixon's Nov. 3 Speech," p. 23.

10. Safire, *Before the Fall*, pp. 175, 178.

11. *Gallup Opinion Index,* Report No. 54, December 1969, p. 3; *New York Times*, November 5, 1969, p. 1; Nixon, *Memoirs*, pp. 410-411.

12. Nixon, *Memoirs*, p. 404; *New York Times*, November 5, 1969, p. 1; Starnes quoted in Robert P. Newman, "Under the Veneer: Nixon's Vietnam Speech of November 3, 1969," *Quarterly Journal of Speech*, 56(April 1970): 177.

13. Hill, "Conventional Wisdom," p. 383; Robert A. Vartabedian, "Nixon's Vietnam Rhetoric: A Case Study of Apologia as Generic Paradox," *Southern Speech Communication Journal*, 50(Summer 1985): 380.

14. Safire, *Before the Fall*, p. 180.

15. Nixon, *Memoirs*, p. 448; Safire, *Before the Fall*, p. 182.

16. Nixon, *Memoirs*, pp. 449-451; Safire, *Before the Fall*, pp. 186-187.

17. Safire, *Before the Fall*, p. 183; Quotations from the speech are taken from "Address to the Nation on the Situation in Southeast Asia," *Public Papers of the Presidents of the United States: Richard Nixon, 1970*, (Washington, D.C.: Government Printing Office, 1971), pp. 405-410.

18. Rowland Evans, Jr. and Robert D. Novak, *Nixon in the White House: The Frustration of Power* (New York: Random House, 1971), pp. 246-247.

19. James D. Barber, *The Presidential Character* (Edgewood Cliffs, N.J.: Prentice Hall, 1977), p. 9; Ruth M. Gonchar and Dan F.

Hahn, "The Rhetorical Predictability of Richard M. Nixon," *Today's Speech*, 10(Fall 1971): 8.

20. *New York Times*, May 2, 1970, pp. 9, 32; Other newspaper editorials are quoted in *New York Times*, May 2, 1970, p. 10; *New Republic*, May 16, 1970; *New York Times*, May 2, 1970, p. 3.

21. *New York Times*, May 4, 1970, p. 8; *Gallup Opinion Index*, Report No. 58, April 1970, p. 18 and Report No. 61, July 1970, p. 5.

22. Nixon, *Six Crises* (Garden City, N.Y.: Doubleday and Co., 1962), p. xv; Nixon, *Memoirs*, p. 454; Price, *With Nixon*, p. 162.

23. Nixon, *Memoirs*, p. 457; Safire, *Before the Fall*, p. 188.

## Chapter 6: Watergate and Resignation Speeches

1. *Gallup Opinion Index*, Report No. 92, February 1973, pp. 2, 6; Report No. 96, June 1973, p. 2.

2. Theodore H. White, *The Making of the President, 1972* (New York: Bantam Books, 1973), pp. 392-393, 398-400; Richard Nixon, *RN: The Memoirs of Richard Nixon* (New York: Grosset & Dunlap, 1978), p. 635.

3. Nixon, *Memoirs*, pp. 826, 849.

4. Raymond Price, *With Nixon* (New York: Viking Press, 1977), p. 98.

5. Price, *With Nixon*, pp. 99-101.

6. Price, *With Nixon*, pp. 102-103; Quotations from the speech are taken from "Address to the Nation About the Watergate Investigations, April 30, 1973" *Public Papers of the Presidents of the United States, Richard Nixon, 1973* (Washington: Government Printing Office, 1975), pp. 328-333; *Time*, May 14, 1973, p. 20.

7. William L. Benoit, "Richard M. Nixon's Rhetorical Strategies in His Public Statements on Watergate," *Southern Speech Communication Journal*, 47(Winter 1982): 192-196.

8. *Time*, May 14, 1973, p. 21.

9. *Gallup Opinion Index*, Report No. 95, May 1973, p. 7; Hugh Sidey, "Guilty Until Proven Innocent?" *Time*, May 14, 1973, p. 19.

10. Price, *With Nixon*, p. 104; *Gallup Opinion Index*, Report No. 95, May 1973, p. 7.

11. *Gallup Opinion Index*, Report No. 96, June 1973, p. 5.

12. Nixon, *Memoirs*, pp. 850-851.

13. Nixon, *Memoirs*, p. 905; *Gallup Opinion Index*, Report No. 98, August 1973, p. 1.

14. *Time*, August 27, 1973, pp. 11-12.

15. Quotations from the speech are taken from "Address to the Nation About the Watergate Investigations, August 15, 1973" *Public Papers, 1973*, pp. 691-698; Barry Brummett, "Presidential Substance: The Address of August 15, 1973," *Western Speech*, 39(Fall 1975): 258.

16. *Time*, August 27, 1973, p. 13; Statistics cited by Frances Lewine, "The President's News Conference of August 22, 1973," *Public Papers, 1973*, p. 712.

17. *Gallup Opinion Index*, Report No. 99, September 1973, pp.3-4 and No. 101, November 1973, p. 5.

18. Price, *With Nixon*, p. 253; Nixon, *Memoirs*, pp. 926-935; Theodore White, *Breach of Faith* (New York: Dell Publishing Co., 1976), pp. 342-343; "The President Should Resign," *Time*, November 12, 1973, pp. 20-21.

19. Howard F. Bremer (ed.), *Richard M. Nixon, 1913-* (Dobbs Ferry, N.Y.: Oceana Publications, 1975), pp. 71-72.

20. Nixon, *Memoirs*, pp. 990-993; *U.S. News & World Report*, April 29, 1974, p. 23.

21. Quotations from the speech are taken from "Address to the Nation Announcing Answer to the House Judiciary Committee Subpoena for Additional Presidential Tape Recordings, April 29, 1974," *Public Papers of the Presidents of the United States, Richard Nixon, 1974* (Washington, D.C.: Government Printing Office, 1975), pp. 389-397.

22. Los Angeles *Times*, April 30, 1974, II, 6.

23. *Gallup Opinion Index*, Report No. 107, May 1974, p. 2.

24. Editorial comments quoted in *Time*, May 20, 1974, pp. 22-23.

25. Ashbrook and Rhodes quoted in White, *Breach of Faith*, p. 378.

26. *Gallup Opinion Index*, Report No. 108, June 1974, p. 8; Anthony J. Lucas, *Nightmare: The Underside of the Nixon Years* (New York: Viking Press, 1976), p. 490.

27. White, *Breach of Faith*, p. 407.

28. Nixon, *Memoirs,* p. 1056.

29. Nixon, *Memoirs*, p. 1057; *Time*, August 19, 1974, p. 16.

30. Price, *With Nixon*, p. 324.

31. Nixon, *Memoirs*, p. 1055; *Time*, August 19, 1974, pp. 20, 63 (*Journal* quoted).

32. Price, *With Nixon*, pp. 337-339.

33. Price, *With Nixon*, p. 340; White, *Breach of Faith*, p. 43; Quotations from the speech are taken from "Address to the Nation Announcing Decision to Resign the Office of President of the United States, August 8, 1974," *Public Papers, 1974*, pp. 626-630.

34. Price, *With Nixon*, pp. 340-341; Theodore Roosevelt, "Citizenship in a Republic," *Presidential Addresses and State Papers* (New York: Review of Reviews, 1910), VIII, 2191.

35. Price, *With Nixon*, p. 341.

36. Price, *With Nixon*, pp. 342-344.

37. Price, *With Nixon*, p. 344.

38. Price, *With Nixon*, p. 345.

39. Gerald L. Wilson, "A Strategy of Explanation: Richard M. Nixon's August 8, 1974, Resignation Address," *Communication Quarterly*, 24(Summer 1976): 18.

40. Nixon, *Memoirs*, p. 1057.

41. Mudd cited in Richard A. Katula, "The Apology of Richard M. Nixon," *Today's Speech*, 23(Fall 1974): 4.

42. *Gallup Opinion Index*, Report No. 95, May 1973, pp. 9-11; Katula, "The Apology of Richard M. Nixon," p. 5.

43. *Newsweek*, August 19, 1974, pp. 48, 14; Wilson, "Strategy of Explanation," p. 20.

44. Nixon, *Memoirs*, p. 1087.

45. Bob Woodward and Carl Bernstein, *The Final Days* (New York: Avon Books, 1976), p. 507;

46. Quotations from the speech are taken from "Remarks on Departure From the White House, August 9, 1974," *Public Papers, 1974*, pp. 630-632.

47. Price, *With Nixon*, p. 351.

48. White, *Breach of Faith*, pp. 48-50.

49. Bruce Herschensohn quoted in Woodward, *Final Days*, p. 508; Walters quoted in Robert L. King, "Transforming Scandal into Tragedy: A Rhetoric of Political Apology," *Quarterly Journal of Speech*, 71(1985): 295.

## Conclusion

1. Jane Milhous Beeson and Merton Wray quoted in Renee K. Schulte (ed.), *The Young Nixon: An Oral Inquiry* (Fullerton, CA.: Oral History Project, 1984), p. 54; Law student quoted in Stewart Alsop, *Nixon & Rockefeller* (Garden City, N.Y.: Doubleday & Co., 1960), p. 238; Finch quoted in Bruce Mazlish, *In Search of Nixon* (New York: Basic Books, 1972), p. 56; Rogers quoted in James D. Barber, *The Presidential Character* (Edgewood Cliffs, N.J.: Prentice-Hall, 1977), p. 384.

2. Alsop, *Nixon & Rockefeller*, p. 148.

3. Alsop, *Nixon & Rockefeller*, p. 149.

4. Eli Chesen, *President Nixon's Psychiatric Profile* (New York: P. H. Wyden, 1973), pp. 99-101.

5. Raymond Price, *With Nixon* (New York: Viking Press, 1977), pp. 42-45.

6. Chesen, *Psychiatric Profile*, pp. 104-105; Richard Nixon, *RN: The Memoirs of Richard Nixon* (New York: Grosset & Dunlap, 1978), pp. 408, 1064-1066.

7. Jules Witcover, *The Resurrection of Richard Nixon* (New York: Putnam, 1970), pp. 374-375.

8. Joe McGinness, *The Selling of the President, 1968* (New York: Pocket Books, 1970), pp. 58-63.

9. McGinness, *Selling of the President*, pp. 154, 160-164.

10. Newton N. Minow, John Martin, and Lee Mitchell, *Presidential Television* (New York: Basic Books, 1973), pp. 56-59.

11. Califano quoted in Minow, *Presidential Television*, p. 64. See also pp. 65-67.

12. Minow, *Presidential Television*, pp. 58-59.

13. Richard Nixon, *Six Crises* (Garden City, N.Y.: Doubleday & Co., 1962), p. 83; "Address to the Nation About the Watergate

Investigations," *Public Papers of the Presidents, Richard Nixon, 1973* (Washington: Government Printing Office, 1974), p. 330.

14. Nixon quoted in Ben Padrow and Bruce Richards, "Richard Nixon: His Speech Preparation," *Today's Speech*, 7(November 1959): 11-12.

15. William Safire, *Before the Fall* (Garden City, N.Y.: Doubleday & Co., 1975), pp. 99-100.

16. Gage William Chapel, "Speechwriting in the Nixon Administration," *Journal of Communication*, 26(Spring 1976): 65-66.

17. *New York Times*, November 4, 1969, p. 17; Wilson quoted in Janet Podell and Steven Anzovin (eds.), *Speeches of the American Presidents* (New York: H. W. Wilson, 1988), p. 663.

18. Padrow, "Richard Nixon," p. 11; Safire, *Before the Fall*, pp. 531-532.

19. Roderick P. Hart, "Absolutism and Situation: Prolegomena to a Rhetorical Biography of Richard M. Nixon," *Communication Monographs*, 43(August 1976): 223.

20. *The Gallup Poll* (New York: Random House, 1972), III, 1659; Statistics in *Six Crises* file, Nixon Pre-presidential papers, National Archives (Los Angeles branch).

21. *The Gallup Poll*, III, 2163; Ralph de Toledano, *One Man Alone: Richard Nixon* (New York: Funk & Wagnalls, 1969), p. 364; Theodore H. White, *The Making of the President, 1972* (New York: Bantam Books, 1973), pp. 459, 466.

22. Walter Fisher, *Human Communication as Narration: Toward a Philosophy of Reasons, Value, and Action* (Columbia: University of South Carolina Press, 1987), p. 47; Theodore White, *The Making of the President, 1960* (New York: Pocket Books, 1961), pp. 332-333, 360-362; Ronald Reagan has confounded his critics in much the same manner. See William F. Lewis, "Telling America's Story: Narrative Form and the Reagan Presidency," *Quarterly Journal of Speech*, 73(1987): 280-302.

23. *Harris Survey Yearbook of Public Opinion, 1973* (New York: Louis Harris, 1976), p. 155.

24. Fawn Brodie, *Richard Nixon: The Shaping of His Character* (Cambridge: Harvard University Press, 1983), pp. 48-49.

25. "Remarks on Departure From the White House," *Public Papers, 1974*, p. 632; Nixon quoted in Safire, *Before the Fall*, p. 154; *Congressional Quarterly*, November 11, 1966, p. 2774; Nixon quoted in David Frost, *"I Gave Them a Sword": Behind the Scenes of the Nixon Interviews* (New York: William Morrow, 1978), p. 270.

26. Richard Nixon, "Memo to President Bush: How to Use TV—and Keep from Being Abused by It," *TV Guide*, 37(January 14, 1989): 26-30; *New York Times*, Feb. 28, 1986, p. B4; William Safire, "Nixon's Second Comeback," San Francisco *Chronicle*, April 18, 1984, p. 53

27. Kenneth Clawson, "A Loyalist's Memoir," Washington *Post*, August 9, 1979, p. D1.

# II
# COLLECTED SPEECHES

# "My Side of the Story": September 23, 1952

My Fellow Americans: I come before you tonight as a candidate for the Vice Presidency and as a man whose honesty and integrity have been questioned.

The usual political thing to do when charges are made against you is to either ignore them or to deny them without giving details.

I believe we've had enough of that in the United States, particularly with the present Administration in Washington, D.C. To me the office of the Vice Presidency of the United States is a great office, and I feel that the people have got to have confidence in the integrity of the men who run for that office and who might obtain it.

I have a theory, too, that the best and only answer to a smear or to an honest misunderstanding of the facts is to tell the truth. And that's why I'm here tonight. I want to tell you my side of the case.

I am sure that you have read the charge and you've heard that I, Senator Nixon, took $18,000 from a group of my supporters.

Now, was that wrong? And let me say that it was wrong—I'm saying, incidentally, that it was wrong and not just illegal. Because it isn't a question of whether it was legal or illegal, that isn't enough. The question is, was it morally wrong?

I say that it was morally wrong if any of that $18,000 went to Senator Nixon for my personal use. I say that it was morally wrong if it was secretly given and secretly handled. And I say that it was morally wrong if any of the contributors got special favors for the contributions that they made.

And now to answer those questions let me say this:

Not one cent of the $18,000 or any other money of that type ever went to me for my personal use. Every penny of it was used to pay for political expenses that I did not think should be charged to the taxpayers of the United States.

It was not a secret fund. As a matter of fact, when I was on "Meet the Press," some of you may have seen it last Sunday—Peter Edson came up to me after the program and he said, "Dick, what about this fund we hear about?" And I said, "Well, there's no secret about it. Go out and see Dana Smith, who was the administrator of the fund."

And I gave him his address, and I said that you will find that the purpose of the fund simply was to defray political expenses that I did not feel should be charged to the Government.

And third, let me point out, and I want to make this particularly clear, that no contributor to this fund, no contributor to any of my campaign, has ever received any consideration that he would not have received as an ordinary constituent.

I just don't believe in that and I can say that never, while I have been in the Senate of the United States, as far as the people that contributed to this fund are concerned, have I made a telephone call for them to an agency, or have I gone down to an agency in their behalf. And the records will show that, the records which are in the hands of the Administration.

But then some of you will say and rightly, "Well, what did you use the fund for, Senator? Why did you have to have it?"

Let me tell you in just a word how a Senate office operates. First of all, a Senator gets $15,000 a year in salary. He gets enough money to pay for one trip a year, a round trip that is, for himself and his family between his home and Washington, D.C.

And then he gets an allowance to handle the people that work in his office, to handle his mail. And the allowance for my State of California is enough to hire thirteen people.

And let me say, incidentally, that that allowance is not paid to the Senator—it's paid directly to the individuals that the Senator puts on his payroll, but all of these people and all of these allowances are for strictly official business. Business, for example, when a constituent writes in and wants you to go down to the Veterans Administration and get some information about his GI policy. Items of that type for example.

But there are other expenses which are not covered by the Government. And I think I can best discuss those expenses by asking you some questions.

Do you think that when I or any other Senator makes a political speech, has it printed, should charge the printing of that speech and the mailing of that speech to the taxpayers? Do you think, for example, when I or any other Senator makes a trip to his home state to make a purely political speech that the cost of that trip should be charged to the taxpayers? Do you think when a Senator makes political broadcasts or political television broadcasts, radio or television, that the expense of those broadcasts should be charged to the taxpayers?

Well, I know what your answer is. It is the same answer that audiences give me whenever I discuss this particular problem. The answer is, "no." The taxpayers shouldn't be required to finance items which are not official business but which are primarily political business.

But then the question arises, you say, "Well, how do you pay for these and how can you do it legally?"

And there are several ways that it can be done, incidentally, and that it is done legally in the United States Senate and in the Congress.

The first way is to be a rich man. I don't happen to be a rich man so I couldn't use that one.

Another way that is used is to put your wife on the payroll. Let me say, incidentally, my opponent, my opposite number for the Vice Presidency on the Democratic ticket, does have his wife on the payroll. And has had her on his payroll for the ten years—the past ten years.

Now just let me say this. That's his business and I'm not critical of him for doing that. You will have to pass judgment on that particular point. But I have never done that for this reason. I have found that there are so many deserving stenographers and secretaries in Washington that needed the work that I just didn't feel it was right to put my wife on the payroll.

My wife's sitting over here. She's a wonderful stenographer. She used to teach stenography and she used to teach shorthand in high school. That was when I met her. And I can tell you folks that she's worked many hours at night and many hours on Saturdays and Sundays in my office and she's done a fine job. And I'm proud to say tonight that in the six years I've been in the House and the Senate of the United States, Pat Nixon has never been on the Government payroll.

There are other ways that these finances can be taken care of. Some who are lawyers, and I happen to be a lawyer, continue to practice law. But I haven't been able to do that. I'm so far away from California that I've been so busy with my Senatorial work that I have not engaged in any legal practice.

And also as far as law practice is concerned, it seemed to me that the relationship between an attorney and the client was so personal that you couldn't possibly represent a man as an attorney and then have an unbiased view when he presented his case to you in the event that he had one before the Government.

And so I felt that the best way to handle these necessary political expenses of getting my message to the American people and the speeches I made, the speeches that I had printed, for the most part, concerned this one message—of exposing this Administration, the communism in it, the corruption in it—the only way that I could do that was to accept the aid which people in my home state of California who contributed to my campaign and who continued to make these contributions after I was elected were glad to make.

And let me say I am proud of the fact that not one of them has ever asked me for a special favor. I'm proud of the fact that not one of them has ever asked me to vote on a bill other than as my own conscience would dictate. And I am proud of the fact that the taxpayers by subterfuge or otherwise have never paid one dime for expenses which I thought were political and shouldn't be charged to the taxpayers.

Let me say, incidentally, that some of you may say, "Well, that's all right, Senator; that's your explanation, but have you got any proof?"

And I'd like to tell you this evening that just about an hour ago we received an independent audit of this entire fund.

I suggested to Gov. Sherman Adams, who is the chief of staff of the Dwight Eisenhower campaign, that an independent audit and legal report be obtained. And I have that audit here in my hand.

It's an audit made by the Price, Waterhouse & Co. firm, and the legal opinion by Gibson, Dunn & Crutcher, lawyers in Los Angeles, the biggest law firm and incidentally one of the best ones in Los Angeles.

I'm proud to be able to report to you tonight that this audit and this legal opinion is being forwarded to General Eisenhower. And I'd like to read to you the opinion that was prepared by Gibson, Dunn & Crutcher and based on all the pertinent laws and statutes, together with the audit report prepared by the certified public accountants.

"It is our conclusion that Senator Nixon did not obtain any financial gain from the collection and disbursement of the fund by Dana Smith; that Senator Nixon did not violate any Federal or state law by reason of the operation of the fund, and that neither the portion of the fund paid by Dana Smith directly to third persons nor the portion paid to Senator Nixon to reimburse him for designated office expenses constituted income to the Senator which was either reportable or taxable as income under applicable tax laws. (signed) Gibson, Dunn & Crutcher by Alma H. Conway."

Now that, my friends, is not Nixon speaking, but that's an independent audit which was requested because I want the American people to know all the facts and I'm not afraid of having independent people go in and check the facts, and that is exactly what they did.

But then I realize that there are still some who may say, and rightly so, and let me say that I recognize that some will continue to smear regardless of what the truth may be, but that there has been understandably some honest misunderstanding on this matter, and there's some that will say:

"Well, maybe you were able, Senator, to fake this thing. How can we believe what you say? After all, is there a possibility that maybe you got some sums in cash? Is there a possibility that you may have feathered your own nest?"

And so now what I am going to do—and incidentally this is unprecedented in the history of American politics—I am going at this time to give this television and radio audience a complete financial history; everything I've earned; everything I've spent; everything I owe. And I want you to know the facts. I'll have to start early.

I was born in 1913. Our family was one of modest circumstances and most of my early life was spent in a store out in East

Whittier. It was a grocery store—one of those family enterprises. The only reason we were able to make it go was because my mother and dad had five boys and we all worked in the store.

I worked my way through college and to a great extent through law school. And then, in 1940, probably the best thing that ever happened to me happened, I married Pat—who is sitting over here. We had a rather difficult time after we were married, like so many of the young couples who may be listening to us. I practiced law; she continued to teach school. Then in 1942 I went into the service.

Let me say that my service record was not a particularly unusual one. I went to the South Pacific. I guess I'm entitled to a couple of battle stars. I got a couple of letters of commendation but I was just there when the bombs were falling and then I returned. I returned to the United States and in 1946 I ran for the Congress.

When we came out of the war, Pat and I—Pat during the war had worked as a stenographer and in a bank and as an economist for a Government agency—and when we came out the total of our savings from both my law practice, her teaching and all the time that I was in the war—the total for that entire period was just a little less than $10,000. Every cent of that, incidentally, was in Government bonds.

Well, that's where we start when I go into politics. Now what have I earned since I went into politics? Well, here it is—I jotted it down, let me read the notes. First of all I've had my salary as a Congressman and as a Senator. Second, I have received a total in this past six years of $1,600 from estates which were in my law firm at the time that I severed my connection with it.

And, incidentally, as I said before, I have not engaged in any legal practice and have not accepted any fees from business that came into the firm after I went into politics. I have made an average of approximately $1,500 a year from nonpolitical speaking engagements and lectures. And then, fortunately, we've inherited a little money. Pat sold her interest in her father's estate for $3,000 and I inherited $1,500 from my grandfather.

We live rather modestly. For four years we lived in an apartment in Park Fairfax, in Alexandria, Va. The rent was $80 a month. And we saved for the time that we could buy a house.

Now, that was what we took in. What did we do with this money? What do we have today to show for it? This will surprise you, because it is so little, I suppose, as standards generally go, of people in public life. First of all, we've got a house in Washington which cost $41,000 and on which we owe $20,000.

We have a house in Whittier, California, which cost $13,000 and on which we owe $3,000 [he meant to say $10,000]. My folks are living there at the present time.

I have just $4,000 in life insurance, plus my G.I. policy which I've never been able to convert and which will run out in two years. I have no insurance whatever on Pat. I have no life insurance on our two youngsters, Patricia and Julie. I own a 1950 Oldsmobile car. We have our furniture. We have no stocks and bonds of any type. We have no interest of any kind, direct or indirect, in any business.

Now, that's what we have. What do we owe? Well, in addition to the mortgage, the $20,000 mortgage on the house in Washington, the $10,000 one on the house in Whittier, I owe $4,500 to the Riggs Bank in Washington, D.C. with interest 4 1/2 per cent.

I owe $3,500 to my parents and the interest on that loan which I pay regularly, because it's the part of the savings they made through the years they were working so hard, I pay regularly 4 per cent interest. And then I have a $500 loan which I have on my life insurance.

Well, that's about it. That's what we have and that's what we owe. It isn't very much but Pat and I have the satisfaction that every dime that we've got is honestly ours. I should say this—that Pat doesn't have a mink coat. But she does have a respectable Republican cloth coat. And I always tell her that she'd look good in anything.

One other thing I probably should tell you because if we don't they'll probably be saying this about me too, we did get something—a gift—after the election. A man down in Texas heard Pat on the radio mention the fact that our two youngsters would like to have a dog. And, believe it or not, the day before we left on this campaign trip we got a message from Union Station in Baltimore saying they had a package for us. We went down to get it. You know what it was.

It was a little cocker spaniel dog in a crate that he'd sent all the way from Texas. Black and white spotted. And our little girl— Tricia, the 6-year old—named it Checkers. And you know, the kids, like all kids, love the dog and I just want to say this right now, that regardless of what they say about it, we're gonna keep it.

It isn't easy to come before a nation-wide audience and air your life as I've done. But I want to say some things before I conclude that I think most of you will agree on. Mr. Mitchell, the chairman of the Democratic National Committee, made the statement that if a man couldn't afford to be in the United States Senate he shouldn't run for the Senate.

And I just want to make my position clear. I don't agree with Mr. Mitchell when he says that only a rich man should serve his Government in the United States Senate or in the Congress. I don't believe that represents the thinking of the Democratic Party, and I know that it doesn't represent the thinking of the Republican Party.

I believe that it's fine that a man like Governor Stevenson who inherited a fortune from his father can run for President. But I also feel that it's essential in this country of ours that a man of modest means can also run for President. Because, you know, remember Abraham Lincoln, you remember what he said: "God must have loved the common people—he made so many of them."

And now I'm going to suggest some courses of conduct.

First of all, you have read in the papers about other funds now. Mr. Stevenson, apparently, had a couple. One of them in which a group of business people paid and helped to supplement the salaries of state employees. Here is where the money went directly into their pockets.

And I think that what Mr. Stevenson should do is come before the American people as I have, give the names of the people that have contributed to that fund; give the names of the people who put this money into their pockets at the same time that they were receiving money from their state government, and see what favors, if any, they gave out for that.

I don't condemn Mr. Stevenson for what he did. But until the facts are in there is a doubt that will be raised.

And as far as Mr. Sparkman is concerned, I would suggest the same thing. He's had his wife on the payroll. I don't condemn him for that. But I think that he should come before the American people and indicate what outside sources of income he has had.

I would suggest that under the circumstances both Mr. Sparkman and Mr. Stevenson should come before the American people as I have and make a complete financial statement as to their financial history. And if they don't, it will be an admission that they have something to hide. And I think that you will agree with me.

Because, folks, remember, a man that's to be President of the United States, a man that's to be Vice President of the United States must have the confidence of all the people. And that's why I'm doing what I'm doing, and that's why I suggest that Mr. Stevenson and Mr. Sparkman since they are under attack should do what I am doing.

Now, let me say this: I know that this is not the last of the smears. In spite of my explanation tonight other smears will be made; others have been made in the past. And the purpose of the smears, I know, is this—to silence me, to make me let up.

Well, they just don't know who they're dealing with. I'm going to tell you this: I remember in the dark days of the Hiss case some of the same columnists, some of the same radio commentators who are attacking me now and misrepresenting my position were violently opposing me at the time I was after Alger Hiss.

But I continued the fight because I knew I was right. And I can say to this great television and radio audience that I have no apologies to the American people for my part in putting Alger Hiss where he is today.

And as far as this is concerned, I intend to continue the fight.

Why do I feel so deeply? Why do I feel that in spite of the smears, the misunderstandings, the necessity for a man to come up here and bare his soul as I have? Why is it necessary for me to continue this fight?

And I want to tell you why. Because, you see, I love my country. And I think my country is in danger. And I think that the only man that can save America at this time is the man that's running for President on my ticket—Dwight Eisenhower.

You say, "Why do I think it's in danger?" and I say look at the record. Seven years of the Truman-Acheson Administration and what's happened? Six hundred million people lost to the

Communists, and a war in Korea in which we have lost 117,000 American casualties.

And I say to all of you that a policy that results in a loss of six hundred million people to the Communists and a war which costs us 117,000 American casualties isn't good enough for America.

And I say that those in the State Department that made the mistakes which caused that war and which resulted in those losses should be kicked out of the State Department just as fast as we can get 'em out of there.

And let me say that I know Mr. Stevenson won't do that. Because he defends the Truman policy and I know that Dwight Eisenhower will do that, and that he will give America the leadership that it needs.

Take the problem of corruption. You've read about the mess in Washington. Mr. Stevenson can't clean it up because he was picked by the man, Truman, under whose Administration the mess was made. You wouldn't trust a man who made the mess to clean it up—that's Truman. And by the same token you can't trust the man who was picked by the man that made the mess to clean it up—and that's Stevenson.

And so I say, Eisenhower, who owes nothing to Truman, nothing to the big city bosses, he is the man that can clean up the mess in Washington.

Take Communism. I say that as far as that subject is concerned, the danger is great to America. In the Hiss case they got the secrets which enabled them to break the American secret State Department code. They got secrets in the atomic bomb case which enabled 'em to get the secret of the atomic bomb, five years before they would have gotten it by their own devices.

And I say that any man who called the Alger Hiss case a "red herring" isn't fit to be President of the United States. I say that a man who like Mr. Stevenson has pooh-poohed and ridiculed the Communist threat in the United States—he said that they are phantoms among ourselves; he's accused us that have attempted to expose the Communists of looking for Communists in the Bureau of Fisheries and Wildlife—I say that a man who says that isn't qualified to be President of the United States.

And I say that the only man who can lead us in this fight to rid the Government of both those who are Communists and those who have corrupted this Government is Eisenhower, because Eisenhower, you can be sure, recognizes the problem and he knows how to deal with it.

Now let me say that, finally, this evening I want to read to you just briefly excerpts from a letter which I received, a letter which, after all this is over, no one can take away from us. It reads as follows:

"Dear Senator Nixon,

"Since I'm only 19 years of age I can't vote in this Presidential election but believe me if I could you and General Eisenhower would certainly get my vote.  My husband is in the Fleet Marines in Korea. He's a corpsman on the front lines and we have a two-month-old son he's never seen.  And I feel confident that with great Americans like you and General Eisenhower in the White House, lonely Americans like myself will be united with their loved ones now in Korea.

"I only pray to God that you won't be too late.  Enclosed is a small check to help you in your campaign.  Living on $85 a month it is all I can afford at present.  But let me know what else I can do."

Folks, it's a check for $10, and it's one that I will never cash.

And just let me say this.  We hear a lot about prosperity these days but I say, why can't we have prosperity built on peace rather than prosperity built on war?  Why can't we have prosperity and an honest government in Washington, D.C., at the same time.  Believe me, we can.  And Eisenhower is the man that can lead this crusade to bring us that kind of prosperity.

And, now, finally, I know that you wonder whether or not I am going to stay on the Republican ticket or resign.

Let me say this: I don't believe that I ought to quit because I'm not a quitter.  And, incidentally, Pat's not a quitter.  After all, her name was Patricia Ryan and she was born on St. Patrick's Day, and you know the Irish never quit.

But the decision, my friends, is not mine.  I would do nothing that would harm the possibilities of Dwight Eisenhower to become President of the United States.  And for that reason I am submitting to the Republican National Committee tonight through this television broadcast the decision which it is theirs to make.

Let them decide whether my position on the ticket will help or hurt.  And I am going to ask you to help them decide.  Wire and write the Republican National Committee whether you think I should stay on or whether I should get off.  And whatever their decision is, I will abide by it.

But just let me say this last word.  Regardless of what happens I'm going to continue this fight.  I'm going to campaign up and down America until we drive the crooks and the Communists and those that defend them out of Washington.  And remember, folks, Eisenhower is a great man.  Believe me.  He's a great man.  And a vote for Eisenhower is a vote for what's good for America.*

---

* Based on *Vital Speeches*, 29 (October 15, 1952): 11-15 and edited using a video tape, *Great American Speeches*,II, Educational Video Group, Greenwood, Indiana.

# "Address to the Nation on the War in Vietnam": November 3, 1969

*Good evening, my fellow Americans:*

Tonight I want to talk to you on a subject of deep concern to all Americans and to many people in all parts of the world—the war in Vietnam.

I believe that one of the reasons for the deep division about Vietnam is that many Americans have lost confidence in what their Government has told them about our policy. The American people cannot and should not be asked to support a policy which involves the overriding issues of war and peace unless they know the truth about that policy.

Tonight, therefore, I would like to answer some of the questions that I know are on the minds of many of you listening to me.

How and why did America get involved in Vietnam in the first place? How has this administration changed the policy of the previous administration?

What has really happened in the negotiations in Paris and on the battlefront in Vietnam?

What choices do we have if we are to end the war?

What are the prospects for peace?

Now, let me begin by describing the situation I found when I was inaugurated on January 20.

—The war had been going on for 4 years.

—31,000 Americans had been killed in action.

—The training program for the South Vietnamese was behind schedule.

—540,000 Americans were in Vietnam with no plans to reduce the number.

—No progress had been made at the negotiations in Paris and the United States had not put forth a comprehensive peace proposal.

—The war was causing deep division at home and criticism from many of our friends as well as our enemies abroad.

In view of these circumstances there were some who urged that I end the war at once by ordering the immediate withdrawal of all American forces.

From a political standpoint this would have been a popular and easy course to follow. After all, we became involved in the war while my predecessor was in office. I could blame the defeat which would be the result of my action on him and come out as the peacemaker. Some put it to me quite bluntly: This was the only way to avoid allowing Johnson's war to become Nixon's war.

But I had a greater obligation than to think only of the years of my administration and of the next election. I had to think of the effect of my decision on the next generation and on the future of peace and freedom in America and in the world.

Let us all understand that the question before us is not whether some Americans are for peace and some Americans are against peace. The question at issue is not whether Johnson's war becomes Nixon's war.

The great question is: How can we win America's peace?

Well, let us turn now to the fundamental issue. Why and how did the United States become involved in Vietnam in the first place?

Fifteen years ago North Vietnam, with the logistical support of Communist China and the Soviet Union, launched a campaign to impose a Communist government on South Vietnam by instigating and supporting a revolution.

In response to the request of the Government of South Vietnam, President Eisenhower sent economic aid and military equipment to assist the people of South Vietnam in their efforts to prevent a Communist takeover. Seven years ago, President Kennedy sent 16,000 military personnel to Vietnam as combat advisers. Four years ago, President Johnson sent American combat forces to South Vietnam.

Now, many believe that President Johnson's decision to send American combat forces to South Vietnam was wrong. And many others—I among them—have been strongly critical of the way the war has been conducted.

But the question facing us today is: Now that we are in the war, what is the best way to end it?

In January I could only conclude that the precipitate withdrawal of American forces from Vietnam would be a disaster not only for South Vietnam but for the United States and for the cause of peace.

For the South Vietnamese, our precipitate withdrawal would inevitably allow the Communists to repeat the massacres which followed their takeover in the North 15 years before.

—They then murdered more than 50,000 people and hundreds of thousands more died in slave labor camps.

—We saw a prelude of what would happen in South Vietnam when the Communists entered the city of Hue last year. During their brief rule there, there was a bloody reign of terror in which 3,000 civilians were clubbed, shot to death, and buried in mass graves.

—With the sudden collapse of our support, these atrocities of Hue would become the nightmare of the entire nation—and particularly for the million and a half Catholic refugees who fled to South Vietnam when the Communists took over in the North.

For the United States, this first defeat in our Nation's history would result in a collapse of confidence in American leadership, not only in Asia but throughout the world.

Three American Presidents have recognized the great stakes involved in Vietnam and understood what had to be done.

In 1963, President Kennedy, with his characteristic eloquence and clarity, said: ". . . we want to see a stable government there, carrying on a struggle to maintain its national independence.

"We believe strongly in that. We are not going to withdraw from that effort. In my opinion, for us to withdraw from that effort would mean a collapse not only of South Viet-Nam, but Southeast Asia. So we are going to stay there."

President Eisenhower and President Johnson expressed the same conclusion during their terms of office.

For the future of peace, precipitate withdrawal would thus be a disaster of immense magnitude.

—A nation cannot remain great if it betrays its allies and lets down its friends.

—Our defeat and humiliation in South Vietnam without question would promote recklessness in the councils of those great powers who have not yet abandoned their goals of world conquest.

—This would spark violence wherever our commitments help maintain the peace—in the Middle East, in Berlin, eventually even in the Western Hemisphere.

Ultimately, this would cost more lives.

It would not bring peace; it would bring more war.

For these reasons, I rejected the recommendation that I should end the war by immediately withdrawing all of our forces. I chose instead to change American policy on both the negotiating front and battlefront.

In order to end a war fought on many fronts, I initiated a pursuit for peace on many fronts.

In a television speech on May 14, in a speech before the United Nations, and on a number of other occasions I set forth our peace proposals in great detail.

—We have offered the complete withdrawal of all outside forces within 1 year.

—We have proposed a cease-fire under international supervision.

—We have offered free elections under international supervision with the Communists participating in the organization and conduct of the elections as an organized political force. And the Saigon Government has pledged to accept the result of the elections.

We have not put forth our proposals on a take-it-or-leave-it basis. We have indicated that we are willing to discuss the proposals that have been put forth by the other side. We have declared that anything is negotiable except the right of the people of South Vietnam to determine their own future. At the Paris peace conference, Ambassador Lodge has demonstrated our flexibility and good faith in 40 public meetings.

Hanoi has refused even to discuss our proposals. They demand our unconditional acceptance of their terms, which are that we withdraw all American forces immediately and unconditionally and that we overthrow the Government of South Vietnam as we leave.

We have not limited our peace initiatives to public forums and public statements. I recognized, in January, that a long and bitter war like this usually cannot be settled in a public forum. That is why in addition to the public statements and negotiation I have explored every possible private avenue that might lead to a settlement.

Tonight I am taking the unprecedented step of disclosing to you some of our other initiatives for peace—initiatives we undertook privately and secretly because we thought we thereby might open a door which publicly would be closed.

I did not wait for my inauguration to begin my quest for peace.

—Soon after my election, through an individual who is directly in contact on a personal basis with the leaders of North Vietnam, I made two private offers for a rapid, comprehensive settlement. Hanoi's replies called in effect for our surrender before negotiations.

—Since the Soviet Union furnishes most of the military equipment for North Vietnam, Secretary of State Rogers, my Assistant for National Security Affairs, Dr. Kissinger, Ambassador Lodge, and I, personally, have met on a number of occasions with representatives of the Soviet Government to enlist their assistance in getting meaningful negotiations started. In addition, we have had extended discussions directed toward that same end with representatives of other governments which have diplomatic relations with North Vietnam. None of these initiatives have to date produced results.

—In mid-July, I became convinced that it was necessary to make a major move to break the deadlock in the Paris talks. I spoke directly in this office, where I am now sitting, with an individual who had known Ho Chi Minh [President, Democratic Republic of Vietnam] on a personal basis for 25 years. Through him I sent a letter to Ho Chi Minh.

I did this outside of the usual diplomatic channels with the hope that with the necessity of making statements for propaganda removed, there might be constructive progress toward bringing the war to an end. Let me read from that letter to you now.

"Dear Mr. President:

"I realize that it is difficult to communicate meaningfully across the gulf of four years of war. But precisely because of this gulf, I wanted to take this opportunity to reaffirm in all solemnity my desire to work for a just peace. I deeply believe that the war in Vietnam has gone on too long and delay in bringing it to an end can benefit no one—least of all the people of Vietnam. . . .

"The time has come to move forward at the conference table toward an early resolution of this tragic war. You will find us forthcoming and open-minded in a common effort to bring the blessings of peace to the brave people of Vietnam. Let history record that at this critical juncture, both sides turned their face toward peace rather than toward conflict and war."

I received Ho Chi Minh's reply on August 30, 3 days before his death. It simply reiterated the public position North Vietnam had taken at Paris and flatly rejected my initiative.

The full text of both letters is being released to the press.

—In addition to the public meetings that I have referred to, Ambassador Lodge has met with Vietnam's chief negotiator in Paris in 11 private sessions.

—We have taken other significant initiatives which must remain secret to keep open some channels of communication which may still prove to be productive.

But the effect of all the public, private, and secret negotiations which have been undertaken since the bombing halt a year ago and since this administration came into office on January 20, can be summed up in one sentence: No progress whatever has been made except agreement on the shape of the bargaining table.

Well now, who is at fault?

It has become clear that the obstacle in negotiating an end to the war is not the President of the United States. It is not the South Vietnamese Government.

The obstacle is the other side's absolute refusal to show the least willingness to join us in seeking a just peace. And it will not do so while it is convinced that all it has to do is to wait for our next concession, and our next concession after that one, until it gets everything it wants.

There can now be no longer any question that progress in negotiation depends only on Hanoi's deciding to negotiate, to negotiate seriously.

I realize that this report on our efforts on the diplomatic front is discouraging to the American people, but the American people are entitled to know the truth—the bad news as well as the good news—where the lives of our young men are involved.

Now let me turn, however, to a more encouraging report on another front.

At the time we launched our search for peace I recognized we might not succeed in bringing an end to the war through negotiation. I, therefore, put into effect another plan to bring peace—a plan which will bring the war to an end regardless of what happens on the negotiating front.

It is in line with a major shift in U.S. foreign policy which I described in my press conference at Guam on July 25. Let me briefly explain what has been described as the Nixon Doctrine—a policy which not only will help end the war in Vietnam, but which is an essential element of our program to prevent future Vietnams.

We Americans are a do-it-yourself people. We are an impatient people. Instead of teaching someone else to do a job, we like to do it ourselves. And this trait has been carried over into our foreign policy In Korea and again in Vietnam, the United States furnished most of the money, most of the arms, and most of the men to help the people of those countries defend their freedom against Communist aggression.

Before any American troops were committed to Vietnam, a leader of another Asian country expressed this opinion to me when I was traveling in Asia as a private citizen. He said: "When you are trying to assist another nation defend its freedom, U.S. policy should be to help them fight the war but not to fight the war for them."

Well, in accordance with this wise counsel, I laid down in Guam three principles as guidelines for future American policy toward Asia:

—First, the United States will keep all of its treaty commitments.

—Second, we shall provide a shield if a nuclear power threatens the freedom of a nation allied with us or of a nation whose survival we consider vital to our security.

—Third, in cases involving other types of aggression, we shall furnish military and economic assistance when requested in accordance with our treaty commitments. But we shall look to the nation directly threatened to assume the primary responsibility of providing the manpower for its defense.

After I announced this policy, I found that the leaders of the Philippines, Thailand, Vietnam, South Korea, and other nations which might be threatened by Communist aggression, welcomed this new direction in American foreign policy.

The defense of freedom is everybody's business—not just America's business. And it is particularly the responsibility of the people whose freedom is threatened. In the previous administration, we Americanized the war in Vietnam. In this administration, we are Vietnamizing the search for peace.

The policy of the previous administration not only resulted in our assuming the primary responsibility for fighting the war, but even more significantly did not adequately stress the goal of strengthening the South Vietnamese so that they could defend themselves when we left.

The Vietnamization plan was launched following Secretary Laird's visit to Vietnam in March. Under the plan, I ordered first a substantial increase in the training and equipment of South Vietnamese forces.

In July, on my visit to Vietnam, I changed General Abrams' orders so that they were consistent with the objectives of our new policies. Under the new orders, the primary mission of our troops is to enable the South Vietnamese forces to assume the full responsibility for the security of South Vietnam.

Our air operations have been reduced by over 20 percent.

And now we have begun to see the results of this long overdue change in American policy in Vietnam.

—After 5 years of Americans going into Vietnam, we are finally bringing American men home. By December 15, over 60,000 men will have been withdrawn from South Vietnam, including 20 percent of all of our combat forces.

—The South Vietnamese have continued to gain in strength. As a result they have been able to take over combat responsibilities from our American troops.

Two other significant developments have occurred since this administration took office.

—Enemy infiltration, infiltration which is essential if they are to launch a major attack, over the last 3 months is less than 20 percent of what it was over the same period last year.

—Most important—United States casualties have declined during the last 2 months to the lowest point in 3 years.

Let me now turn to our program for the future.

We have adopted a plan which we have worked out in cooperation with the South Vietnamese for the complete withdrawal of all U.S. combat ground forces, and their replacement by South Vietnamese forces on an orderly scheduled timetable. This withdrawal will be made from strength and not from weakness. As South Vietnamese forces become stronger, the rate of American withdrawal can become greater.

I have not and do not intend to announce the timetable for our program. And there are obvious reasons for this decision which I am sure you will understand. As I have indicated on several occasions, the rate of withdrawal will depend on developments on three fronts.

One of these is the progress which can be or might be made in the Paris talks. An announcement of a fixed timetable for our withdrawal would completely remove any incentive for the enemy to negotiate an agreement. They would simply wait until our forces had withdrawn and then move in.

The other two factors on which we will base our withdrawal decisions are the level of enemy activity and the progress of the training programs of the South Vietnamese forces. And I am glad to be able to report tonight progress on both of these fronts has been greater than we anticipated when we started the program in June for withdrawal. As a result, our timetable for withdrawal is more optimistic now than when we made our first estimates in June. Now, this clearly demonstrates why it is not wise to be frozen in on a fixed timetable.

We must retain the flexibility to base each withdrawal decision on the situation as it is at that time rather than on estimates that are no longer valid.

Along with this optimistic estimate, I must—in all candor— leave one note of caution. If the level of enemy activity significantly increases we might have to adjust our timetable accordingly.

However, I want the record to be completely clear on one point.

At the time of the bombing halt just a year ago, there was some confusion as to whether there was an understanding on the part of the enemy that if we stopped the bombing of North Vietnam they would stop the shelling of cities in South Vietnam. I want to be sure that there is no misunderstanding on the part of the enemy with regard to our withdrawal program.

We have noted the reduced level of infiltration, the reduction of our casualties, and are basing our withdrawal decisions partially on those factors. If the level of infiltration or our casualties increase while we are trying to scale down the fighting, it will be the result of a conscious decision by the enemy.

Hanoi could make no greater mistake than to assume that an increase in violence will be to its advantage. If I conclude that increased enemy action jeopardizes our remaining forces in Vietnam, I shall not hesitate to take strong and effective measures to deal with that situation.

This is not a threat. This is a statement of policy, which as Commander in Chief of our Armed Forces, I am making in meeting my responsibility for the protection of American fighting men wherever they may be.

My fellow Americans, I am sure you can recognize from what I have said that we really only have two choices open to us if we want to end this war.

—I can order an immediate, precipitate withdrawal of all Americans from Vietnam without regard to the effects of that action.

—Or we can persist in our search for a just peace through a negotiated settlement if possible, or through continued implementation of our plan for Vietnamization if necessary, a plan in which we will withdraw all of our forces from Vietnam on a schedule in accordance with our program, as the South Vietnamese become strong enough to defend their own freedom.

I have chosen this second course. It is not the easy way. It is the right way.

It is a plan which will end the war and serve the cause of peace—not just in Vietnam but in the Pacific and in the world.

In speaking of the consequences of a precipitate withdrawal, I mentioned that our allies would lose confidence in America.

Far more dangerous, we would lose confidence in ourselves. Oh, the immediate reaction would be a sense of relief that our men were coming home. But as we saw the consequences of what we had done, inevitable remorse and divisive recrimination would scar our spirit as a people.

We have faced other crises in our history and have become stronger by rejecting the easy way out and taking the right way in meeting our challenges. Our greatness as a nation has been our capacity to do what had to be done when we knew our course was right.

I recognize that some of my fellow citizens disagree with the plan for peace I have chosen. Honest and patriotic Americans have reached different conclusions as to how peace should be achieved.

In San Francisco a few weeks ago, I saw demonstrators carrying signs reading: "Lose in Vietnam, bring the boys home."

Well, one of the strengths of our free society is that any American has a right to reach that conclusion and to advocate that point of view. But as President of the United States, I would be untrue to my oath of office if I allowed the policy of this Nation to be dictated by the minority who hold that point of view and who try to impose it on the Nation by mounting demonstrations in the street.

For almost 200 years, the policy of this Nation has been made under our Constitution by those leaders in the Congress and the White House elected by all of the people. If a vocal minority, however fervent its cause, prevails over reason and the will of the majority, this Nation has no future as a free society.

And now I would like to address a word, if I may, to the young people of this Nation who are particularly concerned, and I understand why they are concerned, about this war.

I respect your idealism. I share your concern for peace. I want peace as much as you do.

There are powerful personal reasons I want to end this war. This week I will have to sign 83 letters to mothers, fathers, wives, and loved ones of men who have given their lives for America in Vietnam. It is very little satisfaction to me that this is only one-third as many letters as I signed the first week in office. There is nothing I want more than to see the day come when I do not have to write any of those letters.

—I want to end the war to save the lives of those brave young men in Vietnam.

—But I want to end it in a way which will increase the chance that their younger brothers and their sons will not have to fight in some future Vietnam someplace in the world.

—And I want to end the war for another reason. I want to end it so that the energy and dedication of you, our young people, now too often directed into bitter hatred against those responsible for the war, can be turned to the great challenges of peace, a better life for all Americans, a better life for all people on this earth.

I have chosen a plan for peace. I believe it will succeed.

If it does succeed, what the critics say now won't matter. If it does not succeed, anything I say then won't matter.

I know it may not be fashionable to speak of patriotism or national destiny these days. But I feel it is appropriate to do so on this occasion.

Two hundred years ago this Nation was weak and poor. But even then, America was the hope of millions in the world. Today we have become the strongest and richest nation in the world. And the wheel of destiny has turned so that any hope the world has for the survival of peace and freedom will be determined by whether the American people have the moral stamina and the courage to meet the challenge of free world leadership.

Let historians not record that when America was the most powerful nation in the world we passed on the other side of the road and allowed the last hopes for peace and freedom of millions of people to be suffocated by the forces of totalitarianism.

And so tonight—to you, the great silent majority of my fellow Americans—I ask for your support.

I pledged in my campaign for the Presidency to end the war in a way that we could win the peace. I have initiated a plan of action which will enable me to keep that pledge.

The more support I can have from the American people, the sooner that pledge can be redeemed; for the more divided we are at home, the less likely the enemy is to negotiate at Paris.

Let us be united for peace. Let us also be united against defeat. Because let us understand: North Vietnam cannot defeat or humiliate the United States. Only Americans can do that.

Fifty years ago, in this room and at this very desk, President Woodrow Wilson spoke words which caught the imagination of a war-weary world. He said: "This is the war to end war." His dream for peace after World War I was shattered on the hard realities of great power politics and Woodrow Wilson died a broken man.

Tonight I do not tell you that the war in Vietnam is the war to end wars. But I do say this: I have initiated a plan which will end this war in a way that will bring us closer to that great goal to which Woodrow Wilson and every American President in our history has been dedicated—the goal of a just and lasting peace.

As President I hold the responsibility for choosing the best path to that goal and then leading the Nation along it.

I pledge to you tonight that I shall meet this responsibility with all of the strength and wisdom I can command in accordance with hour hopes, mindful of your concerns, sustained by your prayers.

Thank you and goodnight.*

*Public Papers of the Presidents of the United States: Richard Nixon, 1969, (Washington, D.C.: Government Printing Office, 1971), pp. 901-9.

# "Address to the Nation on the Situation in Southeast Asia": April 30, 1970

*Good evening my fellow Americans:*

Ten days ago, in my report to the Nation on Vietnam, I announced a decision to withdraw an additional 150,000 Americans from Vietnam over the next year. I said then that I was making that decision despite our concern over increased enemy activity in Laos, in Cambodia, and in South Vietnam.

At that time, I warned that if I concluded that increased enemy activity in any of these areas endangered the lives of Americans remaining in Vietnam, I would not hesitate to take strong and effective measures to deal with that situation.

Despite that warning, North Vietnam has increased its military aggression in all these areas, and particularly in Cambodia.

After full consultation with the National Security Council, Ambassador Bunker, General Abrams, and my other advisers, I have concluded that the actions of the enemy in the last 10 days clearly endanger the lives of Americans who are in Vietnam now and would constitute an unacceptable risk to those who will be there after withdrawal of another 150,000.

To protect our men who are in Vietnam and to guarantee the continued success of our withdrawal and Vietnamization programs, I have concluded that the time has come for action.

Tonight, I shall describe the actions of the enemy, the actions I have ordered to deal with that situation, and the reasons for my decision.

Cambodia, a small country of 7 million people, has been a neutral nation since the Geneva agreement of 1954—an agreement, incidentally, which was signed by the Government of North Vietnam.

American policy since then has been to scrupulously respect the neutrality of the Cambodian people. We have maintained a skeleton diplomatic mission of fewer than 15 in Cambodia's capital, and that only since last August. For the previous 4 years, from 1965 to 1969, we did not have any diplomatic mission whatever in

Cambodia. And for the past 5 years, we have provided no military assistance whatever and no economic assistance to Cambodia.

North Vietnam, however, has not respected that neutrality.

For the past 5 years—as indicated on this map that you see here—North Vietnam has occupied military sanctuaries all along the Cambodian frontier with South Vietnam. Some of these extend up to 20 miles into Cambodia. The sanctuaries are in red and, as you note, they are on both sides of the border. They are used for hit and run attacks on American and South Vietnamese forces in South Vietnam. These Communist occupied territories contain major base camps, training sites, logistics facilities, weapons and ammunition factories, airstrips, and prisoner-of-war compounds.

For 5 years, neither the United States nor South Vietnam has moved against these enemy sanctuaries because we did not wish to violate the territory of a neutral nation. Even after the Vietnamese Communists began to expand these sanctuaries 4 weeks ago, we counseled patience to our South Vietnamese allies and imposed restraints on our own commanders.

In contrast to our policy, the enemy in the past 2 weeks has stepped up his guerrilla actions and he is concentrating his main forces in these sanctuaries that you see on this map where they are building up to launch massive attacks on our forces and those of South Vietnam.

North Vietnam in the last 2 weeks has stripped away all pretense of respecting the sovereignty or the neutrality of Cambodia. Thousands of their soldiers are invading the country from the sanctuaries; they are encircling the capital of Phnom Penh. Coming from these sanctuaries, as you see here, they have moved into Cambodia and are encircling the capital.

Cambodia, as a result of this, has sent out a call to the United States, to a number of other nations, for assistance. Because if this enemy effort succeeds, Cambodia would become a vast enemy staging area and a springboard for attacks on South Vietnam along 600 miles of frontier—a refuge where enemy troops could return from combat without fear of retaliation.

North Vietnamese men and supplies could then be poured into that country, jeopardizing not only the lives of our own men but the people of South Vietnam as well.

Now confronted with this situation, we have three options.

First, we can do nothing. Well, the ultimate result of that course of action is clear. Unless we indulge in wishful thinking, the lives of Americans remaining in Vietnam after our next withdrawal of 150,000 would be gravely threatened.

Let us go to the map again. Here is South Vietnam. Here is North Vietnam. North Vietnam already occupies this part of Laos. If North Vietnam also occupied this whole band in Cambodia, or the entire country, it would mean that South Vietnam was completely outflanked and the forces of Americans in this area, as well as the South Vietnamese, would be in an untenable military position.

Our second choice is to provide massive military assistance to Cambodia itself.  Now unfortunately, while we deeply sympathize with the plight of 7 million Cambodians whose country is being invaded, massive amounts of military assistance could not be rapidly and effectively utilized by the small Cambodian Army against the immediate threat.  With other nations, we shall do our best to provide the small arms and other equipment which the Cambodian Army of 40,000 needs and can use for its defense.  But the aid we will provide will be limited to the purpose of enabling Cambodia to defend its neutrality and not for the purpose of making it an active belligerent on one side or the other.

Our third choice is to go to the heart of the trouble.  That means cleaning out major North Vietnamese and Vietcong occupied territories—these sanctuaries which serve as bases for attacks on both Cambodia and American and South Vietnamese forces in South Vietnam.  Some of these, incidentally, are as close to Saigon as Baltimore is to Washington.  This one, for example [indicating], is called the Parrot's Beak.  It is only 33 miles from Saigon.

Now faced with these three options, this is the decision I have made.

In cooperation with the armed forces of South Vietnam, attacks are being launched this week to clean out major enemy sanctuaries on the Cambodian-Vietnam border.

A major responsibility for the ground operations is being assumed by South Vietnamese forces.  For example, the attacks in several areas, including the Parrot's Beak that I referred to a moment ago, are exclusively South Vietnamese ground operations under South Vietnamese command with the United States providing air and logistical support.

There is one area, however, immediately above Parrot's Beak, where I have concluded that a combined American and South Vietnamese operation is necessary.

Tonight, American and South Vietnamese units will attack the headquarters for the entire Communist military operation in South Vietnam.  This key control center has been occupied by the North Vietnamese and Vietcong for 5 years in blatant violation of Cambodia's neutrality.

This is not an invasion of Cambodia.  The areas in which these attacks will be launched are completely occupied and controlled by North Vietnamese forces.  Our purpose is not to occupy the areas.  Once enemy forces are driven out of these sanctuaries and once their military supplies are destroyed, we will withdraw.

These actions are in no way directed to the security interests of any nation.  Any government that chooses to use these actions as a pretext for harming relations with the United States will be doing so on its own responsibility, and on its own initiative, and we will draw the appropriate conclusions.

Now let me give you the reasons for my decision.  A majority of the American people, a majority of you listening to me, are for the withdrawal of our forces from Vietnam.  The action I have taken tonight is indispensable for the continuing success of that withdrawal program.

A majority of the American people want to end this war rather than to have it drag on interminably.  The action I have taken tonight will serve that purpose.

A majority of the American people want to keep the casualties of our brave men in Vietnam at an absolute minimum.  The action I take tonight is essential if we are to accomplish that goal

We take this action not for the purpose of expanding the war into Cambodia but for the purpose of ending the war in Vietnam and winning the just peace we all desire.  We have made—we will continue to make every possible effort to end this war through negotiation at the conference table rather than through more fighting on the battlefield.

Let us look again at the record.  We have stopped the bombing of North Vietnam.  We have cut air operations by over 20 percent.  We have announced withdrawal of over 250,000 of our men.  We have offered to withdraw all of our men if they will withdraw theirs.  We have offered to negotiate all issues with only one condition—and that is that the future of South Vietnam be determined not by North Vietnam, and not by the United States, but by the people of South Vietnam themselves.

The answer of the enemy has been intransigence at the conference table, belligerence in Hanoi, massive military aggression in Laos and Cambodia, and stepped-up attacks in South Vietnam, designed to increase American casualties.

This attitude has become intolerable.  We will not react to this threat to American lives merely by plaintive diplomatic protests.  If we did, the credibility of the United States would be destroyed in every area of the world where only the power of the United States deters aggression.

Tonight, I again warn the North Vietnamese that if they continue to escalate the fighting when the United States is withdrawing its forces, I shall meet my responsibility as Commander in Chief of our Armed Forces to take the action I consider necessary to defend the security of our American men.

The action that I have announced tonight puts the leaders of North Vietnam on notice that we will be patient in working for peace; we will be conciliatory at the conference table, but we will not be humiliated.  We will not be defeated.  We will not allow American men by the thousands to be killed by an enemy from privileged sanctuaries.

The time came long ago to end this war through peaceful negotiations.  We stand ready for those negotiations.  We have made major efforts, many of which must remain secret.

I say tonight: All the offers and approaches made previously remain on the conference table whenever Hanoi is ready to negotiate seriously.

But if the enemy response to our most conciliatory offers for peaceful negotiation continues to be to increase its attacks and humiliate and defeat us, we shall react accordingly.

My fellow Americans, we live in an age of anarchy, both abroad and at home. We see mindless attacks on all the great institutions which have been created by free civilizations in the last 500 years. Even here in the United States, great universities are being systematically destroyed. Small nations all over the world find themselves under attack from within and from without.

If, when the chips are down, the world's most powerful nation, the United States of America, acts like a pitiful, helpless giant, the forces of totalitarianism and anarchy will threaten free nations and free institutions throughout the world.

It is not our power but our will and character that is being tested tonight. The question all Americans must ask and answer tonight is this: Does the richest and strongest nation in the history of the world have the character to meet a direct challenge by a group which rejects every effort to win a just peace, ignores our warning, tramples on solemn agreements, violates the neutrality of an unarmed people, and uses our prisoners as hostages?

If we fail to meet this challenge, all other nations will be on notice that despite its overwhelming power the United States, when a real crisis comes, will be found wanting.

During my campaign for the Presidency, I pledged to bring Americans home from Vietnam. They are coming home.

I promised to end this war. I shall keep that promise.

I promised to win a just peace. I shall keep that promise.

We shall avoid a wider war. But we are also determined to put an end to this war.

In this room, Woodrow Wilson made the great decisions which led to victory in World War I. Franklin Roosevelt made the decisions which led to our victory in World War II. Dwight D. Eisenhower made decisions which ended the war in Korea and avoided war in the Middle East. John F. Kennedy, in his finest hour, made the great decision which removed Soviet nuclear missiles from Cuba and the Western Hemisphere.

I have noted that there has been a great deal of discussion with regard to this decision that I have made and I should point out that I do not contend that it is in the same magnitude as these decisions that I have just mentioned. But between those decisions and this decision there is a difference that is very fundamental. In those decisions, the American people were not assailed by counsels of doubt and defeat from some of the most widely known opinion leaders of the Nation.

I have noted, for example, that a Republican Senator has said that this action I have taken means that my party has lost all chance of winning the November elections. And others are saying today that this move against enemy sanctuaries will make me a one-term President.

No one is more aware than I am of the political consequences of the action I have taken. It is tempting to take the easy political path: to blame this war on previous administrations and to bring all of our men home immediately, regardless of the consequences, even though that would mean defeat for the United States; to desert 18 million South Vietnamese people, who have put their trust in us and to expose them to the same slaughter and savagery which the leaders of North Vietnam inflicted on hundreds of thousands of North Vietnamese who chose freedom when the Communists took over North Vietnam in 1954; to get peace at any price now, even though I know that a peace of humiliation for the United States would lead to a bigger war or surrender later.

I have rejected all political considerations in making this decision.

Whether my party gains in November is nothing compared to the lives of 400,000 brave Americans fighting for our country and for the cause of peace and freedom in Vietnam. Whether I may be a one-term President is insignificant compared to whether by our failure to act in this crisis the United States proves itself to be unworthy to lead the forces of freedom in this critical period in world history. I would rather be a one-term President and do what I believe is right than to be a two-term President at the cost of seeing America become a second-rate power and to see this Nation accept the first defeat in its proud 190-year history.

I realize that in this war there are honest and deep differences in this country about whether we should have become involved, that there are differences as to how the war should have been conducted. But the decision I announce tonight transcends those differences.

For the lives of American men are involved. The opportunity for 150,000 Americans to come home in the next 12 months is involved. The future of 18 million people in South Vietnam and 7 million people in Cambodia is involved. The possibility of winning a just peace in Vietnam and in the Pacific is at stake.

It is customary to conclude a speech from the White House by asking support for the President of the United States. Tonight, I depart from that precedent. What I ask is far more important. I ask for your support for our brave men fighting tonight halfway around the world—not for territory—not for glory—but so that their younger brothers and their sons and your sons can have a chance to grow up in a world of peace and freedom and justice.

Thank you and good night.*

---

*Public Papers of the Presidents of the United States: Richard Nixon, 1970, (Washington, D.C.: Government Printing Office, 1971), pp. 405-10.

# "First Address to the Nation about the Watergate Investigations": April 30, 1973

*Good evening:*

I want to talk to you tonight from my heart on a subject of deep concern to every American.

In recent months, members of my Administration and officials of the Committee for the Re-Election of the President—including some of my closest friends and most trusted aides—have been charged with involvement in what has come to be known as the Watergate affair. These include charges of illegal activity during and preceding the 1972 Presidential election and charges that responsible officials participated in efforts to cover up that illegal activity.

The inevitable result of these charges has been to raise serious questions about the integrity of the White House itself. Tonight I wish to address those questions.

Last June 17, while I was in Florida trying to get a few days rest after my visit to Moscow, I first learned from news reports of the Watergate break-in. I was appalled at this senseless, illegal action, and I was shocked to learn that employees of the Re-Election Committee were apparently among those guilty. I immediately ordered an investigation by appropriate Government authorities. On September 15, as you will recall, indictments were brought against seven defendants in the case.

As the investigations went forward, I repeatedly asked those conducting the investigation whether there was any reason to believe that members of my Administration were in any way involved. I received repeated assurances that they there were not. Because of these continuing reassurances, because I believed the reports I was getting, because I had faith in the persons from whom I was getting them, I discounted the stories in the press that appeared to implicate members of my Administration or other officials of the campaign committee.

Until March of this year, I remained convinced that the denials were true and that the charges of involvement by members of the

White House Staff were false. The comments I made during this period, and the comments made by my Press Secretary in my behalf, were based on the information provided to us at the time we made those comments. However, new information then came to me which persuaded me that there was a real possibility that some of these charges were true, and suggesting further that there had been an effort to conceal the facts both from the public, from you, and from me.

As a result, on March 21, I personally assumed the responsibility for coordinating intensive new inquiries into the matter, and I personally ordered those conducting the investigations to get all the facts and to report them directly to me, right here in this office.

I again ordered that all persons in the Government or at the Re-Election Committee should cooperate fully with the FBI, the prosecutors, and the grand jury. I also ordered that anyone who refused to cooperate in telling the truth would be asked to resign from Government service. And, with ground rules adopted that would preserve the basic constitutional separation of powers between the Congress and the Presidency, I directed that members of the White House Staff should appear and testify voluntarily under oath before the Senate committee which was investigating Watergate.

I was determined that we should get to the bottom of the matter, and that the truth should be fully brought out—no matter who was involved.

At the same time, I was determined not to take precipitate action and to avoid, if at all possible, any action that would appear to reflect on innocent people. I wanted to be fair. But I knew that in the final analysis, the integrity of this office—public faith in the integrity of this office—would have to take priority over all personal considerations

Today, in one of the most difficult decisions of my Presidency, I accepted the resignations of two of my closest associates in the White House—Bob Haldeman, John Ehrlichman—two of the finest public servants it has been my privilege to know.

I want to stress that in accepting these resignations, I mean to leave no implication whatever of personal wrongdoing on their part, and I leave no implication tonight of implication on the part of others who have been charged in this matter.

But in matters as sensitive as guarding the integrity of our democratic process, it is essential not only that rigorous legal and ethical standards be observed but also that the public, you, have total confidence that they are both being observed and enforced by those in authority and particularly by the President of the United States. They agreed with me that this move was necessary in order to restore that confidence.

Because Attorney General Kleindienst—though a distinguished public servant, my personal friend for 20 years, with no personal involvement whatever in this matter—has been a close personal and professional associate of some of those who are involved in this case, he and I both felt that it was also necessary to name a new Attorney General.

The Counsel to the President, John Dean, has also resigned.

As the new Attorney General, I have today named Elliot Richardson, a man of unimpeachable integrity and rigorously high principle. I have directed him to do everything necessary to ensure that the Department of Justice has the confidence and the trust of every law-abiding person in this country.

I have given him absolute authority to make all decisions bearing upon the prosecution of the Watergate case and related matters. I have instructed him that if he should consider it appropriate, he has the authority to name a special supervising prosecutor for matters arising out of the case.

Whatever may appear to have been the case before, whatever improper activities may yet be discovered in connection with this whole sordid affair, I want the American people, I want you to know beyond the shadow of a doubt that during my term as President, justice will be pursued fairly, fully, and impartially, no matter who is involved. This office is a sacred trust and I am determined to be worthy of that trust.

Looking back at the history of this case, two questions arise:

How could it have happened?

Who is to blame?

Political commentators have correctly observed that during my 27 years in politics I have always previously insisted on running my own campaigns for office.

But 1972 presented a very different situation. In both domestic and foreign policy, 1972 was a year of crucially important decisions, of intense negotiations, of vital new directions, particularly in working toward the goal which has been my overriding concern throughout my political career—the goal of bringing peace to America, peace to the world.

That is why I decided, as the 1972 campaign approached, that the Presidency should come first and politics second. To the maximum extent possible, therefore, I sought to delegate campaign operations, to remove the day-to-day campaign decisions from the President's office and from the White House. I also, as you recall, severely limited the number of my own campaign appearances.

Who, then, is to blame for what happened in this case?

For specific criminal actions by specific individuals, those who committed those actions must, of course, bear the liability and pay the penalty.

For the fact that alleged improper actions took place within the White House or within my campaign organization, the easiest course would be for me to blame those to whom I delegated the responsibility to run the campaign. But that would be a cowardly thing to do.

I will not place the blame on subordinates—on people whose zeal exceeded their judgment and who may have done wrong in a cause they deeply believed to be right.

In any organization, the man at the top must bear the responsibility. That responsibility, therefore, belongs here, in this office. I accept it. And I pledge to you tonight, from this office, that I will do everything in my power to ensure that the guilty are brought to justice and that such abuses are purged from our political processes in the years to come, long after I have left this office.

Some people, quite properly appalled at the abuses that occurred, will say that Watergate demonstrates the bankruptcy of the American political system. I believe precisely the opposite is true. Watergate represented a series of illegal acts and bad judgments by a number of individuals. It was the system that has brought the facts to light and that will bring those guilty to justice—a system that in this case has included a determined grand jury, honest prosecutors, a courageous judge, John Sirica, and a vigorous free press.

It is essential now that we place our faith in that system—and especially in the judicial system. It is essential that we let the judicial process go forward, respecting those safeguards that are established to protect the innocent as well as to convict the guilty. It is essential that in reacting to the excesses of others, we not fall into excesses ourselves.

It is also essential that we not be so distracted by events such as this that we neglect the vital work before us, before this Nation, before America, at a time of critical importance to America and the world.

Since March, when I first learned that the Watergate affair might in fact be far more serious than I had been led to believe, it has claimed far too much of my time and my attention.

Whatever may now transpire in the case, whatever the actions of the grand jury, whatever the outcome of any eventual trials, I must now turn my full attention—and I shall do so—once again to the larger duties of this office. I owe it to this great office that I hold, and I owe it to you—to my country.

I know that as Attorney General, Elliot Richardson will be both fair and he will be fearless in pursuing this case wherever it leads. I am confident that with him in charge, justice will be done.

There is vital work to be done toward our goal of a lasting structure of peace in the world—work that cannot wait, work that I must do.

Tomorrow, for example, Chancellor Brandt of West Germany will visit the White House for talks that are a vital element of "The Year of Europe," as 1973 has been called. We are already preparing for the next Soviet-American summit meeting later this year.

This is also a year in which we are seeking to negotiate a mutual and balanced reduction of armed forces in Europe, which will reduce our defense budget and allow us to have funds for other purposes at home so desperately needed. It is the year when the United States and Soviet negotiators will seek to work out the second and even more important round of our talks on limiting nuclear arms and of reducing the danger of a nuclear war that would destroy civilization as we know it. It is a year in which we confront the difficult tasks of maintaining peace in Southeast Asia and in the potentially explosive Middle East.

There is also vital work to be done right here in America: to ensure prosperity, and that means a good job for everyone who wants to work; to control inflation, that I know worries every housewife, everyone who tries to balance a family budget in America; to set in motion new and better ways of ensuring progress toward a better life for all Americans.

When I think of this office—of what it means—I think of all the things that I want to accomplish for this Nation, of all the things I want to accomplish for you.

On Christmas Eve, during my terrible personal ordeal of the renewed bombing of North Vietnam, which after 12 years of war finally helped to bring America peace with honor, I sat down just before midnight. I wrote out some of my goals for my second term as President.

Let me read them to you.

"To make it possible for our children, and for our children's children, to live in a world of peace.

"To make this country be more than ever a land of opportunity—of equal opportunity, full opportunity for every American.

"To provide jobs for all who can work, and generous help for those who cannot work.

"To establish a climate of decency and civility, in which each person respects the feelings and the dignity and the God-given rights of his neighbor.

"To make this a land in which each person can dare to dream, can live his dreams—not in fear, but in hope—proud of his community, proud of his country, proud of what America has meant to himself and to the world."

These are great goals. I believe we can, we must work for them. We can achieve them. But we cannot achieve these goals unless we dedicate ourselves to another goal.

We must maintain the integrity of the White House, and that integrity must be real, not transparent. There can be no whitewash at the White House.

We must reform our political process—ridding it not only of the violations of the law but also of the ugly mob violence and other inexcusable campaign tactics that have been too often practiced and too readily accepted in the past, including those that may have been a response by one side to the excesses or expected excesses of the other side. Two wrongs do not make a right.

I have been in public life for more than a quarter of a century. Like any other calling, politics has good people and bad people. And let me tell you, the great majority in politics—in the Congress, in the Federal Government, in the State government—are good people. I know that it can be very easy, under the intensive pressures of a campaign, for even well-intentioned people to fall into shady tactics, to rationalize this on the grounds that what is at stake is of such importance to the Nation that the end justifies the means. And both of our great parties have been guilty of such tactics in the past.

In recent years, however, the campaign excesses that have occurred on all sides have provided a sobering demonstration of how far this false doctrine can take us. The lesson is clear: America, in its political campaigns, must not again fall into the trap of letting the end, however great that end is, justify the means.

I urge the leaders of both political parties, I urge citizens, all of you, everywhere, to join in working toward a new set of standards, new rules and procedures to ensure that future elections will be as nearly free of such abuses as they possibly can be made. This is my goal. I ask you to join in making it America's goal.

When I was inaugurated for a second time this past January 20, I gave each member of my Cabinet and each member of my senior White House Staff a special 4-year calendar, with each day marked to show the number of days remaining to the Administration. In the inscription on each calendar, I wrote these words: "The Presidential term which begins today consists of 1,461 days—no more, no less. Each can be a day of strengthening and renewal for America; each can add depth and dimension to the American experience. If we strive together, if we make the most of the challenge and the opportunity that these days offer us, they can stand out as great days for America, and great moments in the history of the world."

I looked at my own calendar this morning up at Camp David as I was working on this speech. It showed exactly 1,361 days remaining in my term. I want these to be the best days in America's history, because I love America. I deeply believe that America is the hope of the world. And I know that in the quality and wisdom of the leadership America gives lies the only hope for millions of people all over the world that they can live their lives in peace and freedom. We must be worthy of that hope, in every sense of the word. Tonight, I ask for your prayers to help me in everything that I do throughout the days of my Presidency to be worthy of their hopes and of yours.

God bless America and God bless each and every one of you.*

---

*Public Papers of the Presidents of the United States: Richard Nixon, 1973, (Washington, D.C.: Government Printing Office, 1975), pp. 328-33.

# "Second Address to the Nation about the Watergate Investigations": August 15, 1973

*Good evening:*

Now that most of the major witnesses in the Watergate phase of the Senate committee hearings on campaign practices have been heard, the time has come for me to speak out about the charges made and to provide a perspective on the issue for the American people.

For over 4 months, Watergate has dominated the news media. During the past 3 months, the three major networks have devoted an average of over 22 hours of television time each week to this subject. The Senate committee has heard over 2 million words of testimony.

This investigation began as an effort to discover the facts about the break-in and bugging of the Democratic National Headquarters and other campaign abuses.

But as the weeks have gone by, it has become clear that both the hearings themselves and some of the commentaries on them have become increasingly absorbed in an effort to implicate the President personally in the illegal activities that took place.

Because the abuses occurred during my Administration, and in the campaign for my reelection, I accept full responsibility for them.

I regret that these events took place, and I do not question the right of a Senate committee to investigate charges made against the President to the extent that this is relevant to legislative duties.

However, it is my constitutional responsibility to defend the integrity of this great office against false charges. I also believe that it is important to address the overriding question of what we as a nation can learn from this experience and what we should now do. I intend to discuss both of these subjects tonight.

The record of the Senate hearings is lengthy. The facts are complicated, the evidence conflicting. It would not be right for me to try to sort out the evidence, to rebut specific witnesses, or to pronounce my own judgments about their credibility. That is for the committee and for the courts.

I shall not attempt to deal tonight with the various charges in detail. Rather, I shall attempt to put the events in perspective from the standpoint of the Presidency.

On May 22, before the major witnesses had testified, I issued a detailed statement addressing the charges that had been made against the President.

I have today issued another written statement, which addresses the charges that have been made since then as they relate to my own conduct, and which describes the efforts that I made to discover the facts about the matter.

On May 22, I stated in very specific terms—and I state again to every one of you listening tonight these facts—I had no prior knowledge of the Watergate break-in; I neither took part in nor knew about any of the subsequent coverup activities; I neither authorized nor encouraged subordinates to engage in illegal or improper campaign tactics.

That was and that is the simple truth.

In all of the millions of words of testimony, there is not the slightest suggestion that I had any knowledge of the planning for the Watergate break-in. As for the coverup, my statement has been challenged by only one of the 35 witnesses who appeared—a witness who offered no evidence beyond his own impressions and whose testimony has been contradicted by every other witness in a position to know the facts.

Tonight, let me explain to you what I did about Watergate after the break-in occurred, so that you can better understand the fact that I also had no knowledge of the so-called coverup.

From the time when the break-in occurred, I pressed repeatedly to know the facts, and particularly whether there was any involvement of anyone in the White House. I considered two things essential:

First, that the investigation should be thorough and aboveboard; and second, that if there were any higher involvement, we should get the facts out first. As I said at my August 29 press conference last year, "What really hurts in matters of this sort is not the fact that they occur, because over-zealous people in campaigns do things that are wrong. What really hurts is if you try to cover it up." I believed that then, and certainly the experience of this last year has proved that to be true.

I know that the Justice Department and the FBI were conducting intensive investigations—as I had insisted that they should. The White House Counsel, John Dean, was assigned to monitor these investigations, and particularly to check into any possible White House involvement. Throughout the summer of 1972, I continued to press the question, and I continued to get the same answer: I was told again and again that there was no indication that any persons were involved other than the seven who were known to have planned and carried out the operation, and who were subsequently indicted and convicted.

On September 12 at a meeting that I held with the Cabinet, the senior White House Staff and a number of legislative leaders, Attorney General Kleindienst reported on the investigation. He told us it had been the most extensive investigation since the assassination of President Kennedy and that it had established that only those seven were involved.

On September 15, the day the seven were indicted, I met with John Dean, the White House Counsel. He gave me no reason whatever to believe that any others were guilty; I assumed that the indictments of only the seven by the grand jury confirmed the reports he had been giving to that effect throughout the summer.

On February 16, I met with Acting Director Gray prior to submitting his name to the Senate for confirmation as permanent Director of the FBI. I stressed to him that he would be questioned closely about the FBI's conduct of the Watergate investigation. I asked him if he still had full confidence in it. He replied that he did, that he was proud of its thoroughness and that he could defend it with enthusiasm before the committee.

Because I trusted the agencies conducting the investigations, because I believed the reports I was getting, I did not believe the newspaper accounts that suggested a coverup. I was convinced there was no coverup, because I was convinced that no one had anything to cover up.

It was not until March 21 of this year that I received new information from the White House Counsel that led me to conclude that the reports I had been getting for over 9 months were not true. On that day, I launched an intensive effort of my own to get the facts and to get the facts out. Whatever the facts might be, I wanted the White House to be the first to make them public.

At first, I entrusted the task of getting me the facts to Mr. Dean. When, after spending a week at Camp David, he failed to produce the written report I had asked for, I turned to John Ehrlichman and to the Attorney General—while also making independent inquiries of my own.

By mid-April, I had received Mr. Ehrlichman's report and also one from the Attorney General based on new information uncovered by the Justice Department. These reports made it clear to me that the situation was far more serious than I had imagined. It at once became evident to me that the responsibility for the investigation in the case should be given to the Criminal Division of the Justice Department.

I turned over all the information I had to the head of that department, Assistant Attorney General Henry Petersen, a career government employee with an impeccable nonpartisan record, and I instructed him to pursue the matter thoroughly. I ordered all members of the Administration to testify fully before the grand jury.

And with my concurrence, on May 18 Attorney General Richardson appointed a Special Prosecutor to handle the matter, and the case is now before the grand jury.

Far from trying to hide the facts, my effort throughout has been to discover the facts—and to lay those facts before the appropriate law enforcement authorities so that justice could be done and the guilty dealt with. I relied on the best law enforcement agencies in the country to find and report the truth. I believed they had done so—just as they believed they had done so.

Many have urged that in order to help prove the truth of what I have said, I should turn over to the Special Prosecutor and the Senate committee recordings of conversations that I held in my office or on my telephone. However, a much more important principle is involved in this question than what the tapes might prove about Watergate.

Each day, a President of the United States is required to make difficult decisions on grave issues. It is absolutely necessary, if the President is to be able to do his job as the country expects, that he be able to talk openly and candidly with his advisers about issues and individuals. This kind of frank discussion is only possible when those who take part in it know that what they say is in strictest confidence.

The Presidency is not the only office that requires confidentiality. A Member of Congress must be able to talk in confidence with his assistants; judges must be able to confer in confidence with their law clerks and with each other. For very good reasons, no branch of Government has ever compelled disclosure of confidential conversations between officers of other branches of Government and their advisers about Government business.

This need for confidence is not confined to Government officials. The law has long recognized that there are kinds of conversations that are entitled to be kept confidential, even at the cost of doing without critical evidence in a legal proceeding. This rule applies, for example, to conversations between a lawyer and a client, between a priest and a penitent, and between a husband and wife. In each case it is thought so important that the parties be able to talk freely to each other that for hundreds of years the law has said these conversations are "privileged" and that their disclosure cannot be compelled in a court.

It is even more important that the confidentiality of conversations between a President and his advisers be protected. This is no mere luxury, to be dispensed with whenever a particular issue raises sufficient uproar. It is absolutely essential to the conduct of the Presidency, in this and in all future Administrations.

If I were to make public these tapes, containing as they do blunt and candid remarks on many different subjects, the confidentiality of the Office of the President would always be suspect from now on. It would make no difference whether it was to serve the interests of a court, of a Senate committee, or the President himself—the same damage would be done to the principle, and that damage would be irreparable.

Persons talking with the President would never again be sure that recordings or notes of what they said would not suddenly be made public. No one would want to advance tentative ideas that might later seem unsound. No diplomat would want to speak candidly in those sensitive negotiations which could bring peace or avoid war. No Senator or Congressman would want to talk frankly about the Congressional horsetrading that might get a vital bill passed. No one would want to speak bluntly about public figures here and abroad.

That is why I shall continue to oppose efforts which would set a precedent that would cripple all future Presidents by inhibiting conversations between them and those they look to for advice.

This principle of confidentiality of Presidential conversations is at stake in the question of these tapes. I must and I shall oppose any efforts to destroy this principle, which is so vital to the conduct of this great office.

Turning now to the basic issues which have been raised by Watergate, I recognize that merely answering the charges that have been made against the President is not enough. The word "Watergate" has come to represent a much broader set of concerns.

To most of us, Watergate has come to mean not just a burglary and bugging of party headquarters but a whole series of acts that either represent or appear to represent an abuse of trust. It has come to stand for excessive partisanship, for "enemy lists," for efforts to use the great institutions of Government for partisan political purposes.

For many Americans, the term "Watergate" also has come to include a number of national security matters that have been brought into the investigation, such as those involved in my efforts to stop massive leaks of vital diplomatic and military secrets, and to counter the wave of bombings and burnings and other violent assaults of just a few years ago.

Let me speak first of the political abuses.

I know from long experience that a political campaign is always a hard and a tough contest. A candidate for high office has an obligation to his party, to his supporters, and to the cause he represents. He must always put forth his best efforts to win. But he also has an obligation to the country to conduct that contest within the law and within the limits of decency.

No political campaign ever justifies obstructing justice, or harassing individuals, or compromising those great agencies of Government that should and must be above politics. To the extent that these things were done in the 1972 campaign, they were serious abuses, and I deplore them. Practices of that kind do not represent what I believe government should be, or what I believe politics should be. In a free society, the institutions of government belong to the people. They must never be used against the people.

And in the future, my Administration will be more vigilant in ensuring that such abuses do not take place and that officials at every level understand that they are not to take place.

And I reject the cynical view that politics is inevitably or even usually a dirty business. Let us not allow what a few overzealous people did in Watergate to tar the reputation of the millions of dedicated Americans of both parties who fought hard but clean for the candidates of their choice in 1972. By their unselfish efforts, these people make our system work and they keep America free.

I pledge to you tonight that I will do all that I can to ensure that one of the results of Watergate is a new level of political decency and integrity in America—in which what has been wrong in our politics no longer corrupts or demeans what is right in our politics.

Let me turn now to the difficult questions that arise in protecting the national security.

It is important to recognize that these are difficult questions and that reasonable and patriotic men and women may differ on how they should be answered.

Only last year, the Supreme Court said that implicit in the President's constitutional duty is "the power to protect our Government against those who would subvert or overthrow it by unlawful means." How to carry out this duty is often a delicate question to which there is no easy answer.

For example, every President since World War II has believed that in internal security matters, the President has the power to authorize wiretaps without first obtaining a search warrant.

An act of Congress in 1968 had seemed to recognize such power. Last year the Supreme Court held to the contrary. And my Administration is, of course, now complying with that Supreme Court decision. But until the Supreme Court spoke, I had been acting, as did my predecessors—President Truman, President Eisenhower, President Kennedy, and President Johnson—in a reasonable belief that in certain circumstances the Constitution permitted and sometimes even required such measures to protect the national security in the public interest.

Although it is the President's duty to protect the security of the country, we, of course, must be extremely careful in the way we go about this for if we lose our liberties we will have little use for security.

Instances have now come to light in which a zeal for security did go too far and did interfere impermissibly with individual liberty. It is essential that such mistakes not be repeated. But it is also essential that we do not overreact to particular mistakes by tying the President's hands in a way that would risk sacrificing our security, and with it all our liberties.

I shall continue to meet my constitutional responsibility to protect the security of this Nation so that Americans may enjoy their freedom. But I shall and can do so by constitutional means, in ways that will not threaten that freedom.

As we look at Watergate in a longer perspective, we can see that its abuses resulted from the assumption by those involved that their cause placed them beyond the reach of those rules that apply to other persons and that hold a free society together.

That attitude can never be tolerated in our country. However, it did not suddenly develop in the year 1972. It became fashionable in the 1960's as individuals and groups increasingly asserted the right to take the law into their own hands, insisting that their purposes represented a higher morality. Then their attitude was praised in the press and even from some of our pulpits as evidence of a new idealism. Those of us who insisted on the old restraints, who warned of the overriding importance of operating within the law and by the rules, were accused of being reactionaries.

That same attitude brought a rising spiral of violence and fear, of riots and arson and bombings, all in the name of peace and in the name of justice.

Political discussion turned into savage debate. Free speech was brutally suppressed as hecklers shouted down or even physically assaulted those with whom they disagreed. Serious people raised serious questions about whether we could survive as a free democracy.

The notion that the end justifies the means proved contagious. Thus, it is not surprising, even though it is deplorable, that some persons in 1972 adopted the morality that they themselves had rightly condemned and committed acts that have no place in our political system.

Those acts cannot be defended. Those who were guilty of abuses must be punished.

But ultimately, the answer does not lie merely in the jailing of a few overzealous persons who mistakenly thought their cause justified their violations of the law.

Rather, it lies in a commitment by all of us to show a renewed respect for the mutual restraints that are the mark of a free and a civilized society. It requires that we learn once again to work together, if not united in all of our purposes, then at least united in respect for the system by which our conflicts are peacefully resolved and our liberties maintained.

If there are laws we disagree with, let us work to change them, but let us obey them until they are changed. If we have disagreements over Government policies, let us work those out in a decent and civilized way, within the law, and with respect for our differences.

We must recognize that one excess begets another, and that the extremes of violence and discord in the 1960's contributed to the extremes of Watergate.

Both are wrong. Both should be condemned. No individual, no group, and no political party has a corner on the market on morality in America.

If we learn the important lessons of Watergate, if we do what is necessary to prevent such abuses in the future—on both sides—we can emerge from this experience a better and a stronger nation.

Let me turn now to an issue that is important above all else and that is critically affecting your life today and will affect your life and your children's life in the years to come.

After 12 weeks and 2 million words of televised testimony, we have reached a point at which a continued, backward-looking obsession with Watergate is causing this Nation to neglect matters of far greater importance to all of the American people.

We must not stay so mired in Watergate that we fail to respond to challenges of surpassing importance to America and the world. We cannot let an obsession with the past destroy our hopes for the future.

Legislation vital to your health and well-being sits unattended on the Congressional calendar. Confidence at home and abroad in our economy, our currency, our foreign policy is being sapped by uncertainty.

Critical negotiations are taking place on strategic weapons and on troop levels in Europe that can affect the security of this Nation and the peace of the world long after Watergate is forgotten. Vital events are taking place in Southeast Asia which could lead to a tragedy for the cause of peace.

These are matters that cannot wait. They cry out for action now, and either we, your elected representatives here in Washington, ought to get on with the jobs that need to be done—for you—or every one of you ought to be demanding to know why.

The time has come to turn Watergate over to the courts, where the questions of guilt or innocence belong. The time has come for the rest of us to get on with the urgent business of our Nation.

Last November, the American people were given the clearest choice of this century. Your votes were a mandate, which I accepted, to complete the initiatives we began in my first term and to fulfill the promises I made for my second term.

This Administration was elected to control inflation; to reduce the power and size of Government; to cut the cost of Government so that you can cut the cost of living; to preserve and defend those fundamental values that have made America great; to keep the Nation's military strength second to none; to achieve peace with honor in Southeast Asia, and to bring home our prisoners of war; to build a new prosperity, without inflation and without war; to create a structure of peace in the world that would endure long after we are gone.

These are great goals, they are worthy of a great people, and I would not be true to your trust if I let myself be turned aside from achieving those goals.

If you share my belief in these goals—if you want the mandate you gave this Administration to be carried out—then I ask for your help to ensure that those who would exploit Watergate in order to keep us from doing what we were elected to do will not succeed.

I ask tonight for your understanding, so that as a nation we can learn the lessons of Watergate and gain from that experience.

I ask for your help in reaffirming our dedication to the principles of decency, honor, and respect for the institutions that have sustained our progress through these past two centuries.

And I ask for your support in getting on once again with meeting your problems, improving your life, building your future.

With your help, with God's help, we will achieve those great goals for America.

Thank you and good evening.*

*Public Papers of the Presidents of the United States: Richard Nixon, 1973, (Washington, D.C.: Government Printing Office, 1975), pp. 691-8.

# "Address to the Nation Announcing Answer to the House Judiciary Committee Subpoena for Additional Presidential Tape Recordings": April 29, 1974

*Good evening*:

I have asked for this time tonight in order to announce my answer to the House Judiciary Committee's subpoena for additional Watergate tapes, and to tell you something about the actions I shall be taking tomorrow—about what I hope they will mean to you and about the very difficult choices that were presented to me.

These actions will at last, once and for all, show that what I knew and what I did with regard to the Watergate break-in and coverup were just as I have described them to you from the very beginning.

I have spent many hours during the past few weeks thinking about what I would say to the American people if I were to reach the decision I shall announce tonight. And so, my words have not been lightly chosen; I can assure you they are deeply felt.

It was almost 2 years ago, in June 1972, that five men broke into the Democratic National Committee headquarters in Washington. It turned out that they were connected with my reelection committee, and the Watergate break-in became a major issue in the campaign.

The full resources of the FBI and the Justice Department were used to investigate the incident thoroughly. I instructed my staff and campaign aides to cooperate fully with the investigation. The FBI conducted nearly 1,500 interviews. For 9 months—until March 1973—I was assured by those charged with conducting and monitoring the investigations that no one in the White House was involved.

Nevertheless, for more than a year, there have been allegations and insinuations that I knew about the planning of the Watergate break-in and that I was involved in an extensive plot to cover it up. The House Judiciary Committee is now investigating these charges.

On March 6, I ordered all materials that I had previously furnished to the Special Prosecutor turned over to the committee. These included tape recordings of 19 Presidential conversations and more than 700 documents from private White House files.

On April 11, the Judiciary Committee issued a subpoena for 42 additional tapes of conversations which it contended were necessary for its investigation.   I agreed to respond to that subpoena by tomorrow.

In these folders that you see over here on my left are more than 1,200 pages of transcripts of private conversations I participated in between September 15, 1972, and April 27 of 1973 with my principal aides and associates with regard to Watergate.   They include all the relevant portions of all the subpoenaed conversations that were recorded, that is, all portions that relate to the question of what I knew about Watergate or the coverup and what I did about it.

They also include transcripts of other conversations which were not subpoenaed, but which have a significant bearing on the question of Presidential actions with regard to Watergate.   These will be delivered to the committee tomorrow.

In these transcripts, portions not relevant to my knowledge or actions with regard to Watergate are not included, but everything that is relevant is included—the rough as well as the smooth—the strategy sessions, the exploration of alternatives, the weighing of human and political costs.

As far as what the President personally knew and did with regard to Watergate and the coverup is concerned, these materials— together with those already made available—will tell it all.

I shall invite Chairman Rodino and the committee's ranking minority member, Congressman Hutchinson of Michigan, to come to the White House and listen to the actual, full tapes of these conversations, so that they can determine for themselves beyond question that the transcripts are accurate and that everything on the tapes relevant to my knowledge and my actions on Watergate is included. If there should be any disagreement over whether omitted material is relevant, I shall meet with them personally in an effort to settle the matter.   I believe this arrangement is fair, and I think it is appropriate.

For many days now, I have spent many hours of my own time personally reviewing these materials and personally deciding questions of relevancy.   I believe it is appropriate that the committee's review should also be made by its own senior elected officials, and not by staff employees.

The task of Chairman Rodino and Congressman Hutchinson will be made simpler than was mine by the fact that the work of preparing the transcripts has been completed.   All they will need to do is to satisfy themselves of their authenticity and their completeness.

Ever since the existence of the White House taping system was first made known last summer, I have tried vigorously to guard the privacy of the tapes.   I have been well aware that my effort to protect the confidentiality of Presidential conversations has heightened the sense of mystery about Watergate and, in fact, has caused increased suspicions of the President. Many people assume that the tapes must incriminate the President, or that otherwise, he would not insist on their privacy.

But the problem I confronted was this: Unless a President can protect the privacy of the advice he gets, he cannot get the advice he needs.

This principle is recognized in the constitutional doctrine of executive privilege, which has been defended and maintained by every President since Washington and which has been recognized by the courts, whenever tested, as inherent in the Presidency. I consider it to be my constitutional responsibility to defend this principle.

Three factors have now combined to persuade me that a major unprecedented exception to that principle is now necessary:

First, in the present circumstances, the House of Representatives must be able to reach an informed judgment about the President's role in Watergate.

Second, I am making a major exception to the principle of confidentiality because I believe such action is now necessary in order to restore the principle itself, by clearing the air of the central question that has brought such pressures upon it—and also to provide the evidence which will allow this matter to be brought to a prompt conclusion.

Third, in the context of the current impeachment climate, I believe all the American people, as well as their representatives in Congress, are entitled to have not only the facts but also the evidence that demonstrates those facts.

I want there to be no question remaining about the fact that the President has nothing to hide in this matter.

The impeachment of a President is a remedy of last resort; it is the most solemn act of our entire constitutional process. Now, regardless of whether or not it succeeded, the action of the House, in voting a formal accusation requiring trial by the Senate, would put the Nation through a wrenching ordeal it has endured only once in its lifetime, a century ago, and never since America has become a world power with global responsibilities.

The impact of such an ordeal would be felt throughout the world, and it would have its effect on the lives of all Americans for many years to come.

Because this is an issue that profoundly affects all the American people, in addition to turning over these transcripts to the House Judiciary Committee, I have directed that they should all be made public—all of these that you see here.

To complete the record, I shall also release to the public transcripts of all those portions of the tapes already turned over to the Special Prosecutor and to the committee that relate to Presidential actions or knowledge of the Watergate affair.

During the past year, the wildest accusations have been given banner headlines and ready credence as well. Rumor, gossip, innuendo, accounts from unnamed sources of what a prospective witness might testify to, have filled the morning newspapers and then are repeated on the evening newscasts day after day.

Time and again, a familiar pattern repeated itself. A charge would be reported the first day as what it was—just an allegation. But it would then be referred back to the next day and thereafter as if it were true.

The distinction between fact and speculation grew blurred. Eventually, all seeped into the public consciousness as a vague general impression of massive wrongdoing, implicating everybody, gaining credibility by its endless repetition.

The basic question at issue today is whether the President personally acted improperly in the Watergate matter. Month after month of rumor, insinuation, and charges by just one Watergate witness—John Dean—suggested that the President did act improperly.

This sparked the demands for an impeachment inquiry. This is the question that must be answered. And this is the question that will be answered by these transcripts that I have ordered published tomorrow.

These transcripts cover hour upon hour of discussions that I held with Mr. Haldeman, John Ehrlichman, John Dean, John Mitchell, former Attorney General Kleindienst, Assistant Attorney General Petersen, and others with regard to Watergate.

They were discussions in which I was probing to find out what had happened, who was responsible, what were the various degrees of responsibilities, what were the legal culpabilities, what were the political ramifications, and what actions were necessary and appropriate on the part of the President.

I realize that these transcripts will provide grist for many sensational stories in the press. Parts will seem to be contradictory with one another, and parts will be in conflict with some of the testimony given in the Senate Watergate committee hearings.

I have been reluctant to release these tapes, not just because they will embarrass me and those with whom I have talked—which they will—and not just because they will become the subject of speculation and even ridicule—which they will—and not just because certain parts of them will be seized upon by political and journalistic opponents—which they will.

I have been reluctant because, in these and in all the other conversations in this office, people have spoken their minds freely, never dreaming that specific sentences or even parts of sentences would be picked out as the subjects of national attention and controversy.

I have been reluctant because the principle of confidentiality is absolutely essential to the conduct of the Presidency. In reading the raw transcripts of these conversations, I believe it will be more readily apparent why that principle is essential and must be maintained in the future. These conversations are unusual in their subject matter, but the same kind of uninhibited discussion—and it is that—the same brutal candor is necessary in discussing how to bring warring factions to the peace table or how to move necessary legislation through the Congress.

Names are named in these transcripts. Therefore, it is important to remember that much that appears in them is no more than hearsay or speculation, exchanged as I was trying to find out what really had happened, while my principal aides were reporting to me on rumors and reports that they had heard, while we discussed the various, often conflicting stories that different persons were telling.

As the transcripts will demonstrate, my concerns during this period covered a wide range. The first and obvious one was to find out just exactly what had happened and who was involved.

A second concern was for the people who had been, or might become, involved in Watergate. Some were close advisers, valued friends, others whom I had trusted. And I was also concerned about the human impact on others, especially some of the young people and their families who had come to Washington to work in my Administration, whose lives might be suddenly ruined by something they had done in an excess of loyalty or in the mistaken belief that it would serve the interests of the President.

And then, I was quite frankly concerned about the political implications. This represented potentially a devastating blow to the Administration and to its programs, one which I knew would be exploited for all it was worth by hostile elements in the Congress as well as in the media. I wanted to do what was right, but I wanted to do it in a way that would cause the least unnecessary damage in a highly charged political atmosphere to the Administration.

And fourth, as a lawyer, I felt very strongly that I had to conduct myself in a way that would not prejudice the rights of potential defendants.

And fifth, I was striving to sort out a complex tangle, not only of facts but also questions of legal and moral responsibility. I wanted, above all, to be fair.

I wanted to draw distinctions, where those were appropriate, between persons who were active and willing participants on the one hand, and on the other, those who might have gotten inadvertently caught up in the web and be technically indictable but morally innocent.

Despite the confusions and contradictions, what does come through clearly is this:

John Dean charged in sworn Senate testimony that I was "fully aware of the coverup" at the time of our first meeting on September 15, 1972. These transcripts show clearly that I first learned of it when Mr. Dean himself told me about it in this office on March 21—some 6 months later.

Incidentally, these transcripts—covering hours upon hours of conversations—should place in somewhat better perspective the controversy over the 18 1/2 minute gap in the tape of a conversation I had with Mr. Haldeman back in June of 1972.

Now, how it was caused is still a mystery to me and, I think, to many of the experts as well.  But I am absolutely certain, however, of one thing: that it was not caused intentionally by my secretary, Rose Mary Woods, or any of my White House assistants.

And certainly, if the theory were true that during those 18 1/2 minutes, Mr. Haldeman and I cooked up some sort of a Watergate coverup scheme, as so many have been quick to surmise, it hardly seems likely that in all of our subsequent conversations—many of them are here—which neither of us ever expected would see the light of day, there is nothing remotely indicating such a scheme; indeed, quite the contrary.

From the beginning, I have said that in many places on the tapes there were ambiguities—a statement and comments that different people with different perspectives might interpret in drastically different ways—but although the words may be ambiguous, though the discussions may have explored many alternatives, the record of my actions is totally clear now, and I still believe it was totally correct then.

A prime example is one of the most controversial discussions, that with Mr. Dean on March 21—the one in which he first told me of the coverup, with Mr. Haldeman joining us midway through the conversation.  His revelations to me on March 21 were a sharp surprise, even though the report he gave to me was far from complete, especially since he did not reveal at that time the extent of his own criminal involvement.

I was particularly concerned by his report that one of the Watergate defendants, Howard Hunt, was threatening blackmail unless he and his lawyer were immediately given $120,000 for legal fees and family support, and that he was attempting to blackmail the White House, not be threatening exposure on the Watergate matter, but by threatening to reveal activities that would expose extremely sensitive, highly secret national security matters that he had worked on before Watergate.

I probed, questioned, tried to learn all Mr. Dean knew about who was involved, what was involved.  I asked more than 150 questions of Mr. Dean in the course of that conversation.

He said to me, and I quote from the transcripts directly: "I can just tell from our conversation that these are things that you have no knowledge of."

It was only considerably later that I learned how much there was that he did not tell me then—for example, that he himself had authorized promises of clemency, that he had personally handled money for the Watergate defendants, and that he had suborned perjury of a witness.

I knew that I needed more facts.  I knew that I needed the judgments of more people.  I knew the facts about the Watergate coverup would have to be made public, but I had to find out more about what they were before I could decide how they could best be made public.

I returned several times to the immediate problem posed by Mr. Hunt's blackmail threat, which to me was not a Watergate problem, but one which I regarded, rightly or wrongly, as a potential national security problem of very serious proportions. I considered long and hard whether it might in fact be better to let the payment go forward, at least temporarily, in the hope that this national security matter would not be exposed in the course of uncovering the Watergate coverup.

I believed then, and I believe today, that I had a responsibility as President to consider every option, including this one, where production of sensitive national security matters was at issue— protection of such matters. In the course of considering it and of "just thinking out loud," as I put it at one point, I several times suggested that meeting Hunt's demands might be necessary.

But then I also traced through where that would lead. The money could be raised. But money demands would lead inescapably to clemency demands, and clemency could not be granted. I said, and I quote directly from the tape "It is wrong, that's for sure." I pointed out, and I quote again from the tape: "But in the end we are going to be bled to death. And in the end it is all going to come out anyway. Then you get the worst of both worlds. We are going to lose, and people are going to—"

And Mr. Haldeman interrupts me and says: "And look like dopes!"

And I responded, "And in effect look like a coverup. So that we cannot do."

Now, I recognize that this tape of March 21 is one which different meaning could be read in by different people. But by the end of the meeting, as the tape shows, my decision was to convene a new grand jury and to send everyone before the grand jury with instructions to testify.

Whatever the potential for misinterpretation there may be as a result of the different options that were discussed at different times during the meeting, my conclusion at the end of the meeting was clear. And my actions and reactions as demonstrated on the tapes that follow that date show clearly that I did not intend the further payment to Hunt or anyone else be made. These are some of the actions that I took in the weeks that followed in my effort to find the truth, to carry out my responsibilities to enforce the law:

As a tape of our meeting on March 22, the next day, indicates, I directed Mr. Dean to go to Camp David with instructions to put together a written report. I learned 5 days later, on March 26, that he was unable to complete it. And so on March 27, I assigned John Ehrlichman to try to find out what had happened, who was at fault, and in what ways and to what degree.

One of the transcripts I am making public is a call that Mr. Ehrlichman made to the Attorney General on March 28, in which he asked the Attorney General to report to me, the President, directly, any information he might find indicating possible involvement of John Mitchell or by anyone in the White House. I had Mr. Haldeman separately pursue other, independent lines of inquiry.

Throughout, I was trying to reach determinations on matters of both substance and procedure on what the facts were and what was the best way to move the case forward. I concluded that I wanted everyone to go before the grand jury and testify freely and fully. This decision, as you will recall, was publicly announced on March 30, 1973. I waived executive privilege in order to permit everybody to testify. I specifically waived executive privilege with regard to conversations with the President, and I waived the attorney-client privilege with John Dean in order to permit him to testify fully and, I hope, truthfully.

Finally, on April 14—3 weeks after I learned of the coverup from Mr. Dean—Mr. Ehrlichman reported to me on the results of his investigation. As he acknowledged, much of what he had gathered was hearsay, but he had gathered enough to make it clear that the next step was to make his findings completely available to the Attorney General, which I instructed him to do.

And the next day, Sunday, April 15, Attorney General Kleindienst asked to see me, and he reported new information which had come to his attention on this matter. And although he was in no way whatever involved in Watergate, because of his close personal ties, not only to John Mitchell but to other potential people who might be involved, he quite properly removed himself from the case. We agreed that Assistant Attorney General Henry Petersen, the head of the Criminal Division, a Democrat and career prosecutor, should be placed in complete charge of the investigation.

Later that day, I met with Mr. Petersen. I continued to meet with him, to talk with him, to consult with him, to offer him the full cooperation of the White House—as you will see from these transcripts—even to the point of retaining John Dean on the White House Staff for an extra 2 weeks after he admitted his criminal involvement, because Mr. Petersen thought that would make it easier for the prosecutor to get his cooperation in breaking the case if it should become necessary to grant Mr. Dean's demand for immunity.

On April 15, when I heard that one of the obstacles to breaking the case was Gordon Liddy's refusal to talk, I telephoned Mr. Petersen and directed that he should make clear not only to Mr. Liddy but to everyone that—and now I quote directly from the tape of that telephone call—"As far as the President is concerned, everybody in this case is to talk and to tell the truth." I told him if necessary I would personally meet with Mr. Liddy's lawyer to assure him that I wanted Liddy to talk and to tell the truth.

From the time Mr. Petersen took charge, the case was solidly within the criminal justice system, pursued personally by the Nation's top professional prosecutor with the active, personal assistance of the President of the United States.

I made clear there was to be no coverup.

Let me quote just a few lines from the transcripts—you can read them to verify them—so that you can hear for yourself the orders I was giving in this period.

Speaking to Haldeman and Ehrlichman, I said: ". . . It is ridiculous to talk about clemency. They all knew that."

Speaking to Ehrlichman, I said: "We all have to do the right thing. . . We just cannot have this kind of a business. . . ."

Speaking to Haldeman and Ehrlichman, I said: "The boil had to be pricked . . . We have to prick the boil and take the heat. Now that's what we are doing here."

Speaking to Henry Petersen, I said: "I want you to be sure to understand that you know we are going to get to the bottom of this thing."

Speaking to John Dean, I said: "Tell the truth. That is the thing I have told everybody around here."

And then speaking to Haldeman: "And you tell Magruder, 'now Jeb, this evidence is coming in, you ought to go to the grand jury. Purge yourself if you're perjured and tell this whole story.'"

I am confident that the American people will see these transcripts for what they are, fragmentary records from a time more than a year ago that now seems very distant, the records of a President and of a man suddenly being confronted and having to cope with information which, if true, would have the most far-reaching consequences, not only for his personal reputation but, more important, for his hopes, his plans, his goals for the people who had elected him as their leader.

If read with an open and a fair mind and read together with the record of the actions I took, these transcripts will show that what I have stated from the beginning to be the truth has been the truth: that I personally had no knowledge of the break-in before it occurred, that I had no knowledge of the coverup until I was informed of it by John Dean on March 21, that I never offered clemency for the defendants, and that after March 21, my actions were directed toward finding the facts and seeing that justice was done, fairly and according to the law.

The facts are there. The conversations are there. The record of actions is there.

To anyone who reads his way through this mass of materials I have provided, it will be totally, abundantly clear that as far as the President's role with regard to Watergate is concerned, the entire story is there.

As you will see, now that you also will have this mass of evidence I have provided, I have tried to cooperate with the House Judiciary Committee. And I repeat tonight the offer that I have made previously: to answer written interrogatories under oath and, if there are then issues still unresolved, to meet personally with the chairman of the committee and with Congressman Hutchinson to answer their questions under oath.

As the committee conducts its inquiry, I also consider it only essential and fair that my counsel, Mr. St. Clair, should be present to cross-examine witnesses and introduce evidence in an effort to establish the truth.

I am confident that for the overwhelming majority of those who study the evidence that I shall release tomorrow—those who are willing to look at it fully, fairly, and objectively—the evidence will be persuasive and, I hope, conclusive.

We live in a time of very great challenge and great opportunity for America. We live at a time when peace may become possible in the Middle East for the first time in a generation. We are at last in the process of fulfilling the hope of mankind for a limitation on nuclear arms—a process that will continue when I meet with the Soviet leaders in Moscow in a few weeks. We are well on the way toward building a peace that can last, not just for this but for other generations as well.

And here at home, there is vital work to be done in moving to control inflation, to develop our energy resources, to strengthen our economy so that Americans can enjoy what they have not had since 1956: full prosperity without war and without inflation.

Every day absorbed by Watergate is a day lost from the work that must be done—by your President and by your Congress—work that must be done in dealing with the great problems that affect your prosperity, affect your security, that could affect your lives.

The materials I make public tomorrow will provide all the additional evidence needed to get Watergate behind us and to get it behind us now. Never before in the history of the Presidency have records that are so private been made so public. In giving you these records—blemishes and all—I am placing my trust in the basic fairness of the American people. I know in my own heart that through the long, painful, and difficult process revealed in these transcripts, I was trying in that period to discover what was right and to do what was right. I hope and I trust that when you have seen the evidence in its entirety, you will see the truth of that statement.

As for myself, I intend to go forward, to the best of my ability, with the work that you elected me to do. I shall do so in a spirit perhaps best summed up a century ago by another President when he was being subjected to unmerciful attack. Abraham Lincoln said:

"I do the very best I know how—the very best I can; and I mean to keep doing so until the end. If the end brings me out all right, what is said against me won't amount to anything. If the end brings me out wrong, ten angels swearing I was right would make no difference."

Thank you and good evening.*

*Public Papers of the Presidents of the United States: Richard Nixon, 1974, (Washington, D.C.: Government Printing Office, 1975), pp. 389-97.

# "Address to the Nation Announcing Decision to Resign the Office of the President of the United States": August 8, 1974

*Good evening:*

This is the 37th time I have spoken to you from this office where so many decisions have been made that shaped the history of this Nation. Each time I have done so to discuss with you some matter that I believe affected the national interest.

In all the decisions I have made in my public life, I have always tried to do what was best for the Nation. Throughout the long and difficult period of Watergate, I have felt it was my duty to persevere, to make every possible effort to complete the term of office to which you elected me.

In the past few days, however, it has become evident to me that I no longer have a strong enough political base in the Congress to justify continuing that effort. As long as there was such a base, I felt strongly that it was necessary to see the constitutional process through to its conclusion, that to do otherwise would be unfaithful to the spirit of that deliberately difficult process and a dangerously destabilizing precedent for the future.

But with the disappearance of that base, I now believe that the constitutional purpose has been served, and there is no longer a need for the process to be prolonged.

I would have preferred to carry through to the finish, whatever the personal agony it would have involved, and my family unanimously urged me to do so. But the interests of the Nation must always come before any personal considerations.

From the discussions I have had with Congressional and other leaders, I have concluded that because of the Watergate matter, I might not have the support of the Congress that I would consider necessary to back the very difficult decisions and carry out the duties of this office in the way the interests of the Nation will require.

I have never been a quitter. To leave office before my term is completed is abhorrent to every instinct in my body. But as President, I must put the interests of America first. America needs a full-time

President and a full-time Congress, particularly at this time with problems we face at home and abroad.

To continue to fight through the months ahead for my personal vindication would almost totally absorb the time and attention of both the President and the Congress in a period when our entire focus should be on the great issues of peace abroad and prosperity without inflation at home.

Therefore, I shall resign the Presidency effective at noon tomorrow. Vice President Ford will be sworn in as President at that hour in this office.

As I recall the high hopes for America with which we began this second term, I feel a great sadness that I will not be here in this office working on your behalf to achieve those hopes in the next 2 1/2 years. But in turning over direction of the Government to Vice President Ford, I know, as I told the Nation when I nominated him for that office 10 months ago, that the leadership of America will be in good hands.

In passing this office to the Vice President, I also do so with the profound sense of the weight of responsibility that will fall on his shoulders tomorrow and, therefore, of the understanding, the patience, the cooperation he will need from all Americans.

As he assumes that responsibility, he will deserve the help and the support of all of us. As we look to the future, the first essential is to begin healing the wounds of this Nation, to put the bitterness and divisions of the recent past behind us and to rediscover those shared ideals that lie at the heart of our strength and unity as a great and as a free people.

By taking this action, I hope that I will have hastened the start of that process of healing which is so desperately needed in America.

I regret deeply any injuries that may have been done in the course of the events that led to this decision. I would say only that if some of my judgments were wrong—and some were wrong—they were made in what I believed at the time to be the best interest of the Nation.

To those who have stood with me during these past difficult months—to my family, my friends, to many others who joined in supporting my cause because they believed it was right—I will be eternally grateful for your support.

And to those who have not felt able to give me your support, let me say I leave with no bitterness toward those who have opposed me, because all of us, in the final analysis, have been concerned with the good of the country, however our judgments might differ.

So, let us all now join together in affirming that common commitment and in helping our new President succeed for the benefit of all Americans.

I shall leave this office with regret at not completing my term, but with gratitude for the privilege of serving as your President for the past 5 1/2 years. These years have been a momentous time in the history of our Nation and the world. They have been a time of achievement in which we can all be proud, achievements that represent the shared efforts of the Administration, the Congress, and the people.

But the challenges ahead are equally great, and they, too, will require the support and the efforts of the Congress and the people working in cooperation with the new Administration.

We have ended America's longest war, but in the work of securing a lasting peace in the world, the goals ahead are even more far-reaching and more difficult. We must complete a structure of peace so that it will be said of this generation, our generation of Americans, by the people of all nations, not only that we ended one war but that we prevented future wars.

We have unlocked the doors that for a quarter of a century stood between the United States and the People's Republic of China.

We must now ensure that the one quarter of the world's people who live in the People's Republic of China will be and remain not our enemies, but our friends.

In the Middle East, 100 million people in the Arab countries, many of whom have considered us their enemy for nearly 20 years, now look on us as their friends. We must continue to build on that friendship so that peace can settle at last over the Middle East and so that the cradle of civilization will not become its grave.

Together with the Soviet Union, we have made the crucial breakthroughs that have begun the process of limiting nuclear arms. But we must set as our goal not just limiting but reducing and, finally, destroying these terrible weapons so that they cannot destroy civilization and so that the threat of nuclear war will no longer hang over the world and the people.

We have opened the new relation with the Soviet Union. We must continue to develop and expand that new relationship so that the two strongest nations of the world will live together in cooperation, rather than confrontation.

Around the world—in Asia, in Africa, in Latin America, in the Middle East—there are millions of people who live in terrible poverty, even starvation. We must keep as our goal turning away from production for war and expanding production for peace so that people everywhere on this Earth can at last look forward in their children's time, if not in our own time, to having the necessities for a decent life.

Here in America, we are fortunate that most of our people have not only the blessings of liberty but also the means to live full and good and, by the world's standards, even abundant lives. We must press on, however, toward a goal, not only of more and better jobs but of full opportunity for every American and of what we are striving so hard right now to achieve, prosperity without inflation.

For more that a quarter of a century in public life, I have shared in the turbulent history of this era. I have fought for what I believed in. I have tried, to the best of my ability, to discharge those duties and meet those responsibilities that were entrusted to me.

Sometimes I have succeeded and sometimes I have failed, but always I have taken heart from what Theodore Roosevelt once said about the man in the arena, "whose face is marred by dust and sweat and blood, who strives valiantly, who errs and comes short again and again because there is not effort without error and shortcoming, but who does actually strive to do the deed, who knows the great enthusiasms, the great devotions, who spends himself in a worthy cause, who at the best knows in the end the triumphs of high achievements and who at the worst, if he fails, at least fails while daring greatly."

I pledge to you tonight that as long as I have a breath of life in my body, I shall continue in that spirit. I shall continue to work for the great causes to which I have been dedicated throughout my years as a Congressman, a Senator, Vice President, and President, the cause of peace, not just for America but among all nations— prosperity, justice, and opportunity for all of our people.

There is one cause above all to which I have been devoted and to which I shall always be devoted for as long as I live.

When I first took the oath of office as President 5 1/2 years ago, I made this sacred commitment: to "consecrate my office, my energies, and all the wisdom I can summon to the cause of peace among nations."

I have done my very best in all the days since to be true to that pledge. As a result of these efforts, I am confident that the world is a safer place today, not only for the people of America but for the people of all nations, and that all of our children have a better chance than before of living in peace rather than dying in war.

This, more than anything, is what I hoped to achieve when I sought the Presidency. This, more than anything, is what I hope will be my legacy to you, to our country, as I leave the Presidency.

To have served in this office is to have felt a very personal sense of kinship with each and every American. In leaving it, I do so with this prayer: May God's grace be with you in all the days ahead.*

---

*Public Papers of the Presidents of the United States: Richard Nixon, 1974, (Washington, D.C.: Government Printing Office, 1975), pp. 626-30.

# "Remarks on the Departure from the White House": August 9, 1974

*Members of the Cabinet, members of the White House Staff, all of our friends here:*

I think the record should show that this is one of those spontaneous things that we always arrange whenever the President comes in to speak, and it will be so reported in the press, and we don't mind, because they have to call it as they see it.

But on our part, believe me, it is spontaneous.

You are here to say goodby to us, and we don't have a good word for it in English—the best is *au revoir*. We will see you again.

I just met with the members of the White House staff, you know, those who serve here in the White House day in and day out, and I asked them to do what I ask all of you to do to the extent that you can and, of course, are requested to do so: to serve our next President as you have served me and previous Presidents—because many of you have been here for many years—with devotion and dedication, because this office, great as it is, can only be as great as the men and women who work for and with the President.

This house, for example—I was thinking of it as we walked down this hall, and I was comparing it to some of the great houses of the world that I have been in. This isn't the biggest house. Many, and most, in even smaller countries, are much bigger. This isn't the finest house. Many in Europe, particularly, and in China, Asia, have paintings of great, great value, things that we just don't have here and, probably, will never have until we are 1,000 years old or older.

But this is the best house. It is the best house, because it has something far more important than numbers of people who serve, far more important than numbers of rooms or how big it is, far more important than numbers of magnificent pieces of art.

This house has a great heart, and that heart comes from those who serve. I was rather sorry they didn't come down. We said goodby to them upstairs. But they are really great. And I recall after so many times I have made speeches, and some of them pretty tough,

yet, I always come back, or after a hard day—and my days usually
have run rather long—I would always get a lift from them, because I
might be a little down but they always smiled.

And so it is with you. I look around here, and I see so many on
this staff that, you know, I should have been by your offices and
shaken hands, and I would love to have talked to you and found out
how to run the world—everybody wants to tell the President what to
do, and boy, he needs to be told many times—but I just haven't had
the time. But I want you to know that each and every one of you, I
know, is indispensable to this Government.

I am proud of this Cabinet. I am proud of all the members who
have served in our Cabinet. I am proud of our sub-Cabinet. I am
proud of our White House Staff. As I pointed out last night, sure, we
have done some things wrong in this Administration, and the top
man always takes the responsibility, and I have never ducked it. But
I want to say one thing: We can be proud of it—5 1/2 years. No man or
no woman came into this Administration and left it with more of this
world's goods than when he came in. No man or no woman ever
profited at the public expense or the public till. That tells something
about you.

Mistakes, yes. But for personal gain, never. You did what you
believed in. Sometimes right, sometimes wrong. And I only wish
that I were a wealthy man—at the present time, I have got to find a
way to pay my taxes—[laughter]—and if I were, I would like to
recompense you for the sacrifices that all of you have made to serve in
government.

But you are getting something in government—and I want you
to tell this to your children, and I hope the Nation's children will hear
it, too—something in government service that is far more important
than money. It is a cause bigger than yourself. It is the cause of
making this the greatest nation in the world, the leader of the world,
because without our leadership, the world will know nothing but war,
possibly starvation or worse, in the years ahead. With our leadership
it will know peace, it will know plenty.

We have been generous, and we will be more generous in the
future as we are able to. But most important, we must be strong here,
strong in our hearts, strong in our souls, strong in our belief, and
strong in our willingness to sacrifice, as you have been willing to
sacrifice, in a pecuniary way, to serve in government.

There is something else I would like for you to tell your young
people. You know, people often come in and say, "What will I tell my
kids?" They look at government and say, sort of a rugged life, and
they see the mistakes that are made. They get the impression that
everybody is here for the purpose of feathering his nest. That is why I
made this earlier point—not in this Administration, not one single
man or woman.

And I say to them, there are many fine careers. This country
needs good farmers, good businessmen, good plumbers, good
carpenters.

I remember my old man. I think that they would have called him sort of a little man, common man. He didn't consider himself that way. You know what he was? He was a streetcar motorman first, and then he was a farmer, and then he had a lemon ranch. It was the poorest lemon ranch in California, I can assure you. He sold it before they found oil on it. [*laughter*] And then he was a grocer. But he was a great man, because he did his job, and every job counts up to the hilt, regardless of what happens.

Nobody will ever write a book probably, about my mother. Well, I guess all of you would say this about your mother—my mother was a saint. And I think of her, two boys dying of tuberculosis, nursing four others in order that she could take care of my older brother for 3 years in Arizona, and seeing each of them die, and when they died, it was like one of her own.

Yes, she will have no books written about her. But she was a saint.

Now, however, we look to the future. I had a little quote in the speech last night from T.R. As you know, I kind of like to read books. I am not educated, but I do read books—[*laughter*]—and the T.R. quote was a pretty good one.

Here is another one I found as I was reading, my last night in the White House, and this quote is about a young man. He was a young lawyer in New York. He had married a beautiful girl, and they had a lovely daughter, and then suddenly she died, and this is what he wrote. This was in his diary.

He said, "She was beautiful in face and form and lovelier still in spirit. As a flower she grew and as a fair young flower she died. Her life had been always in the sunshine. There had never come to her a single great sorrow. None ever knew her who did not love and revere her for her bright and sunny temper and her saintly unselfishness. Fair, pure and joyous as a maiden, loving, tender and happy as a young wife. When she had just become a mother, when her life seemed to be just begun and when the years seemed so bright before her, then by a strange and terrible fate death came to her. And when my heart's dearest died, the light went from my life forever."

That was T.R. in his twenties. He thought the light had gone from his life forever—but he went on. And he not only became President but, as an ex-President, he served his country, always in the arena, tempestuous, strong, sometimes wrong, sometimes right, but he was a man.

And as I leave, let me say, that is an example I think all of us should remember. We think sometimes when things happen that don't go the right way; we think that when you don't pass the bar exam the first time—I happened to, but I was just lucky; I mean, my writing was so poor the bar examiner said, "We have just got to let the guy through." We think that when someone dear to us dies, we think that when we lose an election, we think that when we suffer a defeat that all is ended. We think, as T.R. said, that the light had left his life forever.

Not true. It is only a beginning, always. The young must know it; the old must know it. It must always sustain us, because the greatness comes not when things go always good for you, but the greatness comes and you are really tested, when you take some knocks, some disappointments, when sadness comes, because only if you have been in the deepest valley can you ever know how magnificent it is to be on the highest mountain.

And so I say to you on this occasion, as we leave, we leave proud of the people who have stood by us and worked for us and served this country.

We want you to be proud of what you have done. We want you to continue to serve in government, if that is your wish. Always give your best, never get discouraged, never be petty; always remember, others may hate you, but those who hate you don't win unless you hate them, and then you destroy yourself.

And so, we leave with high hopes, in good spirit, and with deep humility, and with very much gratefulness in our hearts. I can only say to each and every one of you, we come from many faiths, we pray perhaps to different gods—but really the same God in a sense—but I want to say for each and every one of you, not only will we always remember you, not only will we always be grateful to you but always you will be in our hearts and you will be in our prayers.

Thank you very much.*

---

*Public Papers of the Presidents of the United States: Richard Nixon, 1974, (Washington, D.C.: Government Printing Office, 1975), pp. 630-2.

# Chronology of Speeches

Speech to Committee of 100 to select Republican Congressional candidate, Whittier, California, November 2, 1945.

Campaign for House, remarks in the 12th District, California, Fall, 1946.

First Nixon-Voorhis Debate, Pasadena, California, September 13, 1946.

Second Nixon-Voorhis Debate, Whittier, California, September 20, 1946.

Third Nixon-Voorhis Debate, Pomona, California, October 11, 1946.

Fourth Nixon-Voorhis Debate, Monrovia, California, October 23, 1946.

Fifth Nixon-Voorhis Debate, San Gabriel, California, October 28, 1946.

House speech: Issuing of contempt citation for Gerhart Eisler, Washington, D.C., February 18, 1947.

House speech: Labor-Management Relations Act, Washington, D.C., April 16, 1947.

Debate with John F. Kennedy: Taft-Hartley Act, McKeesport, Pennsylvania, April 21, 1947.

House speech: Contempt citations, Washington, D.C., April 22, 1947.

Extended House remarks: Labor Law Symposium, Washington, D.C., May 27, 1947.

House remarks: Central Valley Project, Washington, D.C., June 26, 1947.

House remarks: Bipartisan foreign policy, Washington, D.C., July 2, 1947.

Extended House remarks: Labor-Management Relations Act, Washington, D.C., July 9, 1947.

House remarks: Employers Liability Act, Washington, D.C., July 17, 1947.

House remarks: Hollywood writers, Washington, D.C., November 24, 1947.

Extended House remarks: Eulogy of Lee J. Noftzger, Washington, D.C., January 12, 1948.

Extended House remarks: Outlawing the Communist Party, Washington, D.C., February 3, 1948.
House remarks: Ed Condon case, Washington, D.C., March 11, 1948.
House remarks: Ed Condon case, Washington, D.C., April 22, 1948.
House remarks: Subversive Activities Control Bill, Washington, D.C., May 14, 18-19, 1948.
House remarks: Praise of retiring Clarence F. Lea and Alfred J. Elliott, Washington, D.C., June 11, 1948.
House remarks: Readjustment Act, Washington, D.C., June 19, 1948.
Speeches for GOP ticket, cross-country, August-November, 1948.
Speech to *Herald-Tribune* Forum on House Un-American Activities Committee, New York City, October 19, 1948.
House speech: Flood-control project, Washington, D.C., March 25, 1949.
Speech on anticommunist legislation, New York City, April 13, 1949.
House remarks: Labor Relations Act, Washington, D.C., April 27-29, 1949.
House remarks: Wood Labor Bill, Washington, D.C., May 3, 1949.
Radio interview on Hiss case, Washington, D.C., July 9, 1949.
Extended House remarks: Judge Samuel Kaufman's conduct of the Hiss case, Washington, D.C., July 12, 1949.
Extended House remarks: Overtime pay, Washington, D.C., July 20, 1949.
Speech announcing candidacy for Senate, Pomona, California, November 3, 1949.
House speech: Hiss case, Washington, D.C., January 26, 1950.
Extended House remarks: Licensing motion picture industry and Hoover Commission Report, Washington, D.C., March 22, 1950.
Speech to Republican Assembly on foreign policy, San Francisco, California, March 25, 1950.
Speech defending Dr. J. Robert Oppenheimer, Oakdale, California, May 10, 1950.
Speech to American Legion on Korea, Sacramento, California, August 16, 1950.
House remarks: Communist Registration Act, Washington, D.C., August 29, 1950.
Extended House remarks: Communists in the labor movement, Washington, D.C., September 18, 1950.
Campaign speeches, every county, California, Fall, 1950.
Speech to Women's Republican Club, New York City, January 27, 1951.
Senate remarks: Immigration, Washington, D.C., March 14, 1951.
Senate speech: Harry Truman's firing of General Douglas MacArthur, Washington, D.C., April 11, 1951.
Senate remarks: MacArthur's firing, Washington, D.C., April 24, 1951.
Senate remarks: Protection of witnesses, Washington, D.C., April 26, 1951.

Speech to Iron and Steel Institute, New York City, May 24, 1951.
Senate remarks: Central Arizona Project, Washington, D.C., May 28, 1951.
Senate remarks: Arizona Project, Washington, D.C., June 4-5, 1951.
Speech to Young Republicans, Boston, June 28, 1951.
Senate remarks: Nomination of William K. Devers to the Home Loan Board, Washington, D.C., June 29, 1951.
Senate remarks: Agricultural Yearbook, Washington, D.C., July 26, 1951.
Senate remarks: Taft-Hartley Act, Washington, D.C., August 21, 1951.
Senate remarks: Defense production, Washington, D.C., August 23, 1951.
Senate remarks: State Department, Washington, D.C., August 24, 1951.
Extended Senate remarks: Public transportation, Washington, D.C., October 8, 1951.
Speech to Ambassadors Club, St. Louis, Missouri, November 7, 1951.
Speech to New York Women's Clubs: Truman Administration, Elmira, New York, November 12, 1951.
Speech to Republican Central Committee: Internal Revenue Service, San Diego, California, November 16, 1951.
Speech at New York Republican Dinner, New York City, May 8, 1952.
Speech accepting Republican nomination for vice-president, Chicago, Illinois, July 11, 1952.
Campaign for vice-president: ninety-two speeches, cross-country, Fall, 1952.
"Checkers" speech, Los Angeles, California, September 23, 1952.
Campaign speeches, Missoula, Montana and Wheeling, West Virginia, September 24, 1952.
Radio address: Yalta Agreement, New York City, October 5, 1952.
Speech at Gannon University, Erie, Pennsylvania, October 10, 1952.
Televised speech: Hiss case, New York City, October 13, 1952.
Televised campaign speech, Los Angeles, California, October 29, 1952.
Remarks: Honoring Herbert Hoover, New York City, March 19, 1953.
Speech to Newspaper Publishers Association: Accomplishments of Eisenhower Administration, New York City, April 23, 1953.
Speech to Business Advisory Council: Federal budget, Hot Springs, Virginia, May 9, 1953.
Speech to General Federation of Women's Clubs: Treaty ratification, Washington, D.C., May 25, 1953.
Speech: Russia and world peace, Philadelphia, Pennsylvania, July 4, 1953.
Remarks: Commemoration of Civil War battle, Gettysburg, Pennsylvania, July 5, 1953.
Remarks to Workers for the Blind, Washington, D.C., July 15, 1953.
Remarks at Boy Scout Jamboree, Newport Beach, California, July 19, 1953.

Speech to Veterans of Foreign Wars: Defense expenditures, Milwaukee, Wisconsin, August 5, 1953.

Speech to American Legion: Military preparedness, St. Louis, Missouri, August 31, 1953.

Speech to American Federation of Labor: Taft-Hartley revisions, St. Louis, Missouri, September 23, 1953.

Remarks, various locations, Honolulu, Hawaii, October 9, 1953.

Speech at Teheran University, Teheran, Iran, December 11, 1953.

Speech to Trade Journal Association, Washington, D.C., January 16, 1954.

Remarks at Westmoreland Community Church, Washington, D.C., January 31, 1954.

Remarks to Republican Party: Need for Democratic support, New Haven, Connecticut, February 11, 1954.

Remarks to state Republican party, Oakland, California, February 12, 1954.

Speech to Philadelphia Bulletin Forum, Philadelphia, March 9, 1954.

Televised speech denying that Joseph McCarthy was splitting Republican party, Washington, D.C., March 13, 1954.

"Off the record" remarks to Society of Newspaper Editors on Vietnam, Washington, D.C., April 16, 1954.

Speech to U.S. Chamber of Commerce on Soviet challenge, Washington, D.C., April 28, 1954.

Speech to GOP state convention, New York City, May 26, 1954.

Commencement address at Whittier College, Whittier, California, June 12, 1954.

Speech at Republican fundraiser, Milwaukee, Wisconsin, June 26, 1954.

Address to Veterans of Foreign Wars on communist threat, Philadelphia, Pennsylvania, August 2, 1954.

Remarks at Republican rally, Wichita, Kansas, September 16, 1954.

Remarks at GOP fundraiser, St. Louis, Missouri, September 17, 1954.

Speech to Young Republicans, Huron, South Dakota, September 18, 1954.

Televised speech at Valley College, Van Nuys, California, October 13, 1954.

Speech to newspaper publishers on the economy, Chicago, Illinois, October 20, 1954.

Speech at Augustana College, Rock Island, Illinois, October 21, 1954.

Televised speech (heckler held), San Mateo, California, October 19, 1954.

Televised campaign speech, Denver, Colorado, November 1, 1954.

Remarks to Chamber of Deputies, Mexico City, February 11, 1955.

Address to graduates of Pan American Agricultural School, El Zamorano, Honduras, February 18, 1955.

Address to Legislative Assembly on commonwealth status, San Juan, Puerto Rico, February 28, 1955.

Address to joint session of the Dominican Republic legislature, Ciudad Trujillo, Dominican Republic, March 1, 1955.

Speech to World Affairs Council on Latin America, Los Angeles, California, March 14, 1955.

Speech to Executives Club on atomic weapons, Chicago, Illinois, March 17, 1955.

Commencement address, Temple University, Philadelphia, Pennsylvania, June 16, 1955.

Speech in Harlem on racial equality, New York City, June 24, 1955.

Address to American Bar Association on world situation, Philadelphia, Pennsylvania, August 25, 1955.

Speech to Veterans of Foreign Wars on China, Boston, August 29, 1955.

Speech at National Plowing Contest, Wabash, Indiana, September 17, 1955.

Remarks on Eisenhower's illness, Washington, D.C., September 26, 1955.

Remarks at Herald Tribune Forum, New York City, October 17, 1955.

Address to Investment Bankers Association on the economy, New York City, October 19, 1955.

Speech at Republican fundraiser, Chicago, Illinois, January 20, 1956.

Remarks at inauguration of President Kubitschek, Volta Redonda, Brazil, February 3, 1956.

Televised speech to Republican clubs, New York City, February 13, 1956.

Remarks to Republican women leaders, Washington, D.C., March 7, 1956.

Commencement address at Lafayette College on Soviet tactics, Easton, Pennsylvania, June 7, 1956.

Remarks to Young Republicans on Eisenhower's illness, Washington, D.C., June 8, 1956.

Remarks celebrating Philippine independence, Manila, July 4, 1956.

Speech to three religious groups on school integration, Ridgecrest, North Carolina, August 5, 1956.

Speech accepting Republican nomination for vice president, San Francisco, California, August 23, 1956.

Speech to American Legion, Los Angeles, California, September 6, 1956.

Campaign for vice-president, 119 formal speeches, thirty-six states, Fall, 1956.

Speech at Republican rally, Gettysburg, Pennsylvania, September 12, 1956.

Televised interview with newsmen from 8 cities; Speech to Zionist Organization of America on the Middle East, Washington, D.C., October 7, 1956.

Speech at Al Smith Dinner, New York City, October 18, 1956.

Televised campaign address, Washington, D.C., November 5, 1956.

Speech to Automobile Manufacturers, New York City, December 6, 1956.

Remarks to Radio-Television Correspondents Association, Washington, D.C., March 23, 1957.

Speech to Jewish groups on Hungary, Chicago, Illinois, April 30, 1957.

Speech at DePauw University, Greencastle, Indiana, May 11, 1957.

Remarks to GOP on party unity, Hartford, Connecticut, May 14, 1957.

Speech to Iron and Steel Institute, New York City, May 23, 1957.

Commencement Address at Bethany College, Bethany, West Virginia, June 2, 1957.

Speech to GOP workers on party unity, Washington D.C., June 6, 1957.

Commencement Address at Michigan State University, East Lansing, Michigan, June 9, 1957.

Speech to Young Republicans, Washington, D.C., June 21, 1957.

Speech to National Kiwanis on exchanges with Soviet Union, Atlantic City, New Jersey, June 27, 1957.

Speech to mayors on assistance to cities, New York City, September 9, 1957.

Speech to Development Conference, San Francisco, California, October 15, 1957.

Campaign speeches for Malcomb S. Forbes, eight cities, New Jersey, October 23, 1957.

Speech to National Council of Catholic Youth on communism, Philadelphia, Pennsylvania, November 24, 1957.

News Conference on Eisenhower's illness, Washington, D.C., November 27, 1957.

Speech to National Association of Manufacturers on foreign aid, New York City, December 6, 1957.

Speech accepting Ives Award for civil rights work; Speech at scholarship dinner for Yeshiva University, New York City, December 15, 1957.

Speech at GOP fundraiser on defense, New York City, January 20, 1958.

Speech to Women's National Republican Club on party unity, New York City, January 25, 1958.

Address to American Newspaper Publishers on the economic recovery, New York City, April 24, 1958.

Remarks on return from Latin America, Washington, D.C., May 15, 1958.

Remarks to American Management Association on labor laws, New York City, May 20, 1958.

Address to National Press Club, Washington, D.C., May 21, 1958.

Address to editors on Middle East, Minneapolis, Minnesota, July 19, 1958.

Address to Harvard Business School, Boston, September 6, 1958.

Campaign speeches for GOP candidates, twenty-four states, Fall, 1958.

Remarks at fundraiser, Indianapolis, Indiana, September 29, 1958.

Televised campaign speech, Los Angeles, California, September 30, 1958.

Speech to English Speaking Union, London, November 26, 1958.

Address to Fordham College alumni on Anastas Mikoyan's visit to United States, New York City, January 27, 1959.

Speech honoring Oregon Centennial, Portland, Oregon, February 14, 1959.

Remarks at GOP luncheon, Los Angeles, California, February 16, 1959.

Remarks to federal attorneys on cold war, Washington, D.C., April 7, 1959.

Speech to GOP National Committee, Washington, D.C., April 10, 1959.

Address to American Academy of Political Science on how to settle international disputes, New York City, April 13, 1959.

Speech to American Society of Newspaper Editors on future plans, Washington, D.C., April 18, 1959.

Remarks at Republican fundraiser, Washington, D.C., June 8, 1959.

Commencement address at Whittier College, Whittier, California, June 13, 1959.

Speech to National Educational Association on the Soviet Union, Colorado Springs, Colorado, June 20, 1959.

Dedication of power project, Massena, New York, June 27, 1959.

Remarks at opening of Soviet Exposition, New York City, June 29, 1959.

Dedication of Sports Arena, Los Angeles, California, July 4, 1959.

Remarks at baseball dinner, Pittsburgh, Pennsylvania, July 6, 1959.

Remarks at airport arrival, Moscow, USSR, July 23, 1959.

Remarks at opening of American Exhibition in the Soviet Union, Moscow, USSR, July 24, 1959.

Luncheon speech on U.S.-Soviet relations, Degtyarsk, USSR, July 30, 1959.

Televised speech to Soviet Union, Moscow, USSR, August 1, 1959.

Remarks on arriving in Poland, Warsaw, August 2, 1959.

Remarks at bond dinner, Spring Lake, New Jersey, August 13, 1959.

Speech to Football Writers Association, Chicago, Illinois, August 14, 1959.

Speech to American Legion, Minneapolis, Minnesota, August 25, 1959.

Speech to Veterans of Foreign Wars, Los Angeles, California, August 31, 1959.

Speech to the American Dental Society, New York City, September 14, 1959.

Address at Thiel College, Greenville, Pennsylvania, September 21, 1959.

Remarks at Khrushchev's departure, Andrews Air Force Base, September 27, 1959.

Dedication of dam, Hopkinton, New Hampshire, October 3, 1959.

Speech at University of Chicago, Chicago, Illinois, October 5, 1959.

Speech to Central Treaty Organization on the Soviet Union, Washington, D.C., October 7, 1959.

Speech to Council on World Affairs, Dallas, Texas, October 9, 1959.

Speech honoring "Rosary Hour," Los Angeles, California, November 4, 1959.

Speech at Los Angeles City College on Soviet educational challenge, Los Angeles, California, November 6, 1959.

Speech to Sigma Delta Chi on trip to Soviet Union, Indianapolis, Indiana, November 13, 1959.

Remarks at Golf Award Dinner, New York City, January 26, 1960.

Speech at Republican fundraiser, Chicago, Illinois, January 27, 1960.

Speech at Lincoln Day dinner, Milwaukee, Wisconsin, February 8, 1960.

Remarks to Boy Scouts, Washington, D.C., February 10, 1960.

Remarks at Winter Olympics, Squaw Valley, Idaho, February 18, 1960.

Speech at University of Notre Dame on the economy, South Bend, Indiana, February 23, 1960.

Speech to American Veterans, Washington, D.C., March 2, 1960.

Remarks to Variety Club and to Chamber of Commerce, New York City, March 16, 1960.

Remarks to Republican women, Washington, D.C., April 4, 1960.

Address to American Society of Newspaper Editors on the summit, Washington, D.C., April 23, 1960.

Televised interview: "Open End" with David Susskind (3:45 length), New York City, May 15, 1960.

Campaign speech for Les Arends, Melvin, Illinois, May 27, 1960.

Remarks opening British Exhibit, New York City, June 10, 1960.

Remarks to Texas Press Association, Houston, Texas, June 19, 1960.

Speech on farm policy, Minot, North Dakota, June 20, 1960.

Speech to National Jaycees, St. Louis, Missouri, June 21, 1960.

Acceptance of GOP nomination for president, Chicago, Illinois, July 28, 1960.

Campaign for president, speeches in 188 cities, 50 states, Fall, 1960.

Campaign speech at Whittier College, Whittier, California, August 2, 1960.

Campaign speech, Greensboro, North Carolina, August 17, 1960.

Speech to Veterans of Foreign Wars on American leadership in the world, Detroit, Michigan, August 24, 1960.

Televised campaign speech, Des Moines, Iowa, September 16, 1960.

Speech to Brotherhood of Carpenters, Chicago, Illinois, September 26, 1960.

First Kennedy-Nixon Debate, Chicago, Illinois, September 26, 1960.

Second Kennedy-Nixon Debate, Washington, D.C., October 7, 1960.

Speech at Mormon Tabernacle, Salt Lake City, Utah, October 10, 1960.

Third Kennedy-Nixon Debate, Los Angeles, California, October 13, 1960.

Speech to World Newspaper Forum, Los Angeles, California, October 14, 1960.

Speech to American Legion, Miami, Florida, October 18, 1960.

Remarks at Al Smith Dinner, New York City, October 19, 1960.

Speech to Business Economists, New York City, October 20, 1960.

Fourth Kennedy-Nixon Debate, New York City, October 21, 1960.
Speech at Muhlenburg College, Allentown, Pennsylvania, October 22, 1960.
Speech to Sigma Delta Chi, Toledo, Ohio, October 26, 1960.
Televised campaign speech, Chicago, Illinois, October 29, 1960.
Televised campaign speech, New York City, November 2, 1960.
Televised campaign speech, Fresno, California, November 4, 1960.
Televised campaign speech, Los Angeles, California, November 6, 1960.
Televised campaign speech, Chicago, Illinois, November 7, 1960.
Taped televised salute to outgoing President Eisenhower, Washington, D.C., January 5, 1961.
Senate: Farewell to Congress, Washington, D.C., January 6, 1961.
Remarks at GOP farewell dinner, Washington, D.C., January 9, 1961.
Remarks to Republican Central Committee, Sacramento, California, March 11, 1961.
Speech to Executives' Club on communism, Chicago, Illinois, May 5, 1961.
Speech at Republican fundraiser, Des Moines, Iowa, May 6, 1961.
Speech to Press Club on foreign policy; Speech to Republican rally, Detroit, Michigan, May 9, 1961.
Speech to GOP about welfare costs, Columbus, Ohio, May 10, 1961.
Speech at Republican dinner on atomic test ban, Los Angeles, California, June 1, 1961.
Speech at GOP fundraiser, Hershey, Pennsylvania, June 26, 1961.
Speech to Pharmaceutical Association, New York City, June 27, 1961.
News Conference announcing candidacy for governor, Los Angeles, California, September 27, 1961.
Campaign speech at Coronado Hotel to county Republicans, San Diego, California, October 28, 1961.
Speech to Onondaga County GOP, Syracuse, New York, October 30, 1961.
Speech to Northern California GOP, San Francisco, California, November 13, 1961.
Speech to GOP Assembly, Santa Maria, California, December 2, 1961.
Remarks at Whittier College, Whittier, California, January 9, 1962.
Interview with Jack Paar, New York City, February 8, 1962.
Campaign speeches, ten counties, California, February 13-16, 1962.
Speech to Retail Grocers Association, Los Angeles, California, May 17, 1962.
Remarks to Commonwealth Club, San Francisco, California, May 18, 1962.
Campaign telethon, Los Angeles, California, May 30, 1962.
Speech to GOP leaders, Gettysburg, Pennsylvania, June 30, 1962.
Independence Day Address, Aalborg, Denmark, July 4, 1962.
Campaign telethon, Salinas, California, September 29, 1962.
Televised taped answers to questions with Edmund Brown, San Francisco, California, September 30, 1962.

"Debate" with Governor Brown, San Francisco, California, October 1, 1962.
Speech to Los Angeles Press Club, Los Angeles, California, October 4, 1962.
Campaign speeches, northern counties, California, October 18-19, 1962.
Televised speech on Cuba, San Diego, California, October 27, 1962.
Campaign telethon, Los Angeles, California, November 3, 1962.
Televised campaign address attacking "smears" by Brown, Los Angeles, California, November 5, 1962.
"Last" news conference, Beverly Hills, California, November 7, 1962.
Address to American Society of Newspaper Editors on foreign policy Washington, D.C., April 20, 1963.
Remarks at farewell luncheon, Los Angeles, California, June 7, 1963.
Televised interview, Paris, France, August 1, 1963.
Speech to American Club, Paris, France, October 24, 1963.
Remarks to Industrial Realtors, New York City, November 11, 1963.
Televised remarks on JFK death, New York City, November 23, 1963.
Remarks on Herbert H. Lehman, New York City, December 5, 1963.
Televised interview with Walter Cronkite, New York City, January 23, 1964.
Speech at Pfeiffer College on foreign leaders, Salisbury, North Carolina, February 3, 1964.
Speech to Germantown GOP Club, Philadelphia, February 10, 1964.
Speech at Lincoln Day Dinner on racial boycotts, Cincinnati, Ohio, February 12, 1964.
Speech to Masons on communism, New York City, March 8, 1964.
Speech to Sons of St. Patrick, Eastchester, New York, March 14, 1964.
Speech to Society of Newspaper Editors on Southeast Asia, Washington, D.C., April 18, 1964.
Televised remarks via Telstar II, New York City, May 27, 1964.
Remarks at fundraiser, Nassau County, New York, June 3, 1964.
Remarks at fundraisers, various cities, Michigan, June 8, 1964.
Remarks at fundraiser, Baltimore, Maryland, June 9, 1964.
Remarks at fundraiser, Milwaukee, Wisconsin, June 13, 1964.
Speech to Apparel Manufacturers, Atlanta, Georgia, June 15, 1964.
Speech to National Coal Association, New York City, June 16, 1964.
Introduction of Barry Goldwater at the Republican national convention, San Francisco, California, July 16, 1964.
Remarks at Republican Unity Conference, Hershey, Pennsylvania, August 12, 1964.
Speech to state GOP convention, Detroit, Michigan, September 19, 1964.
More than 100 speeches in thirty-six states for GOP candidates, Fall, 1964.
Speech at Catawba College on foreign policy, Salisbury, North Carolina, October 10, 1964.
Tribute to Barry Goldwater at National Republican Committee meeting, Chicago, Illinois, January 22, 1965.

Address to Executives' Club on Vietnam, New York City, January 26, 1965.

Speech at GOP fundraiser, Philadelphia, Pennsylvania, February 10, 1965.

Remarks to Republican women, Washington, D.C., April 3, 1965.

Remarks at Moscow University, Moscow, USSR, April 10, 1965.

Speech at GOP fundraiser, Phoenix, Arizona, April 14, 1965.

Speech to National Industrial Conference Board on the economy, New York City, April 15, 1965.

Speech at Republican fundraiser, Cleveland, Ohio, June 9, 1965.

Remarks to Young Republicans, Miami Beach, Florida, June 18, 1965.

Speech at Hoover Library, West Branch, Iowa, August 10, 1965.

Speech to Australian Press Club, Canberra, September 9, 1965.

Remarks to World Conference on Peace through Law on Vietnam, Washington, D.C., September 15, 1965.

Remarks at fundraiser for Robert H. Finch, Los Angeles, California, September 23, 1965.

Remarks to Republican Central Committee, San Francisco, California, September 25, 1965.

Remarks at various GOP fundraisers, Virginia, October 6, 1965.

Speech at fundraiser honoring Dwight Eisenhower, Chicago, Illinois, October 14, 1965.

Campaign speeches for Wayne Dumont, New Jersey, October 24, 1965.

Speech to Western States Republicans, Albuquerque, New Mexico, November 5, 1965.

TV Interview: "Face the Nation," New York City, November 21, 1965.

Address to National Association of Manufacturers on Vietnam, New York City, December 3, 1965.

Speech to Women's Republican Club, New York City, January 29, 1966.

Remarks at GOP fundraiser, Washington, D.C., February 3, 1966.

Speech at Republican State Convention, Billings, Montana, March 26, 1966.

Speech at Tulane University, New Orleans, Louisiana, April 16, 1966.

Argument before Supreme Court, Washington, D.C., April 27, 1966.

Remarks on Vietnam, Durham, North Carolina, April 30, 1966.

Speech to Republican women campaign workers, Washington, D.C.; Speech at Millsaps College, Jackson, Mississippi, May 6, 1966.

Speech at Republican fundraiser, Kansas City, Kansas, May 14, 1966.

Speeches at fundraisers, Washington, D.C., May 26, 1966.

Speech at fundraiser, Jamestown, New York, June 1, 1966.

Commencement address at University of Rochester, Rochester, New York, June 5, 1966.

Remarks at fundraiser on lawlessness, Chicago, Illinois, June 10, 1966.

Speech at fundraiser for Ronald Reagan, Los Angeles, California, June 23, 1966.

Speech to American Medical Association, Chicago, Illinois, June 26, 1966.
Speech to National Jaycees, Detroit, Michigan, June 28, 1966.
Speech at fundraiser on foreign policy, Chicago, Illinois, June 30, 1966.
Remarks to leading conservatives, Washington, D.C., August 24, 1966.
Speech to American Legion, Washington, D.C., August 31, 1966.
Campaign speeches for GOP, sixty-one Congressional districts, Fall, 1966.
Speech to Overseas Press Club, New York City, September 13, 1966.
Argument before Supreme Court, Washington, D.C., October 18, 1966.
Televised taped campaign speech, New York City, November 6, 1966.
Remarks to National Board of Boys Clubs of America, New York City, November 28, 1966.
Speech on foreign policy, Gainesville, Florida, January 20, 1967.
Speech to Feed Manufacturers on Latin America, Chicago, Illinois, May 23, 1967.
Speech to World Affairs Council on the Middle East, Philadelphia, Pennsylvania, May 31, 1967.
Lakeside Speech, Bohemian Grove, California, July 29, 1967.
Speech to National Industrial Conference Board on recent trips, New York City, September 12, 1967.
Campaign speeches, various cities, New Hampshire, October 25, 1967.
Speech to Executives Club on Vietnam, Chicago, Illinois, October 27, 1967.
Tribute to Glenn R. Davis, Waukesha, Wisconsin, October, 18, 1967.
Address at Law School on draft, Madison, Wisconsin, November 17, 1967.
Taped televised remarks on Vietnam, Portland, Oregon, November 28, 1967.
Speech to National Association of Manufacturers on Vietnam, New York City, December 8, 1978
Speech at fundraiser for Jacob Javits, New York City, December 11, 1967.
Taped televised remarks with Mayor Samuel Yorty, Los Angeles, California, December 14, 1967.
Speech to Chamber of Commerce on civil rights, Richmond, Virginia, January 12, 1968.
Speech to Women's National Republican Club on the Pueblo incident, New York City, January 27, 1968.
Speech opening campaign for Republican presidential nomination, Manchester, New Hampshire, February 2, 1968.
Speech at University of New Hampshire, Durham, New Hampshire, February 14, 1968.
Speech at Republican fundraiser, Washington, D.C., March 5, 1968.
Broadcast of taped radio speech on civil disorder, March 7, 1968.

Radio speech on civil rights, Milwaukee, Wisconsin, March 28, 1968.

Speech to Republican women on Lyndon Johnson's withdrawal from presidential race, Cincinnati, Ohio, April 2, 1968.

Speech to Society of Newspaper Editors, Washington, D.C., April 19, 1968.

Speech on black capitalism, Minneapolis, Minnesota, April 20, 1968.

Radio speech on urban problems, Indianapolis, Indiana, May 2, 1968.

Speech at Concordia College, Fort Wayne, Indiana, May 3, 1968.

Speech at GOP fundraiser, Newark, New Jersey, May 17, 1968.

Campaign speeches and telethon, Oregon, May 24-26, 1968.

Remarks at Republican fundraiser, Phoenix, Arizona, May 29, 1968.

Commencement Address at Finch College, New York City, June 14, 1968.

Remarks to National Newspaper Publishers Association, Minneapolis, Minnesota, June 21, 1968.

Remarks at Republican fundraiser, Lansing, Michigan, June 26, 1968.

Radio address on federal power, Washington, D.C., June 27, 1968.

Remarks at Public Square rally, Cleveland, Ohio, July 19, 1968.

Televised taped interview with six citizens , Los Angeles, California, July 21, 1968.

Speech to Association of Counties, Washington, D.C., July 31, 1968.

Speech accepting Republican presidential nomination, Miami Beach, Florida, August 8, 1968.

Presidential campaign, speeches in 118 cities, 30 states, Fall, 1968.

Speech to Veterans of Foreign Wars, Detroit, Michigan, August 19, 1968.

Taped interview shown in three states, Chicago, Illinois, September 4, 1968.

Speech to B'nai B'rith on Mideast, Washington, D.C., September 8, 1968.

Speech to GOP rally, White Plains, New York, September 10, 1968.

Televised taped interview shown, South Carolina, North Carolina, Indiana, September 12, 1968.

Radio address on nature of presidency, New York City, September 19, 1968.

Televised taped interview shown, New York, Pennsylvania, New Jersey, September 20-21, 1968.

Televised taped interview shown in twelve Southern states, Atlanta, Georgia, October 3, 1968.

Radio address on the federal bureaucracy, New York City, October 6, 1968.

Speech to United Press Editors, Washington, D.C., October 7, 1968.

Televised taped interview, Dallas, Texas, October 13, 1968.

Remarks at Al Smith Dinner, New York City, October 16, 1968.

Radio address on conservation; Televised taped interview shown in New England, Boston, October 18, 1968.

Radio address on foreign policy, Chicago, Illinois, October 19, 1968.

Radio address on education, New York City, October 20, 1968.

Radio address on job training, Cincinnati, Ohio, October 21, 1968.

Campaign speeches, various cities, Ohio and Michigan, October 22-23, 1968.

Radio address on arms control; campaign speeches, various cities, Pennsylvania, October 24, 1968.

Televised taped interview shown in ten Eastern states, New York City, October 25, 1968.

Radio address on federal-state relations, October 26, 1968.

Interview on "Face the Nation"; radio address on Vietnam, New York City, October 27, 1968.

Radio address on electoral system, Cleveland, Ohio, October 30, 1968.

Rally at Madison Square Garden, New York City, October 31, 1968.

Radio address on "law and order," November 2, 1968.

Interview on "Meet the Press"; four-hour telethon, Los Angeles, California, November 3-4, 1968.

Remarks honoring James Francis Cardinal McIntyre, Los Angeles, California, December 5, 1968.

Remarks to Western Governors, Palm Springs, California, December 6, 1968.

Televised introduction of Cabinet, Washington, D.C., December 11, 1968.

First Inaugural Address, Washington, D.C., January 20, 1969.

First News Conference, Washington, D.C., January 27, 1969.

Remarks at the State Department, Washington, D.C., January 30, 1969.

Remarks at Prayer Breakfast, Washington, D.C., January 30, 1969.

Remarks at Justice Department, Washington, D.C., January 30, 1969.

Remarks at Defense Department, Washington, D.C., January 31, 1969.

Remarks at the Departments of Housing and Urban Development and Agriculture, Washington, D.C., February 3, 1969.

Remarks at Labor Department, Washington, D.C., February 4, 1969.

Second News Conference, Washington, D.C., February 6, 1969.

Remarks to participants in the Senate Youth Program, Washington, D.C., February 7, 1969.

Remarks at Department of Commerce, Washington, D.C., February 7, 1969.

Speech at Department of Transportation, Washington, D.C., February 11, 1969.

Remarks at Departments of Health, Education, and Welfare and Treasury, Washington, D.C., February 14, 1969.

Remarks at Department of Interior, Washington, D.C., February 19, 1969.

Remarks about European trip, Washington, D.C., February 22, 1969.

Remarks to the North Atlantic Council, Brussels, February 24, 1969.

Remarks to Bundestag, Bonn, West Germany, February 26, 1969.

Third News Conference, Washington, D.C., March 4, 1969.

Remarks to the CIA, McLean, Virginia, March 7, 1969.

Fourth News Conference, Washington, D.C., March 14, 1969.
Remarks to the International Alliance of Businessmen, the American Legion, and the Gridiron Club, Washington, D.C., March 15, 1969.
Remarks to National Association of Broadcasters, Washington, D.C., March 25, 1969.
Eulogy of Dwight D. Eisenhower, Washington, D.C., March 30, 1969.
Address to the North Atlantic Council, Washington, D.C., April 10, 1969.
Remarks to the Organization of American States, Washington, D.C., April 14, 1969.
Remarks to Republican Women's Conference, Washington, D.C., April 16, 1969.
Fifth News Conference, Washington, D.C., April 18, 1969.
Remarks to U.S. Chamber of Commerce, Washington, D.C., April 29, 1969.
Remarks at Republican Victory Dinner, Washington, D.C., May 7, 1969.
Address to the Nation on Vietnam, Washington, D.C., May 14, 1969.
Remarks to newsmen about the nomination of Warren Burger as Chief Justice, Washington, D.C., May 22, 1969.
Remarks to the Organization of African Unity and Remarks at the FBI Graduation, Washington, D.C., May 25, 1969.
Address at George Beadle State College on antiwar demonstrations, Madison, South Dakota, June 3, 1969.
Commencement Address at the Air Force Academy, Colorado Springs, Colorado, June 4, 1969.
Sixth News Conference, Washington, D.C., June 19, 1969.
Remarks to National Field Service Students, Washington, D.C., July 22, 1969.
Remarks to newsmen, announcing Nixon Doctrine, Guam, July 25, 1969.
Address to the Nation on welfare, Washington, D.C., August 8, 1969.
Address to the National Governors' Conference on revenue sharing, Colorado Springs, Colorado, September 1, 1969.
Eulogy of Everett Dirksen, Washington, D.C., September 9, 1969.
Seventh News Conference and Remarks to the National Federation of Republican Women, Washington, D.C., September 26, 1969.
Remarks about the People-to-People Program, Washington, D.C., October 14, 1969.
Address to the Nation on cost of living, Washington, D.C., October 17, 1969.
Remarks to newsmen about the nomination of Clement Haynsworth to the Supreme Court, Washington, D.C., October 20, 1969.
Remarks at Prayer Breakfast, Washington, D.C., October 22, 1969.
Remarks at Civic Center, Salem, Virginia, October 28, 1969.
Remarks in various cities, New Jersey, October 29, 1969.
Remarks to the Inter-American Press Association, Washington, D.C., October 31, 1969.

Address to the Nation on Vietnam, Washington, D.C., November 3, 1969.

Remarks to the House and to the Senate about Vietnam, Washington, D.C., November 13, 1969.

Remarks to businessmen, Washington, D.C., November 21, 1969.

Remarks to senior citizens, Washington, D.C., November 21, 1969.

Remarks at Conference on Food, Nutrition, and Health, Washington, D.C., December 2, 1969.

Remarks to Governors' Conference, Washington, D.C., December 3, 1969.

Televised interview at Arkansas-Texas football game half-time, Fayetteville, Arkansas, December 6, 1969.

Eighth News Conference and Remarks to Mexican Farm Bureau, Washington, D.C., December 8, 1969.

Remarks at National Football Foundation dinner, New York City, December 9, 1969.

Address to the Nation on progress in Vietnam, Washington, D.C., December 15, 1969.

State of the Union Address, Washington, D.C., January 22, 1970.

Ninth News Conference, Washington, D.C., January 30, 1970.

Remarks at annual Prayer Breakfast, Washington, D.C., February 5, 1970.

Remarks following meeting of the Environmental Council, Chicago, Illinois, February 6, 1970.

Remarks on the environment, Washington, D.C., February 10, 1970.

Remarks at Governors' Conference, Washington, D.C., February 25, 1970.

Remarks to French reporters, Washington, D.C., February 26, 1970.

Remarks about Non-Proliferation Treaty, Washington, D.C., March 5, 1970.

Remarks to Veterans of Foreign Wars, Washington, D.C., March 10, 1970.

Unscheduled News Conference, Washington, D.C., March 21, 1970.

Remarks: Strikes in postal system, Washington, D.C., March 23, 1970.

Remarks to Municipal Law Officers, Washington, D.C., April 8, 1970.

Remarks about Supreme Court nominees, Washington, D.C., April 9, 1970.

Address to the Nation on progress toward peace in Vietnam, Washington, D.C., April 20, 1970.

Address to the Nation on the Situation in Southeast Asia, Washington, D.C., April 30, 1970.

Tenth News Conference, Washington, D.C., May 8, 1970.

Remarks at Billy Graham Crusade, Knoxville, Tennessee, May 28, 1970.

Remarks to the Nation on the Cambodian Situation, Washington, D.C., June 3, 1970.

Remarks to Presidential Scholars of 1970, Washington, D.C., June 4, 1970.

Remarks to U.S. Attorneys' Conference, Washington, D.C., June 11, 1970.

Address to the Nation on economic policy, Washington, D.C., June 17, 1970.

Remarks to the U.S. Jaycees, St. Louis, Missouri, June 25, 1970.

Televised interview about foreign policy, Los Angeles, California, July 1, 1970.

Remarks at impromptu news briefing, Washington, D.C., July 20, 1970.

Remarks in the Civic Center, Fargo, North Dakota, July 24, 1970.

Eleventh News Conference, Los Angeles, California, July 30, 1970.

Remarks to newsmen, Denver, Colorado, August 3, 1970.

Remarks about public education, New Orleans, Louisiana, August 14, 1970.

Televised interview, CBS Morning News, San Clemente, California, August 31, 1970.

Speech at Kansas State University, Manhattan, Kansas, September 16, 1970.

Remarks at Citizenship Day Reception, Chicago, Illinois, September 17, 1970.

Remarks to students from the North American College, Vatican City, September 28, 1970.

Address to the Nation about a new initiative for peace in Southeast Asia, Washington, D.C., October 7, 1970.

Remarks at White House Conference on Drug Abuse, Washington, D.C., October 14, 1970.

Campaign for Republican Congressional candidates, Vermont, New Jersey, Pennsylvania, Wisconsin, Ohio, North Dakota, Missouri, Tennessee, North Carolina, Indiana, October 17-20, 1970.

Remarks at East Tennessee State University, Johnson City, Tennessee, October 20, 1970.

Address to UN General Assembly, New York City, October 23, 1970.

Campaign for Republican Congressional candidates, Maryland, Florida, Texas, Illinois, Minnesota, California, Arizona, New Mexico, Nevada, Utah, October 24-30, 1970.

Taped remarks for GOP candidates, Washington, D.C., November 1, 1970.

Remarks to reporters on election day, San Clemente, California, November 3, 1970.

Remarks about the election results, San Clemente, California, November 4, 1970.

Twelfth News Conference, Washington, D.C., December 10, 1970.

Remarks to White House Conference on Children, Washington, D.C., December 13, 1970.

Remarks at the Lighting of the Nation's Christmas Tree, Washington, D.C., December 16, 1970.

Remarks at Research Center, Beltsville, Maryland, December 17, 1970.

Televised interview with network representatives, Washington, D.C., January 4, 1971.

Remarks at University of Nebraska, Lincoln, Nebraska, January 14, 1971.

Dedication of Eisenhower National Republican Center, Washington, D.C., January 15, 1971.

State of the Union Address, Washington, D.C., January 22, 1971.

Tribute to Richard Russell, Atlanta, Georgia, January 23, 1971.

Remarks at Prayer Breakfast, Washington, D.C., February 2, 1971.

Remarks to the American College of Cardiology, Washington, D.C., February 4, 1971.

Remarks to American Legion, Washington, D.C., February 16, 1971.

Thirteenth News Conference, Washington, D.C., February 17, 1971.

Remarks at Wilson Center, Washington, D.C., February 18, 1971.

Radio address on foreign policy, Washington, D.C., February 25, 1971.

Remarks to Iowa State Legislature and to farm media representatives, Des Moines, Iowa, March 1, 1971.

Fourteenth News Conference, Washington, D.C., March 4, 1971.

Remarks to the National Conference on the Judiciary, Williamsburg, Virginia, March 11, 1971.

Commencement Address at Naval Officer Candidate School, Newport, Rhode Island, March 12, 1971.

Eulogy of Whitney M. Young, Lexington, Kentucky, March 17, 1971.

Televised interview with Howard K. Smith, Washington, D.C., March 22, 1971.

Address to the Nation on the situation in Southeast Asia, Washington, D.C., April 7, 1971.

Radio interview with American Society of Newspaper Editors, Washington, D.C., April 16, 1971.

Remarks to Republican Governors, Williamsburg, Virginia, April 19, 1971.

Remarks to the Daughters of the American Revolution, Washington, D.C., April 19, 1971.

Remarks to U.S. Chamber of Commerce, Washington, D.C., April 26, 1971.

Fifteenth News Conference, Washington, D.C., April 29, 1971.

Sixteenth News Conference, San Clemente, California, May 1, 1971.

Radio address on agriculture, Palm Springs, California, May 2, 1971.

Remarks to farm leaders, Washington, D.C., May 7, 1971.

Remarks at LBJ Library, Austin, Texas, May 22, 1971.

Remarks at waterway dedication, Mobile, Alabama, May 25, 1971.

Remarks to Southern news media, Birmingham, Alabama, May 25, 1971.

Remarks to the Councils of the Arts, Washington, D.C., May 26, 1971.

Remarks to Corps of Cadets, West Point, New York, May 29, 1971.

Seventeenth News Conference, Washington, D.C., June 1, 1971.

Dedication of river navigation system, Tulsa, Oklahoma, June 5, 1971.

Remarks to Eastern media, Rochester, New York, June 18, 1971.

Remarks to American Medical Association, Atlantic City, New Jersey, June 22, 1971.
Dedication of Hannah Nixon birthplace, Vernon, Indiana, June 24, 1971.
Remarks to National Retired Teachers Association and American Association of Retired Persons, Chicago, Illinois, June 25, 1971.
Remarks at FBI graduation, Washington, D.C., June 30, 1971.
Remarks to Midwestern news media, Kansas City, Missouri, July 6, 1971.
Announcement of trip to China, Burbank, California, July 15, 1971.
Remarks at NFL Hall of Fame Dinner, Canton, Ohio, July 30, 1971.
Televised interview with Frank Gifford, Canton, Ohio, July 31, 1971.
Dedication of Rathbun Dam, Centerville, Iowa, July 31, 1971.
Eighteenth News Conference, Washington, D.C., August 4, 1971.
Remarks to delegates of Girls Nation, Washington, D.C., August 6, 1971.
Address to the Nation about proposed economic policy, Washington, D.C., August 15, 1971.
Remarks to the Knights of Columbus, New York City, August 17. 1971.
Remarks at Lincoln house, Springfield, Illinois, August 18, 1971.
Remarks to Veterans of Foreign Wars, Dallas, Texas, August 19, 1971.
Remarks at Loma Linda University, Loma Linda, California, August 20, 1971.
Dedication of Air Force Museum, Dayton, Ohio, September 3, 1971.
Remarks to Milk Producers, Chicago, Illinois, September 3, 1971.
Radio Address on Labor Day, Camp David, Maryland, September 6, 1971.
Address to Congress on the economy, Washington, D.C., September 9, 1971.
Nineteenth News Conference, Washington, D.C., September 16, 1971.
Remarks at Economic Club, Detroit, Michigan, September 23, 1971.
Speech to International Monetary Fund and International Bank, Washington, D.C., September 29, 1971.
Address to the Nation on inflation, Washington, D.C., October 7, 1971.
Twentieth News Conference, Washington, D.C., October 12, 1971.
Remarks about Billy Graham, Charlotte, North Carolina, October 15, 1971.
Address to the Nation about Supreme Court Nominees, Lewis F. Powell and William H. Rehnquist, Washington, D.C., October 21, 1971.
Remarks to Federation of GOP Women, Washington, D.C., October 22, 1971.
Radio Address on Veterans Day, Camp David, Maryland, October 24, 1971.
Remarks at "Salute to the President" dinner, Camp David, Maryland, October 24, 1971.

Remarks at "Salute to the President" dinner, Chicago, Illinois, November 9, 1971.

Twenty-first News Conference, Washington, D.C., November 12, 1971.

Remarks to AFL-CIO, Bal Harbour, Florida, November 19, 1971.

Remarks to Washington Redskins, Loudoun Co., Virginia, November 23, 1971.

Remarks to National 4-H Club, Chicago, Illinois, December 1, 1971.

Remarks to Conference on Aging, Washington, D.C., December 2, 1971.

Televised interview with Dan Rather, Washington, D.C., January 2, 1972.

Remarks at National Steel and Shipbuilding Company, San Diego, California, January 3, 1972.

State of the Union Address, Washington, D.C., January 20, 1972.

Address to the Nation on Vietnam, Washington, D.C., January 25, 1972.

Remarks at Prayer Breakfast, Washington, D.C., February 1, 1972.

Remarks to White House Conference on the "Industrial World Ahead," Washington, D.C., February 7, 1972.

Radio Address on foreign policy, Washington, D.C., February 9, 1972.

Twenty-second News Conference and Remarks to National Center for Voluntary Action, Washington, D.C., February 10, 1972.

Remarks on return from China, Andrews AFB, February 28, 1972.

Remarks to Veterans of Foreign Wars, Washington, D.C., March 7, 1972.

Address to the Nation on equal educational opportunity and school busing, Washington, D.C., March 16, 1972.

Twenty-third News Conference, Washington, D.C., March 24, 1972.

Remarks to National Catholic Educational Association, Philadelphia, Pennsylvania, April 6, 1972.

Address to Canadian Parliament, Ottawa, Canada, April 14, 1972.

Remarks to Organization of American States, Washington, D.C., April 15, 1972.

Address to the Nation on Vietnam, Washington, D.C., April 26, 1972.

Remarks at John Connally's ranch, Floresville, Texas, April 30, 1972.

Address to the Nation on the situation in Southeast Asia, Washington, D.C., May 8, 1972.

Remarks to reporters about trip to USSR, Washington, D.C., May 19, 1972.

Televised Address to Soviet people, Moscow, USSR, May 28, 1972.

Address on return from the USSR, Washington, D.C., June 1, 1972.

Twenty-fourth News Conference, Washington, D.C., June 22, 1972.

Twenty-fifth News Conference, Washington, D.C., June 29, 1972.

Radio address on the Bicentennial, Washington, D.C., July 4, 1972.

Twenty-sixth News Conference, Washington, D.C., July 27, 1972.

Remarks to Young Voters Rally, Miami, Florida, August 22, 1972.

Acceptance of Republican nomination for president, Miami, Florida, August 23, 1972.

Remarks to American Legion, Chicago, Illinois, August 24, 1972.

Remarks at Eisenhower High School, Utica, Michigan, August 24, 1972.

Twenty-seventh News Conference, San Clemente, California, August 29, 1972.

Remarks to Conference on International Narcotics Control, Washington, D.C., September 18, 1972.

Remarks to Young Labor for Nixon, Washington, D.C., September 23, 1972.

Remarks to Governors of the International Monetary Fund, Washington, D.C., September 25, 1972.

Twenty-eighth News Conference, Washington, D.C., October 5, 1972.

Radio address on the budget, Camp David, Maryland, October 7, 1972.

Remarks at Columbus Day dinner, Washington, D.C., October 8, 1972.

Remarks to Southern supporters, Atlanta, Georgia, October 12, 1972.

Radio address on crime, Camp David, Maryland, October 15, 1972.

Remarks to families of POWs, Washington, D.C., October 16, 1972.

Remarks to foreign labor leaders, Washington, D.C., October 17, 1972.

Radio address on philosophy of government, Camp David, Maryland, October 21, 1972.

Radio address on Veterans, Camp David, Maryland, October 22, 1972.

Radio address on education, Washington, D.C., October 25 1972.

Radio address: "One America," Washington, D.C., October 18, 1972.

Radio address on defense policy, Washington, D.C., October 29, 1972.

Radio address on the elderly, Camp David, Maryland, October 30, 1972.

Radio address on urban affairs, Washington, D.C., November 1, 1972.

Address to the Nation on the future, Washington, D.C., November 2, 1972.

Radio address on health care, Washington, D.C., November 3, 1972.

Radio address on foreign policy, Washington, D.C.; Radio address: "The Birthright of an American Child," San Clemente, California, November 5, 1972.

Remarks on election eve, San Clemente, California, November 6, 1972.

Remarks on being reelected, Washington, D.C., November 7, 1972.

Remarks at Victory Rally, Washington, D.C., November 8, 1972.

Remarks on second term, Camp David, Maryland, November 27, 1972.

Second Inaugural Address, Washington, D.C., January 20, 1973.

Address to the Nation announcing the end of the Vietnam War, Washington, D.C., January 23, 1973.

Radio address on the budget, Washington, D.C., January 28, 1973.

Twenty-ninth News Conference, Washington, D.C., January 31, 1973.

Remarks at Annual Prayer Breakfast, Washington, D.C., February 1, 1973.

State of the Union Address, Washington, D.C., February 2, 1973.

Radio address on the environment, Washington, D.C., February 14, 1973.

Remarks to the South Carolina General Assembly, Columbia, South Carolina, February 20, 1973.

Radio address on the economy, Washington, D.C., February 21, 1973.

Radio address on human resources, Washington, D.C., February 24, 1973.

Thirtieth News Conference, Washington, D.C., March 2, 1973.

Radio address on building communities, Washington, D.C., March 4, 1973.

Radio address on law enforcement and drug abuse prevention, Washington, D.C., March 4, 1973.

Remarks to Foreign Service Women, Washington, D.C., March 13, 1973.

Thirty-first News Conference, Washington, D.C., March 15, 1973.

Address to the Nation about Vietnam and domestic problems, Washington, D.C., March 29, 1973.

Remarks to Legislative Conference, Washington, D.C., March 30, 1973.

Remarks to White House Correspondents Association, Washington, D.C., April 14, 1973.

Remarks to Building and Construction Workers, Washington, D.C., April 16, 1973.

Remarks at Stennis Naval Technical Training Center, Meridan, Mississippi, April 27, 1973.

Address to the Nation on the Watergate investigations, Washington, D.C., April 30, 1973.

Radio address on foreign policy, Washington, D.C., May 3, 1973.

Remarks at GOP fundraising dinner, Washington, D.C., May 9, 1973.

Remarks about federal election reform, Washington, D.C., May 16, 1973.

Remarks to returned POWs, Washington, D.C., May 24, 1973.

Commencement address at Florida Technological University, Orlando, Florida, June 8, 1973.

Address to the Nation on price controls, Washington, D.C., June 13, 1973.

Remarks at Everett Dirksen Leadership Research Center, Pekin, Illinois, June 15, 1973.

Radio address on the economy, San Clemente, California, July 1, 1973.

Remarks on return from hospital, Washington, D.C., July 20, 1973.

Address to the Nation about the Watergate investigations, Washington, D.C., August 15, 1973.

Remarks to the Veterans of Foreign Wars, New Orleans, Louisiana, August 20, 1973.

Thirty-second News Conference, San Clemente, California, August 22, 1973

Thirty-third News Conference, Washington, D.C., September 5, 1973.

Remarks on energy policy, Washington, D.C., September 8, 1973.

Radio address on legislative goals, Washington, D.C., September 9, 1973.

Remarks at Crime Conference, Washington, D.C., September 11, 1973.

Thirty-fourth News Conference, Washington, D.C., October 3, 1973.

Remarks at Conference on Exports, Washington, D.C., October 11, 1973.

Announcement of Gerald R. Ford's nomination as vice-president, Washington, D.C., October 12, 1973.

Thirty-fifth News Conference, Washington, D.C., October 26, 1973.

Address to the Nation on energy, Washington, D.C., November 7, 1973.

Remarks to Nevada State Society, Washington, D.C., November 8, 1973.

Remarks to the Society of Realtors, Washington, D.C., November 15, 1973.

Remarks at Walter George School of Law, Macon, Georgia, November 18, 1973.

Address to the Nation about national energy planning, Washington, D.C., November 25, 1973.

Remarks to the Seafarers Union, Washington, D.C., November 26, 1973.

Remarks at lighting of the nation's Christmas tree, Washington, D.C., December 14, 1973.

Remarks about Egyptian-Israeli Agreement, Washington, D.C., January 14, 1974.

Radio address on the energy crisis, Washington, D.C., January 19, 1974.

State of the Union Address, Washington, D.C., January 30, 1974.

Remarks at annual Prayer Breakfast, Washington, D.C., January 31, 1974.

Remarks to Hospital Association, Washington, D.C., February 5, 1974.

Radio address about transportation, Washington, D.C., February 9, 1974.

Remarks at Energy Conference, Washington, D.C., February 11, 1974.

Remarks at Lincoln Memorial, Washington, D.C., February 11, 1974.

Remarks at Cedars of Lebanon Health Care Center, Miami, Florida, February 14, 1974.

Remarks for "Honor America Day," Huntsville, Alabama, February 18, 1974.

Radio address on right of privacy, Washington, D.C., February 23, 1974.

Thirty-sixth News Conference, Washington, D.C., February 25, 1974.

Remarks on Vietnam veterans, Washington, D.C., February 26, 1974.

Remarks to Young Republicans, Washington, D.C., February 28, 1974.

Thirty-seventh News Conference, Washington, D.C., March 6, 1974.

Radio address on campaign reform, Washington, D.C., March 8, 1974.

Radio address on the Bicentennial, Key Biscayne, Florida, March 10, 1974.

Remarks to Veterans of Foreign Wars, Washington, D.C., March 12, 1974.

Remarks to Executives' Club, Chicago, Illinois, March 15, 1974.

Remarks at Grand Ole Opry, Nashville, Tennessee, March 16, 1974.

Remarks at Johnson Space Center, Houston, Texas, March 20, 1974.

Radio address on education, Camp David, Maryland, March 23, 1974.

Speech to Agricultural Editors, Washington, D.C., March 26, 1974.

Remarks at GOP fundraiser, Washington, D.C., March 27, 1974.

Remarks honoring Vietnam veterans, Washington, D.C., March 29, 1974.

Radio address on veterans' affairs, Key Biscayne, Florida, March 31, 1974.

Campaign remarks in four cities, Michigan, April 10, 1974.

Remarks to Daughters of the American Revolution, Washington, D.C., April 18, 1974.

Remarks to Economic Council, Jackson, Mississippi, April 25, 1974.

Address to the Nation about subpoena for presidential tape recordings, Washington, D.C., April 29, 1974.

Remarks to U.S. Chamber of Commerce, Washington, D.C., April 30, 1974.

Remarks at state Republican rally, Phoenix, Arizona, May 3, 1974.

Commencement Address at Oklahoma State University, Stillwater, Oklahoma, May 11, 1974.

Radio address on health insurance, Key Biscayne, Florida, May 20, 1974.

Radio address on the economy, Key Biscayne, Florida, May 25, 1974.

Radio address on Memorial Day, Key Biscayne, Florida, May 27, 1974.

Commencement Address at the U.S. Naval Academy, Annapolis, Maryland, June 5, 1974.

Remarks to Committee for Fairness to the President, Washington, D.C., June 9, 1974.

Remarks on signing statement of cooperation, Cairo, Egypt, June 14, 1974.

Televised address to people of the Soviet Union, Moscow, USSR, July 2, 1974.

Address to the Nation on returning from the Soviet Union, Loring Air Force Base, Maine, July 3, 1974.

Remarks at dinner, honoring the president, Bel Air, California, July 25, 1974.

Address to the Nation announcing resignation, Washington, D.C., August 8, 1974.

Remarks on departure from the White House, Washington, D.C., August 9, 1974.

Televised interviews with David Frost, San Clemente, California, May 4, 12, 19, 25, and September 8, 1977.

Speech at GOP fundraiser, Corona Del Mar, California, October 7, 1977.

Remarks at returned POWs reunion, San Clemente, California, May 27, 1978.

Address dedicating recreation complex, Hyden, Kentucky, July 2, 1978.

Televised interview with Sam Yorty criticizing Carter policies, Los Angeles, California, August 18, 1978.

Remarks at Republican fundraiser, San Clemente, California, August 27, 1978.

Veterans Day speech, Biloxi, Mississippi, November 11, 1978.

Televised call-in interview show, Paris, France, November 28, 1978.

Speech to Oxford Union Debate Society on changing world, Oxford, England, November 30, 1978.

Remarks at party for astronauts, San Clemente, California, July 15, 1979.

Televised interview with Jerry Dunphy on foreign policy, Los Angeles, California, November 26, 1979.

Televised interview on Iranian hostages, Paris, France, April 21, 1980.

Televised interview with Barbara Walters on "20-20," New York City, May 10, 1980.

Five-part televised interview on "Today" show, New York City, September 8-12, 1980.

Courtroom testimony in FBI break-in case, Washington, D.C., October 29, 1980.

Speech at GOP fundraiser, Columbus, Ohio, February, 18, 1981.

Speech at Republican fundraiser, Seattle, Washington, May 10, 1981.

Remarks at Republican fundraiser, New York City, June 15, 1981.

Speech at Republican fundraiser, Anaheim, California, April 21, 1982.

Televised interviews with Jerry Dunphy, Los Angeles, California, November 3-7, 1982.

Remarks at reunion of 1972 staff, Washington, D.C., November 6, 1982.

Remarks honoring Hyman Rickover, Washington, D.C., February 28, 1983.

Speech to Council on U.S.-China Trade, Washington, D.C., June 1, 1983.

Remarks to Kissinger Commission on Latin American policy, Washington, D.C., September 28, 1983.

Radio interview: ABC Talk Radio, New York City, February 3, 1984.

Speech to Economics Club: USSR, New York City, March 14, 1984.

Taped televised interviews with Frank Gannon on "60 Minutes" and "The American Parade," New York City, April 8, 10, 15, 1984.

Speech to American Society of Newspaper Editors on the USSR, Washington, D.C., May 9, 1984.

Speech at Chapman College on the Soviet Union, Orange, California, May 15, 1984.

Brief remarks at Smithsonian on twentieth anniversary of "kitchen debate" with Khrushchev, Washington, D.C., July 25, 1984.

Speech at University of International Business and Economics, Beijing, China, September 4, 1985.

Remarks at National Black Republicans award dinner, New York City, October 17, 1985.

Remarks to "Pumpkin Papers Irregulars," New York City, October 31, 1985.

Address to World Affairs Council, Los Angeles, California, March 6, 1986.

Speech to Association of Community Cancer Centers, Washington, D.C., April 5, 1986.

Speech to American Newspaper Publishers Association on foreign policy, San Francisco, California, April 21, 1986.

Remarks at GOP fundraiser, Newport Beach, California, April 22, 1986.

Remarks to Goodwill Games athletes, Moscow, USSR, July 13, 1986.

Speech to Republican Governors' Conference on foreign policy, Parsippany, New Jersey, December 9, 1986.

Speech accepting membership in the French Academy of Fine Arts, Paris, France, May 20, 1987.

Televised interview: "Meet the Press," Washington, D.C., April 10, 1988.

Speech to Society of Newspaper Editors, Washington, D.C., April 15, 1988.

Remarks at drug rehabilitation center, Bethel, New York, October 19, 1988.

Testimony to Senate Select Committee on Indian Affairs: Treaty Obligations, Washington, D.C., January 30, 1989.

# Bibliography

The bibliography is divided into four sections: (1) Library holdings and special collections; (2) Books and articles written by Nixon; (3) Annotated studies of Nixon's speaking; (4) Biographies and case studies of Nixon

## Library and Special Collections

Richard M. Nixon: Pre-presidential Papers. National Archives and Record Service, Laguna Niguel, California.
> The collection contains more than 840 boxes of general correspondence from Nixon's early political career to 1966. Additional files chronicle Nixon's personal appearances and trips to foreign countries. Some audio tapes, especially from the 1964 campaign, are available. The correspondence files have an alphabetical directory.

Richard M. Nixon: Presidential Papers and Tapes. National Archives. Washington, D.C.
> Congress gave custody of all Nixon's presidential papers to the National Archives. Thus far 5 million of the 40 million pages accumulated by Nixon and his staff have been made available to the public. Eventually visitors will be able to listen to 4000 hours of Nixon's presidential conversations preserved on 880 tapes.

Richard M. Nixon Collection. Wardman Library, Whittier College, Whittier, California.
> Nixon's *alma mater* houses a significant collection of books and typescripts about Nixon, as well as the 41 boxes of letters and telegrams sent to the Republican National Committee after the "Checkers" speech. A large clipping file awaits cataloging. The Whittier College newspaper, *Quaker Campus*, and the yearbook, *Acropolis*, from Nixon's days as a student are available.

Richard M. Nixon Project. Oral History Program. California State University, Fullerton, Fullerton, California.
> More than 190 interviews with family, friends, and acquaintances of Richard and Pat Nixon were recorded between 1969 and 1977. Those interviewed knew the Nixons in Southern California before Nixon entered politics. A complete list of interviews and the materials discussed can be found in Shirley E. Stephenson, *Oral History Collection: CSU Fullerton* (Fullerton, CA: CSU, Fullerton, 1985). A small, but useful, clipping collection and a few taped speeches are also housed in the CSU, Fullerton Library.

Earl Warren Oral History Project. Bancroft Library, University of California, Berkeley.
> This collection includes "Richard M. Nixon in the Warren Era," a series of five interviews with leaders of Nixon's campaigns between 1946 and 1968. Amelia Fry interviewed Earl Adams, Ray Crocker, Roy Day, John W. Dinkelspiel, and Frank Jorgensen in 1975.

Richard M. Nixon Presidential Library, Yorba Linda, California.
> The $25 million library is under construction next to the house in which Nixon was born. Because of Congressional action, the library will probably never house his presidential papers, but it is likely that the pre-presidential papers, his White House diaries, and personal papers since he left office will be kept here.

Miscellaneous Special Collections.
> Texts of many of Nixon's important speeches can be found in the bimonthly *Vital Speeches* or in the annual *Representative American Speeches* (New York: H. W. Wilson). All of his presidential addresses are reported in the *Weekly Compliation of Presidential Documents* and in *Public Papers of the Presidents: Richard Nixon* (6 volumes). A video tape of Nixon's "Checkers" speech is in Volume I and his resignation speech in Volume III of *Great Speeches for Criticism & Evaluation* (Greenwood, IN: Educational Video Group, 1987). Video tapes of the Kennedy-Nixon Debates can be obtained from the John F. Kennedy Library, Boston, Massachusetts. The Television News Archive of Vanderbilt University, Nashville, Tennessee, offers video tapes of Nixon's televised presidential addresses.

**The Writings of Richard Nixon**

"Asia After Vietnam." *Foreign Affairs* 46(October 1967): 111-125.
"Cuba, Castro, and John F. Kennedy." *Reader's Digest* 85(November 1964): 281-284+.
"Four Academic Freedoms." *Saturday Review* 49(August 27, 1966): 12-13+.
*Four Great Americans: Tributes Delivered by President Richard Nixon.* Garden City, NY: Doubleday, 1973.

"The Greater Menace." *Educational Record* 39(January 1958): 15-19.

"Hard-Headed Detente." *New York Times,* August 18, 1982, p. A21.

"Khruschev's Hidden Weaknesses." *Saturday Evening Post,* October 12, 1963, pp. 23-29.

*Leaders.* New York: Warner Books, 1982.

"The Lessons of the Alger Hiss Case." *Human Events* 46(March 15, 1986): 10-12.

"Let's Give Business a Square Deal." *Nation's Business* 54(April 1966): 46-47+.

"Memo to President Bush: How to Use TV—and Keep from Being Abused by It." *TV Guide* 37(January 14, 1989): 26-30.

"Needed in Vietnam: The Will to Win." *Reader's Digest* 85(August 1964): 37-43.

*A New Road for America: Major Policy Statements March 1970 to October 1971.* Garden City, NY: Doubleday, 1972.

*1999: Victory Without War.* New York: Simon and Schuster, 1988.

*No More Vietnams.* New York: Arbor House, 1985.

"On Economic Power." *New York Times,* August 19, 1982, p. A27.

"Plea for an Anti-Communist Faith." *Saturday Review* 35(March 24, 1952): 12-13.

*Public Papers of the Presidents of the United States, Richard M. Nixon.* 6 volumes. Washington, DC: Government Printing Office, 1971-1975.

*Real Peace.* Boston: Little, Brown, 1984.

*The Real War.* New York: Warner Books, 1980.

*RN: The Memoirs of Richard Nixon.* New York: Grosset & Dunlap, 1978.

*Setting the Course, the First Year: Major Policy Statements by President Richard Nixon.* New York: Funk & Wagnalls, 1970.

*Six Crises.* New York: Doubleday, 1962.

"The Strange Case of Alger Hiss." *Reader's Digest* 81(November 1962): 88-93+.

"Superpower Summitry." *Foreign Affairs* 65(Fall 1985): 1-11.

"Unforgettable John Foster Dulles." *Reader's Digest* 91(July 1967): 99-104.

"What Has Happened to America?" *Reader's Digest* 91(October 1967): 49-54.

*The White House Transcripts.* New York: Viking Press, 1974.

"Why Not Negotiate in Vietnam?" *Reader's Digest* 87(December 1965): 49-54.

## Communication studies

Baskerville, Barnet. "The Illusion of Proof." *Western Speech* 25(Fall 1961): 236-242.

Baskerville analyzed the 1952 fund speech to determine the probative value of the proof offered by Nixon for his innocence. Two-thirds of the speech had nothing to do with the charges against Nixon, but most listeners agreed that Nixon had vindicated himself.  The public accepted the illusion of proof for the real thing.

Baskerville, Barnet.  "The New Nixon" in Donald C. Bryant (ed), "Rhetoric and the Campaign of 1956." *Quarterly Journal of Speech* 43(February 1957): 38-43.
Nixon's rhetoric in the 1956 campaign revealed a conscious attempt to change his image.  Baskerville found much less innuendo in Nixon's speeches and milder criticism of his opponents.  Nixon proved to be a "distinct asset" to Eisenhower's campaign, but he engaged in "the rhetoric of plausibility," showing more concern for the attractiveness of his comments than for their truthfulness.

Baskerville, Barnet.  "The Nixon Affair" in Frederick W. Haberman (ed.), "The Election of 1952: A Symposium." *Quarterly Journal of Speech* 38(December 1952): 397-414.
The persuasive appeal of Nixon's fund speech was in its "outward reasonableness, its apparent frank facing of issues and fearless presentation of all facts despite personal embarassment."  The speech was a "study in appearances as opposed to realities."  Both political parties subordinated ethical considerations to political expediency.

Baudhuin, E. Scott.  "From Campaign to Watergate: Nixon's Communication Image." *Western Speech* 38(Summer 1974): 182-189.
Nixon's "credibility image" during the Watergate affair was compared to what had previously been observed during the 1972 presidential election.  Baudhuin wished to determine whether credibility components remained invariant.  The four basic factors of Nixon's image—"character," "authoritativeness," "interpersonal attractiveness," and "dynamism"—remained comparable with the earlier study.  On the "character" or "trustworthiness" dimension, however, Nixon suffered a considerable drop in evaluation.

Benoit, William L.  "Richard M. Nixon's Rhetorical Strategies in his Public Statements on Watergate." *Southern Speech Communication Journal* 47(Winter 1982): 192-211.
Benoit identified nine rhetorical strategies used by Nixon during the Watergate crisis and traced their development.  He found them unpersuasive, often inconsistent, and sometimes unethical.  Benoit concluded that Nixon's strategies were "ineffective in turning the tide of public opinion."

Brock, Bernard and James F. Klumpp.  "Richard Nixon's Anti-Impeachment Campaign: America's Paradise Lost." *Exetasis* 1(May 1, 1974): 1-16.
The authors analyzed Nixon's April 29, 1974, address on Watergate.  They found that by juxtaposing his credibility to that of John Dean, Nixon took a great risk.  They also evaluated some intrinsic characteristics of the speech, noting that some of Nixon's strategies were contradictory.  Nixon did not

artistically apply principles based on the theories of rhetorical situation, quest story, or dramatism.

Brummett, Barry. "Presidential Substance: The Address of August 15, 1973." *Western Speech* 39(Fall 1975): 249-259.

Brummett applied Kenneth Burke's concepts of identification and substance to Nixon's televised address of August 15, 1973. By defining his motivations as contextual, Nixon was unable to foster identification with the public. In his attempt to surmount his association with disreputable colleagues and to justify his actions based on executive privilege, Nixon discouraged identification with the man in the office.

Campbell, Karlyn K. "An Exercise in the Rhetoric of Mythical America" in Campbell, *Critiques of Contemporary Rhetoric* (Belmont, CA: Wadsworth, 1972): 50-57.

Campbell analyzed Nixon's November 3, 1969, speech using four criteria she found in the speech itself: truth, credibility, unity, and ethical principles. She concluded that the president failed to meet his own criteria and that his speech perpetuated myths about America's role in the world.

Carpenter, Ronald H. and Robert V. Seltzer. "Nixon, *Patton*, and a Silent Majority Sentiment about the Viet Nam War: The Cinematophic Bases of a Rhetorical Stance." *Central States Speech Journal* 25(Summer 1974): 105-110.

Nixon may have been influenced by his viewing of the movie *Patton* to undertake the Cambodian incursion. His Pattonesque statement that he would not accept America's first military defeat may have been influential in shaping a favorable public reaction to his policy.

Chapel, Gage William. "Speechwriting in the Nixon Administration." *Journal of Communication* 26(Spring 1976): 65-72.

Chapel interviewed presidential speechwriter Aram Bakshian who revealed how the writing staff (usually seven or eight people) was organized and where the ideas for speeches originated. Nixon's strengths as well as his limitations as a speaker were noted. Bakshian explained the difference between three types of writing—the formal manuscript speech, "remarks," and "talking points."

Church, Russell T. "President Richard M. Nixon's Crisis Rhetoric, 1969-1972." Dissertation. Temple University, 1977.

Church compared three of Nixon's speeches delivered in crisis situations with speeches delivered on noncrisis occasions. Among his findings were: (1) Nixon's crisis speeches were more concretely detailed than his noncrisis efforts; (2) Nixon stressed threats to life and values in his crisis efforts; (3) Nixon was inconsistent in his assumption of personal responsibility. Nixon's tone was often belligerent and inflammatory.

Condit, Celeste Michelle. "Richard Milhous Nixon" in Bernard K. Duffy and Halbert Ryan (eds.), *American Orators of the*

*Twentieth Century: Critical Studies and Sources.* Westport, CT: Greenwood Press, 1987.

Condit offered an overview of Nixon as a political persuader. He "was one of the most skillful of America's modern-day political rhetors." Selected critical studies were listed and a short chronology of his major speeches was provided.

Cooper, Martha. "Ethos, a Cloth Coat and a Cocker Spaniel" in Lloyd Rohler and Roger Cook (eds.), *Great Speeches for Criticism & Analysis.* Greenwood, IN: Alistair Press, 1988.

The "Checkers" speech was an example of the skillful construction of ethos, the personal character of the speaker. Nixon successfully presented an image of himself as a man of good sense, good character, and good will. In doing so he successfully persuaded three audiences, the public at large, Eisenhower and his advisors, and the press.

Cooper, Martha. "Rhetorical Criticism and Foucault's Philosophy of Discursive Events." *Central States Speech Journal* 39(Spring 1988): 1-17.

By first reviewing his philosophy of "incorporeal materialism" and by contrasting his view with those of other rhetoricians, Cooper examined Foucault's notion of discursive events. Foucault's analysis focused on "what knowledge, power, or ethical posture is created when someone apologizes." Cooper offered Nixon's "Checkers" speech to illustrate such an analysis.

Cushman, Donald P. "A Comparative Study of President Truman's and President Nixon's Justification for Committing Troops to Combat in Korea and Cambodia." Dissertation. University of Wisconsin-Madison.

Cushman examined the commonalities and differences in Truman's and Nixon's transformation of their reasons for acting into public justifications for sending troops into combat. Truman's justification was direct; Nixon's was not. Truman revealed the reasons for his decision; Nixon did not.

Fisher, Walter R. "Reaffirmation and Subversion of the American Dream." *Quarterly Journal of Speech.* 59(April 1973): 160-167.

The 1972 presidential election was a contest between rival definitions of the American Dream. Nixon personified the materialistic myth that promises "if one employs one's energies and talents to the fullest, one will reap the rewards of status, wealth, and power." McGovern personified the moralistic myth that "endeavors to invest all public institutions with guarantees that all men will be treated equally and . . . serves to inspire cooperative efforts to benefit those who are less fortunate than others." Fisher examined the symbolic message of the election and its foreshadowing of the future.

Freeman, Douglas N. "Freedom of Speech Within the Nixon Administration." *Communication Quarterly* 24(Winter 1976): 3-10.

Domestic and foreign policy decisionmaking were "impaired because dissent within the governmental bureaucracy was suppressed." During the Nixon administration, decisions were made by "a handful of key advisors without Congressional consultation or consideration of alternative points of view." The resignations of Walter Hinkel and Daniel Moynihan and the firing of Archibald Cox were examples of how dissenters were treated in the Nixon administration.

Freeman, William. " 'Maudlin Friday' Revisited: Nixon's Farewell Address to His Staff, August 9, 1974." *Exetasis* 1(August 1974): 13-21.

Nixon's farewell was replete with personal references to the past because Nixon was attempting to come to grips with a personal disaster that was becoming clear to him for the first time. Similar recollections were used by Nixon at times when he faced political defeat—the presidential elections of 1960 and 1968. Unaccustomed to revealing himself in public, Nixon attempted to "wrap himself in the security of the already experienced past."

Gibson, James W. and Patricia K. Felkins. "A Nixon Lexicon." *Western Speech* 38(Summer 1974): 190-198.

The authors examined the language used by Nixon in the "Checkers" speech and in two speeches on Watergate to determine the general nature of his language and to see if personal characteristics influenced his language. The three speeches were compared on seven dimensions—difficulty, sensitivity, knowledge, legality, virtue, affiliation, and power. A varimax factor rotation yielded two clusters, "strength" and "consciousness." Factor one accounted for 76 percent of the variance and factor two for 24 percent, confirming what other writers have said about these three speeches.

Gonchar, Ruth M. and Dan F. Hahn. "The Rhetorical Predictability of Richard M. Nixon." *Today's Speech* 19(Fall 1971): 3-13

To a great extent, Nixon's rhetoric was predictable because he "personalized" the presidency and because of his concepts of leadership. Nixon justified the rightness of his actions by suggesting that they were important, difficult, selfless, and/or had good results. He justified his own role as president by demonstrating that he was fulfilling the requirements of his office. When criticized, Nixon vindicated his position by contending that there were no errors in his policies, or that the blame lay elsewhere. Nixon's rhetoric was not unique, but it was predictable.

Gregg, Richard B. and Gerard Hauser. "Richard Nixon's April 30, 1970 Address on Cambodia: The 'Ceremony' of Confrontation." *Speech Monographs* 40(April 1973): 167-181.

The authors found, based on a content analysis, that in the last third of Nixon's speech, his insistence that America should be judged on its willingness to expend its power was a reflection of

the potlatch ceremony of the Kwakiutl Indians.  From this
perspective they discovered in the speech "the kind of
transitional thinking that is part of the search for new schemes
and behavior in the world of nuclear stalemate."

Hahn, Dan F. and Ruth M. Gonchar.  "The Watergate Strategies of
Richard Nixon During the 1972 Campaign."  *The
Communicator* 10(Spring 1980): 64-75.
Nixon used no new rhetorical strategies to deal with the
Watergate incident during the presidential campaign.  He
simply denied the facts and the signifigance of the facts.  At the
same time he issued a number of anti-McGovern ads,
maximizing negative information about his opponent.  The
authors concluded that "crises will not be perceived as crises if
handled by non-crisis rhetoric."

Hahn, Dan F. and Ruth M.Gonchar.  "Richard Nixon and
Presidential Mythology." *Journal of Applied Communication
Research* 1(Winter-Spring 1973): 25-48.
Nixon's presidential rhetoric utilized three myths: "(1) all
problems are caused by outgroups (the emergent enemy); (2)
our leaders are benevolent heroes who will lead us out of
danger (personal involvement, the lone struggle, effort); and (3)
the function of the citizen is to sacrifice and work hard to do the
bidding of the leaders (appeal to faith, effort)."  Nixon
successfully used the myths to identify problems, propose
solutions, and to enhance himself.

Harrell, Jackson, B.L. Ware and Wil A. Linkugel.  "Failure of
Apology in American Politics:  Nixon on Watergate." *Speech
Monographs* 42(November 1975): 245-261.
Nixon's rhetorical efforts concerning Watergate in 1973 failed.
His enormous backlog of support, as measured by Gallup polls,
dissipated in the course of one year.  He "consistently failed to
project the needed image of openness, honesty, and
forthrightness."  His appeals to national security and executive
privilege proved unpopular.  His assertions of innocence
needed support that he could not offer.

Harris, Barbara Ann.  "The Inaugural of Richard Milhous Nixon: A
Reply to Robert L. Scott." *Western Speech* 34 (Summer 1970):
231-234.
Harris claimed that Robert Scott failed to restrict himself to
intrinsic factors of analysis, as he had promised, in an earlier
essay.  Since he looked at some extrinsic factors, he should
have examined all the significant ones.  His assertion that
Nixon was striving for eloquence but failed to achieve it
assumed that eloquence was possible.  Harris found in the
Inaugural Address a continuation of the rhetorical techniques
used by Nixon in his presidential campaign.

Hart, Roderick P.  "Absolutism and Situation:  Prolegomena to a
Rhetorical Biography of Richard M. Nixon." *Communication
Monographs* 43(August 1976): 204-228.

Hart noted "how Richard Nixon modulated the firmness with which he made his oral, public statements, how such adaptations may reflect the particular cast of his public personality, and how his use of verbal absolutism may illuminate [his] psychological propensities." Using a specially devised test of verbal absolutism on seventy-nine speeches on various topics to different types of audiences, Hart concluded that Nixon was peculiarly responsive to the rhetorical situations he faced during his public career: "at least as far as verbal absolutism is concerned, Nixon was a textbook persuader—certain when hosting friendly elements, equivocal otherwise."

Hart, Roderick P. *Verbal Style and the Presidency: A Computer-Based Analysis*. Orlando, FL: Academic Press, 1984.

Hart applied computer based language analysis to 38 of Nixon's presidential speeches and compared the results to what he had learned about other presidents and other presidential candidates. Nixon's speeches were high in realism and activity, but lacked complexity and variety. Nixon's use of human interest and symbolism were the highest of any president studied. Hart suggested that for Nixon public speaking was a performance: "It was to be planned for, practiced, monitored, and then evaluated."

Highlander, John P. and Lloyd Watkins. "A Closer Look at the Great Debates." *Western Speech* 26(Winter 1962): 39-48.

Six major issues emerged during the Kennedy-Nixon debates: (1) American prestige abroad; (2) The extent of government intervention in the economy; (3) The cost of government programs; (4) Medical care for the aged; (5) Quemoy and Matsu; and (6) Cuba. The authors concluded that Nixon should have made a greater effort to capture liberal voters, that each of the candidates adequately represented his political party, that Kennedy's vigorous delivery was more attention-getting than Nixon's more conversational tone, that the time limits did not allow for analysis of issues, and that Kennedy gained support as the result of his showing in the first debate.

Hill, Forbes. "Conventional Wisdom—Traditional Form—The President's Message of November 3, 1969." *Quarterly Journal of Speech* 58(December 1972): 373-386.

Hill offered a strict neo-Aristotelian analysis of Nixon's speech to discover if Nixon used the best possible means of gaining a favorable decision from a specified group of auditors in a specific situation. He concluded that Nixon was a "superior technician" who chose those values and premises that would create a psychological climate in his audience favorable to his policy of Vietnamization.

Hillbruner, Anthony. "Archetype and Signature: Nixon and the 1973 Inaugural." *Central States Speech Journal* 25(Fall 1974): 169-181.

Nixon's Inaugural was the result of a great deal of hard work and study. His speech "was effective, even admirable in its use of archetype and enthymematic suggestion." The weakness of the speech was in its call for personal rather than social responsibility. The author predicted that future presidents will study Nixon's effort for ideas on "the efficacious use of rhetorical means to complement their political ends."

Hillbruner, Anthony. "Rhetoric and Politics: The Making of the President, 1960." *Western Speech* 29(Spring 1965): 91-102.
Hillbruner examined Theodore White's *The Making of the President, 1960* as a work of rhetorical analysis and criticism. White seemed to condemn Nixon unduly while going overboard in his praise of Kennedy. Nevertheless, Hillbruner praised White's delineation of the speechmaking background and his understanding of the particular audiences each candidate was addressing.

Jablonski, Carol J. "Richard Nixon's Irish Wake: A Case of Generic Transference." *Central States Speech Journal* 30(Summer 1979): 164-173.
By turning his announcement of Gerald Ford as the vice presidential designate into a ceremonial occasion, Nixon was able "to reassert his prestige as President in a non-apologetic fashion." Nixon's tactic allowed him to disassociate himself from Agnew's disgrace while responding to the crisis it caused. Jablonski calls Nixon's speech an example of "generic transference," the superimposing of an established rhetorical form onto an unprecedented rhetorical situation.

Jampol, Kenneth. "I Shall Resign the Presidency." *Exetasis* 1(August 1974): 3-11.
Nixon's resignation speech failed on most counts. Nixon did not satisfy the expectations of Congress and the public that he would provide a complete accounting of his role in Watergate. He did not admit guilt to the indictments of the House Judiciary Committee. He did not unite the country. His speech was a "self-serving and obfuscating swan song."

Kane, Peter E. "Evaluating the 'Great Debates' " *Western Speech* 30(Spring 1966): 89-96.
Network news broadcasters failed to give more than passing coverage to the debates. The four joint appearances were no more important than other campaign appearances by the candidates. Newspaper coverage of the debates, however, was significantly greater than for other campaign activities. Although James Michener and Theodore White have suggested the debates were a major factor in determining the winner of the election, surveys taken immediately after the debates indicated that their effect on the results was "negligible."

Katula, Richard A. "The Apology of Richard M. Nixon." *Today's Speech* 23(Fall 1975): 1-5.

Katula's analysis of Nixon's August 8, 1974, speech concluded that the speech failed because Nixon did not address the questions that forced the speech. The "strategies of denial of content and transcendence to a larger context were largely unsuccessful in securing closure with his audience."

Kaufer, David S. "The Ironist and Hypocrite as Presidential Symbols: A Nixon-Kennedy Analog." *Communication Quarterly* 27(Fall 1979): 20-26.
Kaufer contrasted the presidential images of Nixon and Kennedy. Nixon, he argued, exemplified a hypocritical power symbol and Kennedy an ironic one. In a democracy, powerholders must take a detached perspective toward their power. Kaufer suggested that "those who resort to hypocrisy to maintain their station betray . . . their lack of detachment and hence their unfitness to rule."

Keele, Gary D. "An Examination of Image in Presidential Campaigning: The Humphrey-Nixon Campaign of 1968." Dissertation. University of Southern California, 1977.
Nixon and Humphrey communicated substantially different images in the areas of economic affairs, crime and disorder, and race relations. In each of these areas Nixon's image corresponded more closely to the position held by the voters. Few differences were found in the images of the candidates concerning Vietnam or other areas of foreign policy.

King, Andrew A. and Floyd Douglas Anderson. "Nixon, Agnew and the 'Silent Majority': A Case Study in the Rhetoric of Polarization." *Western Speech* 35(Fall 1971): 243-255.
The authors presented an analysis of the rhetorical strategies that Nixon used in 1969 and 1970 to create, broaden, and mobilize his constituency and showed how these strategies polarized the country. Nixon "manufactured a constituency" that he labelled the "Silent Majority" by uniting a number of diverse groups against a common foe. Nixon's strategy had only "limited success."

King, Robert L. "Transforming Scandal into Tragedy: A Rhetoric of Political Apology." Quarterly Journal of Speech 71(August 1985): 289-301.
King argued that "*tragedy* as a generic term has acquired a cluster of meaning in the popular imagination" and that some political apologists have improperly applied these meanings to themselves. Comments about Nixon's resignation speech and Edward Kennedy's speech on Chappaquiddick were seen as examples of the term's misuse because the speakers avoided the moral implications of true tragedy.

Larson, Barbara A. "Criticism and the Campaign Concept of Persuasion: A Case Study Analysis of Method" *Central States Speech Journal* 24(Spring 1973): 52-59.
Larson analyzed Nixon's 1972 State of the Union Address. She noted a duality of function and purpose in the address, the

external factors influencing the speech, and the specific context in which the president responded. The "defensive-refutative" nature of the speech previewed Nixon's campaign strategy and reaffirmed the scope and value of the programs he supported.

Larson, Charles U. (ed.). "A Pentadic Analysis of Richard Nixon and Watergate." *Speaker and Gavel* 15(Fall 1977): 1-15.
Five short essays examined Nixon's Watergate speeches through different elements of Kenneth Burke's Pentad. Richard Crable looked at scene; Bernard Brock at act: David Ling at agent; Larson himself at agency; and Ruth Gonchar at purpose. Although the critics sometimes disagreed, the symposium helped explain the motives of the major Watergate figures.

Linkugel, Wil A. and Dixie Lee Cody. "Nixon, McGovern, and the Female Electorate." *Today's Speech* 21(Fall1973): 25-32.
The authors examined how Nixon and McGovern adapted their 1972 presidential campaign rhetoric toward women's issues. Nixon stood on his record and attempted to show McGovern as a "radical challenger" to basic American institutions. McGovern's attempt to gain feminist support only intensified his image as a dissident candidate.

Litfin, A. Duane. "Network Responses to a Presidential Address." *Western Speech* 36(Winter 1972): 24-30.
Litfin found that the network analyses of Nixon's November 3, 1969, address were "relatively useful and unbiased coverage of the event." He noted, however, that the programs would have been more valuable to the public had the participants limited their use of opinion and provided more facts. Too much speculation was offered.

McGuckin, Henry E. "A Value Analysis of Richard Nixon's 1952 Campaign-Fund Speech." *Southern Speech Journal* 33(Summer 1968): 259-269.
Offering historical and experimental evidence, McGuckin concluded that Nixon was "reasonably successful" in persuading a significant portion of his audience. Nixon enhanced his ethos and moved his audience by identifying with basic American cultural values, such as puritan morality, equality, patriotism, and courage.

Miller, N. Edd (ed.). "Presidential Campaign 1960: A Symposium, Part II." *Quarterly Journal of Speech* 46(December 1960): 355-364. The Nixon campaign concentrated on three issues: foreign policy, American prestige abroad, and the relative experience of the candidates. A fourth issue, Kennedy's religion, was not formally discussed but held public attention. Nixon formulated a basic campaign speech that was adapted to local conditions. This technique proved highly effective on the stump, but Nixon was less effective in the televised debates whose format imposed a straight jacket on discussion of the issues.

Newman, Robert P. "Under the Veneer: Nixon's Vietnam Speech of November 3, 1969." *Quarterly Journal of Speech* 56(April 1970): 169-178.

Neither Nixon's rhetorical strategies nor his substantive arguments were sound. Nixon's speech was "shoddy rhetoric" pleasing only to "white, nonurban, uptight voters." Nevertheless a Gallup telephone poll taken immediately after the speech found 77 percent approving the speech and Nixon's overall performance rating rose dramatically after the speech.

Padrow, Ben and Bruce Richards. "Richard Nixon . . . His Speech Preparation." *Today's Speech* 7(November 1959): 11-12.

The authors questioned Vice-President Nixon about his speech-making practices. They asked him about his background, his preparation, delivery techniques, and how he analyzed audiences. Nixon's responses were quoted verbatim and the authors found them to be "a strange admixture of sureness and unsureness."

Porter, Laurinda W. "The White House Transcripts: Group Fantasy Events Concerning the Mass Media." *Central States Speech Journal* 27 (Winter 1976): 272-279.

Through content analysis, Porter found four important fantasy themes about the media emerging in the White House Transcripts. Members of the White House staff invented fantasies about how to control Nixon's image in the press, the reality of their own actions, how to orchestrate the channel choice and timing of their messages, and relations with individual members of the news-gathering institutions. Their group norm "of ignoring the criticism of their enemies" prevented them from choosing the best alternatives for action.

Rosenfield, L.W. "A Case Study in Speech Criticism: The Nixon-Truman Analog." *Speech Monographs* 35(November 1968): 435-450.

Rosenfield compared the "Checkers" speech to a speech given by Truman defending his handling of the Harry Dexter White case. He found that the most curious shortcoming of Nixon's speech, when compared to Truman's, was its endurance in the public mind. Nixon's speech "demolished his opposition's case, but injured his standing as a public man." Traces of Nixon's speech continued to plague him long after the speech was delivered.

Rosenfield, Lawrence W. "August 9, 1974: The Victimage of Richard Nixon." *Communication Quarterly* 24(Fall 1976): 19-23.

Using blunt and derogatory language, Rosenfield described Nixon's speech to his staff on leaving the White House as "revealingly banal." He argued that Nixon failed to evoke an image of heroism or a mood of tragic pity.

Ryan, Halford R.  "Senator Richard M. Nixon's Apology for the 'Fund' " in Ryan (ed.), *Oratorical Encounters*. New York: Greenwood Press, 1988: 99-120.

> Ryan found that the fund speech contained "the artful application of a number of persuasive devices." Relying on a classical pattern of organization, Nixon made his speech "an offensive defense."  Nixon's delivery of the speech was "extraordinarily effective" and his diction suggested a "guileless stylist."  Newspaper reaction to the speech was mixed, with some writers feeling that the question of the fund's propriety had not been answered.

Samovar, Larry A.  "Ambiguity and Unequivocation in the Kennedy-Nixon Television Debates."  *Quarterly Journal of Speech* 48(October 1962): 277-279.

> Ambiguity was present in the four Kennedy-Nixon debates. Ambiguous passages dealt with farm policy, civil rights, Quemoy and Matsu, and American prestige abroad. Unequivocal pasages concerned Berlin, Cuba, and national prestige.  Voters tended to read meaning into passages presented by a favored source and to report lack of meaning in passages from an unfavored one.

Samovar, Larry A.  "Ambiguity and Unequivocation in the Kennedy-Nixon Television Debates: A Rhetorical Analysis."  *Western Speech* 29(Fall 1963): 211-218.

> Samovar found considerable ambiguity in the debates, on topics such as civil rights, Quemoy and Matsu, American prestige, and foreign policy.  Ambiguity arose from "weaving rebuttal into your own policy statement, jargon, emotional language, a lack of development, weak or no transitions, unanswered rhetorical questions, and contradictory statements."  Direct statements, redundancy, and evidence aided clarity.

Scott, Robert L. "Response to Barbara Ann Harris." *Western Speech* 34(Summer 1970): 235-236.

> Scott admitted that he was unable to remain strictly within his intrinsic criteria of Nixon's 1968 Inaugural Address in his earlier essay, but argued that useful insight was obtained. Nixon sensed a demand for eloquence and Scott believed that a close listening to the delivery of the speech demonstrates Nixon's attempt to attain eloquence.

Scott, Robert L.  "Rhetoric that Postures: An Intrinsic Reading of Richard M. Nixon's Inaugural Address." *Western Speech* 34 (Winter 1970): 46-52.

> Based on criteria for evaluation inferred from the speech itself, Scott argued that Nixon's 1968 Inaugural Address was a "failure."  This "failure was compounded of euphemism and fundamental satisfaction with things as they are."

Smith, Craig Allen. "President Richard M. Nixon and the Watergate Scandal" in Halford Ryan (ed.), *Oratorical Encounters* (Westport, CT: Greenwood Press, 1988): 201-226.

Nixon's Watergate defenses illustrated the danger of redefining charges and narrowing the critical focus.  When Nixon accepted nominal responsibility for his associates and promised to conduct a complete investigation, he unnecessarily implicated himself in the coverup.   His April 30 address brought him "personally into the Watergate affair, raised doubts about his early denials, stripped him of his top aides . . . and limited the basis for future challenges to the new attorney general."   Smith concluded: "It is difficult to imagine a less productive speech."

Smith, Craig R. "Richard Nixon's 1968 Acceptance Speech as a Model of Dual Audience Adaptation." *Today's Speech* 19(Fall 1971): 15-22.
Nixon's 1968 acceptance speech was well received by the convention audience of supporters and by the national television audience.  The speech was fashioned on the basis of position papers on what issues were important to Americans and what positions they preferred on these issues.  Nixon allayed hostility by avoiding controversial arguments and by attempting to win over the unconvinced.  Nixon's popularity jumped immediately after the speech.

Stelzner, Herman G.  "The Quest Story and Nixon's November 3, 1969 Address." *Quarterly Journal of Speech* 57(April 1971): 163-172.
Stelzner examined Nixon's speech as a nonliterary version of a quest story, a "search for something the truth or falsity of which is known only upon the conclusion of the search."  He concluded that the speech was not a good quest story: "It is not altogether convincing, there are too many loose ends and too many unanswered questions.  It is peopled by flat characters and its language is dull and unimaginative."

Stupp, Vicki O'Donnell.  "The Debate Techniques of Richard Milhous Nixon From 1947 to 1960." Master's thesis. Pennsylvania State University, 1961.
Stupp's purpose was to describe the debating techniques used by Nixon in speeches taken from sequential stages of his political career.  Nixon used a number of techniques probably learned in his collegiate debating career.   Careful organization, adaptation to opposing arguments, and strong factual support were found. Nixon, however, twisted the words of his opponents and drew false implications about what was said.

Trent, Judith S.   "The New Nixon: A Comparison of the Types of Sentences Used in His 1960 and 1968 Campaigns." *Michigan Speech Association Journal* 6(1971): 12-23.
Compared to his campaign speeches in 1960, Nixon's 1968 speeches "contained more simple sentences and a complete absence of rambling or drifting into compound-complex sentences."  The differences may be explained as a result of a deliberate change in Nixon's method of speech preparation.

The 1968 style showed an "edited" Nixon, a Nixon attempting to be "perfectly clear."

Trent, Judith S. "Richard Nixon's Method of Identification in the Presidential Campaigns of 1960 and 1968: A Content Analysis." *Today's Speech* 19(Fall 1971): 23-30.

Trent compared five of Nixon's manuscript speeches from the 1960 presidential campaign with five speeches from the 1968 campaign to determine any differences in the methods Nixon used to build identification with his audience. She found that "Nixon's use of every form of identification decreased significantly in the 1968 campaign." The seven forms studied were obvious relations, common ground, American values, and the four possible combinations of these factors.

Vancil, David L. and Sue D. Pendell. "The Myth of Viewer-Listener Disagreement in the First Kennedy-Nixon Debate." *Central States Speech Journal* 38(Spring 1987): 16-27.

That Nixon won the first Kennedy-Nixon debate according to those who listened on the radio but lost according to those who saw it on television is a myth. The only empirical study that suggested such a Nixon win on the radio "has serious flaws in every dimension examined."

Vartabedian, Robert A. "A Case Study in Contemporary Apologia: The Self-Defense Rhetoric of Richard Nixon" Dissertation. University of Oklahoma, 1981.

Vartabedian applied the B. L. Ware and Wil Linkugel system of analysis to four Nixon speeches: "Checkers," "A Vietnam Plan," "Cambodia," and the "Watergate Scandal." With the exception of the "Checkers" speech, in which he used denial and differentiation, Nixon relied primarily on differentiation and bolstering for persuasive effect. Nixon bolstered his image by identifying himself with the office of president and contrasted the propriety of his actions with the actions of others. These techniques worked when he was speaking about Vietnam, but they were not successful in the Watergate speech.

Vartabedian, Robert A. "Nixon's Vietnam Rhetoric: A Case Study of Apologia as Generic Paradox." *Southern Speech Communication Journal* 50(Summer 1985): 366-381.

Vartabedian found that Nixon used unexpected apologetic strategies in his Vietnam addresses. Their use helps to explain Nixon's success. Relying primarily on bolstering and differentiation strategies, Nixon focused public response on his apparently "sincere and politically selfless efforts for peace."

Vatz, Richard E. and Theodore Otto Windt, Jr. "The Defeats of Judges Haynsworth and Carswell: Rejection of Supreme Court Nominees." *Quarterly Journal of Speech* 60(December 1974): 477-488.

The authors examined the rhetoric used to justify rejection of two Supreme court nominees. Haynsworth's opponents accused him of being insensitive to the relationship between private finances and judicial decisions.  Carswell's opponents accused him of being "a mediocre judge unfit for service on the Supreme Court."   Nixon's speech after the defeat of his candidates distorted the Senate debate over confirmation

Wilson, Gerald L.  "A Strategy of Explanation: Richard M. Nixon's August 8, 1974, Resignation Speech."  *Communication Quarterly* 24(Summer 1976): 14-20.

Using the genre of apologia as a framework, Wilson examined Nixon's televised resignation speech.  Nixon used the strategies of differentiation and bolstering well, but his speech suffered from an omission of recognition of the "gravity of the misdeed" and the "congruity of the statements with reality." Only those who continued to follow the president "with blind faith" would be satisfied by Nixon's speech.

## Biographies and Case Studies

Abrahamsen, David.  *Nixon vs. Nixon: A Psychological Inquest.* New York: Farrar, Straus, and Giroux, 1976.

Adler, Bill.  *Wit and Humor of Richard Nixon.*  New York: Popular Library, 1969.

Allen, Gary.  *Richard Nixon: The Man Behind the Mask.*  Boston: Western Island Press, 1971.

Alsop, Stewart.  *Nixon and Rockefeller: A Double Portrait.*  Garden City, NY: Doubleday, 1960.

Ambrose, Stephen E.  *Nixon: The Education of a Politician, 1913-1962.* New York: Simon and Schuster, 1987.

Andrews, Phillip.  *This Man Nixon: The Life Story of California Senator Richard M. Nixon.*  Philadelphia: Winston, 1952.

Anson, Robert S.  *Exile: The Unquiet Oblivion of Richard M. Nixon.* New York: Simon and Schuster, 1984.

Arnold, William A.  *Back When It All Began: The Early Nixon Years.*  New York: Vantage Press, 1975.

Atkins, Ollie.  *Triumph and Tragedy: The White House Years.*  New York: Playboy Press, 1977.

Balch, John T.  "Richard Nixon vs. H. Jerry Voorhis For Congress, 1946."  Typescript. Department of History, California State University, Fresno.

Barber, James D.  *The Presidential Character: Predicting Performance in the White House.*  Englewood Cliffs, NJ: Prentice-Hall, 1972.

Ben-Veniste, Richard and George Frampton.  *Stonewall: The Inside Story of the Watergate Prosecution.*  New York: Simon & Schuster, 1977.

Brandenburgh, Donald C.  "A Comparative Study of Social Rank and 'The Nixon Papers' "  Master's thesis. Department of Sociology, Whittier College, 1960.

Brashear, Ernest.  "Who is Richard Nixon?"  *New Republic* 127(September 8, 1952): 9-11.

Bremer, Howard F. (ed.). *Richard M. Nixon, 1913-*. Dobbs Ferry, NY: Oceana, 1975.

Breslin, Jimmy. *How the Good Guys Finally Won: Notes from an Impeachment Summer*. New York: Ballantine Books, 1976.

Brodie, Fawn M. *Richard Nixon: The Shaping of His Character*. New York: Norton, 1981.

Bullock, Paul. *Jerry Voorhis: The Idealist as Politician*. New York: Vantage Press, 1978.

_____. "Rabbits and Radicals: Richard Nixon's 1946 Campaign Against Jerry Voorhis." *Southern California Quarterly* 55(Fall 1973): 319-359.

Casper, Dale E. *Richard M. Nixon: A Bibliographic Exploration*. New York: Garland, 1988.

Chesen, Eli S. *President Nixon's Psychiatric Profile*. New York: Wyden, 1973.

Chester, Lewis et al. *An American Melodrama: The Presidential Campaign of 1968*. New York: Viking Press, 1969.

Clawson, Kenneth. "A Loyalist's Memoir." Washington *Post*, October 9, 1979, p. D1.

Converse, Philip E. and Howard Schuman. " 'Silent Majorities' and the Vietnam War." *Scientific American* 222(June 1970): 17-25.

Costello, William. *The Facts About Nixon: An Unauthorized Biography*. New York: Viking Press, 1960.

Culbert, David. "Television's Nixon: The Politician and His Image." *American History/American Television*, ed. John E. O'Connor. New York: Frederick Ungar, 1983.

David, Lester. *The Lonely Lady of San Clemente: The Story of Pat Nixon*. New York: Thomas Crowell, 1978.

de Toledano, Ralph. *Nixon*. New York: Henry Holt, 1956.

_____. *One Man Alone: Richard Nixon*. New York: Funk and Wagnalls, 1969.

Dean, John. *Blind Ambition*. New York: Simon & Schuster, 1976.

Donahue, Bernard F. "The Political Use of Religious Symbols: A Case Study of the 1972 Presidential Campaign." *Review of Politics* 37(January 1975): 48-65.

Douglas, Helen Gahagan. *A Full Life*. Garden City, NY: Doubleday, 1982.

Drew, Elizabeth. *Washington Journal: The Events 1973-1974*. New York: Random House, 1975.

Ehrlichman, John. *Witness to Power: The Nixon Years*. New York: Simon and Schuster, 1982.

Eisenhower, Julie Nixon. *Pat Nixon: The Untold Story*. New York: Simon and Schuster, 1986.

Ellsworth, John W. "Rationality and Campaigning: A Content Analysis of the 1960 Presidential Campaign Debates." *Western Political Quarterly* 18(December 1960): 794-802.

Ervin, Sam J. *The Whole Truth: The Watergate Conspiracy*. New York: Random House, 1980.

Evans, Rowland and Robert Novak. *Nixon in the White House: The Frustration of Power*. New York: Random House, 1971.

Frost, David. *"I Gave Them a Sword": Behind the Scenes of the Nixon Interviews*. New York: Morrow, 1978.

_____. *The Presidential Debates, 1968*. New York: Stein and Day, 1968.

Gardner, Richard. "Richard Nixon: The Story of a Fighting Quaker." Typescript. Whittier College Library.

Garza, Hedda. *The Watergate Investigation Index: House Judiciary Committee Hearings and Report on Impeachment*. Wilmington, DE: Scholarly Resources, 1985.

Goldman, Eric F. "The 1947 Kennedy-Nixon 'Tube City' Debate," *Saturday Review*, 4(October 16, 1976): 12-13.

Goulden, Joseph C. "Warming up for Watergate: The 1962 Nixon-Brown California Gubernatorial Election." *Nation* 216(May 28, 1973): 688-691.

Haldeman, H. R. *The Ends of Power*. New York: Times Books, 1978.

Halterman, William H. *Nixon in Retrospect, 1946-1962*. New York: Research Data Publications, 1973.

Harris, Mark. *Mark the Glove Boy, or the Last Days of Richard Nixon*. New York: Macmillan, 1964.

Higgins, George V. "The Friends of Richard Nixon," *Atlantic* 234(November 1974): 41-52.

_____. *The Friends of Richard Nixon*. Boston: Little, Brown, and Co., 1975.

Hoffman, Paul. *The New Nixon*. New York: Tower Publications, 1970.

Honan, William H. "The Men Behind Nixon's Speeches." *New York Times Magazine*, January 19, 1969, pp. 20-21+.

Hoyt, Edwin P. *The Nixons: An American Family*. New York: Random House, 1972.

Hughes, Arthur J. *Richard M. Nixon*. New York: Dodd, Mead, 1972.

Jackson, Donald. "The Young Nixon." *Life*, November 6, 1970, pp. 54-66.

Jaworski, Leon. *The Right and the Power: The Prosecution of Watergate*. New York: Reader's Digest Press, 1976.

Keogh, James. *President Nixon and the Press*. New York: Funk & Wagnalls, 1972.

_____. *This is Nixon*. New York: G. P. Putnam's Sons, 1956.

Kissinger, Henry. *White House Years*. Boston: Little, Brown, & Co., 1979.

_____. *Years of Upheaval*. Boston: Little, Brown, & Co., 1982.

Klein, Herbert S. *Making It Perfectly Clear*. Garden City, NY: Doubleday, 1980.

Knappman, Edward W. and Evan Drossman. *Watergate and the White House*. 3 volumes. New York: Facts on File, 1974.

Kornitzer, Bela. *The Real Nixon: An Intimate Biography*. New York: Rand-McNally, 1960.

Kraus, Sidney (ed.). *The Great Debates.*. Bloomington, IN: Indiana University Press, 1962.

Lasky, Victor. *It Didn't Start with Watergate.* New York: Dell Publishing Co., 1977.

Lucas, J. Anthony. *Nightmare: The Underside of the Nixon Years.* New York: Viking Press, 1976.

Lurie, Leonard. *The Running of Richard Nixon.* New York: Coward, McCann, and Geoghegan, 1972.

McCarley, Carroll E. "The California Campaigns of Richard Nixon: Strategies and Issues." Master's thesis. Department of History, San Francisco State College, 1970.

McGinniss, Joe. *The Selling of the President, 1968.* New York: Trident Press, 1969.

Magruder, Jeb. *An American Life: One Man's Road to Watergate.* New York: Barnes and Noble, 1974.

Mankiewicz, Frank. *Perfectly Clear: Nixon from Whittier to Watergate.* New York: Harper & Row, 1973.

_____. *The Final Crisis of Richard M. Nixon.* New York: Quadrangle, 1975.

Mazlish, Bruce. *In Search of Nixon: A Psychohistorical Inquiry.* New York: Basic Books, 1972.

Mazo, Earl. *Richard Nixon: A Political and Personal Portrait.* New York: Harper & Row, 1959.

Mazo, Earl and Stephen Hess. *Nixon: A Political Portrait.* New York: Harper & Row, 1968.

Mazon, Mauricio. "Young Richard Nixon: A Study in Political Precosity." *Historian* 41(November 1978): 21-40.

Miller, William Lee. "The Debating Career of Richard M. Nixon." *The Reporter*, April 19, 1956, pp. 11-17.

Minow, Newton N., John Martin, and Lee Mitchell. *Presidential Television.* New York: Basic Books, 1973.

Mollenhoff, Clark R. *Game Plan for Disaster: An Ombudsman's Report on the Nixon Years.* New York: W. W. Norton, 1976.

Morgan, Lael. "Whittier '34: Most Likely to Succeed." Los Angeles *Times*, May 10, 1970: (*This Week* section), pp. 34-38.

*New York Times. End of a Presidency.* New York; Holt, Rinehart, Winston, 1974.

_____. *The Watergate Hearings: Break-in and Cover-up.* New York: Viking Press, 1973.

_____. *The White House Transcripts.* New York: Viking Press, 1974.

Nixon, Hannah M. "Richard Nixon: A Mother's Story." *Good Housekeeping* 150(June 1960): 54-57.

Nixon, Patricia Ryan (as told to Joe Alex Morris). "I Say He's a Wonderful Guy." *Saturday Evening Post*, September 6, 1952, pp. 17-19+

O'Brien, Robert W. and Elizabeth Jones. "The Night Nixon Spoke: A Study in Political Effectiveness." Typescript. Whittier College Library, 1969.

*Orange County Salutes Richard Nixon.* Newport Beach, CA: Orange County Illustrated, 1969.

Osborne, John. *The Fifth Year of the Nixon Watch.* New York: Liveright Press, 1974.

————. *The Fourth Year of the Nixon Watch.* New York: Liveright Press, 1973.

————. *The Last Nixon Watch.* Washington, DC: New Republic, 1975.

————. *The Nixon Watch.* New York: Liveright Press, 1970.

————. *The Second Year of the Nixon Watch.* New York: Liverignt Press, 1971.

————. *The Third Year of the Nixon Watch.* New York: Liveright Press, 1972.

Pearl, Arthur. *Landslide: The How and Why of Nixon's Victory.* Secaucus, NJ: Citadel Press, 1973.

Price, Raymond. *With Nixon.* New York; Viking Press, 1977.

Rather, Dan and Gary P. Gates. *The Palace Guard.* New York; Harper & Row, 1974.

"Record of the Nixon Affair: Legal Opinion, List of Contributors, Audit, Speeches, Statements, and Documents." *US News and World Report,* October 3, 1952, pp. 61-70.

"Richard M. Nixon in the Warren Era." Typescript. Berkeley, CA: Regional Oral History Office, 1980.

Robinson, David. "Nixon in Crisis-Land: The Rhetoric of Six Crises." *Journal of American Culture* 8(Spring 1985): 79-85.

Rosenberg, Kenyon C. and Judith K. Rosenberg. *Watergate: An Annotated Bibliography.* Littleton, CO: Libraries Unlimited, 1975.

Rowse, Arthur E. *Slanted News: A Case Study of the Nixon and Stevenson Fund Stories.* Boston: Beacon Press, 1957.

Safire, William. *Before the Fall: An Insider's View of the Pre-Watergate White House.* New York: Doubleday, 1975.

Schell, Jonathan. *The Time of Illusion.* New York: Alfred Knopf, 1976.

Schlesinger, Arthur M., Jr. *Kennedy or Nixon.* New York: Macmillan, 1960.

————. *The Imperial Presidency.* Boston: Houghton Mifflin, 1973.

Schulte, Renee K. (ed.) *The Young Nixon: An Oral Inquiry.* Fullerton, CA: California State University, 1978.

Scobie, Ingrid Winther. "Helen Gahagan Douglas and Her 1950 Senate Race with Richard Nixon." *Southern California Quarterly* 58(Spring 1976): 113-126.

Semple, Robert B., Jr. "Nixon's Nov. 3 Speech: Why He Took the Gamble Alone." *New York Times,* January 19, 1970, p. 23.

Sevareid, Eric. (ed.) *Candidates 1960: Behind the Headlines in the Presidential Race.* New York: Basic Books, 1960.

Sirica, John J. *To Set the Record Straight: The Break-in, the Tapes, the Conspirator, the Pardon.* New York: Norton, 1979.

Smith, Myron, Jr. *Watergate: An Annotated Bibliography*. Metuchen, NJ: Scarecrow Press, 1983.

Spalding, Henry D. *The Nixon Nobody Knows*. Middle Village, NY: Jonathan David, 1972.

Spear, Joseph C. *Presidents and the Press: The Nixon Legacy*. Cambridge, MA: MIT Press, 1984.

Stratton, William M. "A Content Analysis of the Response to 'The Nixon Speech' " Master's thesis. Department of Sociology, Whittier College, 1964.

Sulzberger, Cyrus L. *The World of Richard Nixon*. New York: Prentice Hall, 1987.

U.S. Congress. House. Committee on the Judiciary. *Debate on the Articles of Impeachment*. Hearings. Washington, DC: Government Printing Office, 1976.

U.S. Congress. House. Committee on the Judiciary. *Impeachment of Richard M. Nixon President of the United States: Report of the Committee on the Judiciary*. Washington, DC: Government Printing Office, 1974.

U.S. Congress. House. Special Committee on Campaign Expenditures. *Campaign Expenditures* Hearings. 7 parts. Washington, DC: Government Printing Office, 1946.

U.S. Congress. Senate. Committee on Commerce. *Freedom of Communications*. 6 parts. Washington, D.C.: Government Printing Office, 1961.

U.S. Congress. Senate. Select Committee on Presidential Campaign Activities. *The Final Report of the Committee. . . .* Washington, DC: Government Printing Office, 1974.

Voorhis, Horace Jeremiah. *Confessions of a Congressman*. Garden City, NY: Doubleday, 1947.

_____. *The Strange Case of Richard Nixon*. New York: Popular Library, 1973.

Washington *Post*. *The Fall of a President*. New York: Delacorte Press, 1974.

Whalen, Richard. *Catch the Falling Flag*. Boston: Houghton Mifflin, 1972.

White, Theodore. *Breach of Faith: The Fall of Richard Nixon*. New York: Atheneum, 1975.

_____. *The Making of the President, 1960*. New York: Atheneum, 1961.

_____. *The Making of the President, 1964*. New York: Atheneum, 1965.

_____. *The Making of the President, 1968*. New York: Atheneum, 1969.

_____. *The Making of the President, 1972*. New York: Atheneum, 1973.

Wills, Garry. *Nixon Agonistes*. Boston: Houghton-Mifflin, 1970.

Wilson, Richard. "Is Nixon Fit to be President?" *Look*, February 24, 1953, pp. 33-42.

Witcover, Jules. *The Resurrection of Richard Nixon*. New York: G.P. Putnam's Sons, 1970.

Woods, Rose Mary. "Nixon's My Boss." *Saturday Evening Post*, December 28, 1957, pp. 20-21+.

Woodstone, Arthur. *Nixon's Head*. New York: St. Martin's Press, 1972.

Woodward, Bob and Carl Bernstein. *The Final Days*. New York: Simon and Schuster, 1976.

# Index

## ABOUT THE AUTHOR

HAL W. BOCHIN is Professor of Speech Communication at California State University, Fresno. He is co-author of *Hiram Johnson: A Bio-Bibliography* (Greenwood Press, 1988), and has contributed articles and essays to *American Orators Before 1900* (Greenwood Press, 1987), *In Search of Justice,* and *Communication Education.*

**Great American Orators**

Defender of the Union: The Oratory of Daniel Webster
*Craig R. Smith*

Harry Emerson Fosdick: Persuasive Preacher
*Halford R. Ryan*

Eugene Talmadge: Rhetoric and Response
*Calvin McLeod Logue*

The Search of Self-Sovereignty: The Oratory of Elizabeth Cady Stanton
*Beth M. Waggenspack*

Henry Ward Beecher: Peripatetic Preacher
*Halford R. Ryan*